# THE
# PARTIAL CRITICS

## LEE T. LEMON

D1711643

New York  OXFORD UNIVERSITY PRESS
1965

23831

R. P. BLACKMUR: From *Language as Gesture*, copyright 1940 by Richard P. Blackmur. Reprinted by permission of Harcourt, Brace & World, Inc., and George Allen & Unwin Ltd.

MAUD BODKIN: From *Archetypal Patterns in Poetry*. Reprinted by permission of Oxford University Press, Inc.

CLEANTH BROOKS: From *The Well Wrought Urn*. Reprinted by permission of Harcourt, Brace & World, Inc., and Dobson Books Ltd.

JOHN CROWE RANSOM: Eight lines from "Piazza Piece" from Poems and Essays. Reprinted by permission of Alfred A. Knopf, Inc. From The World's Body. Reprinted by permission of Charles Scribner's Sons.

HERBERT READ: From The Nature of Literature (English title: Collected Essays in Literary Criticism). Reprinted by permission of Horizon Press and Faber and Faber Ltd.

CARL SANDBURG: "Fog" from Chicago Poems, copyright 1916 by Holt, Rinehart and Winston, Inc., renewed 1944 by Carl Sandburg. Reprinted by permission of Holt, Rinehart and Winston, Inc., and Faber and Faber Ltd.

WALLACE STEVENS: "God Is Good. It Is a Beautiful Night" and "Study of Two Pears" from The Collected Poems of Wallace Stevens. Reprinted by permission of Alfred A. Knopf, Inc., and Faber and Faber Ltd. From The Necessary Angel. Reprinted by permission of Alfred A. Knopf, Inc.

ALLEN TATE: From Collected Essays, copyright 1960 by Allen Tate. Reprinted by permission of Alan Swallow, Publisher.

ALFRED NORTH WHITEHEAD: From Process and Reality, copyright 1929 by The Macmillan Company, renewed 1957 by Evelyn Whitehead. Reprinted by permission of The Macmillan Company.

W. K. WIMSATT and MONROE C. BEARDSLEY: From The Verbal Icon. Reprinted by permission of University of Kentucky Press.

YVOR WINTERS: From In Defense of Reason, copyright 1947, 1960 by Yvor Winters. Reprinted by permission of Alan Swallow, Publisher, and Routledge & Kegan Paul Ltd.

To: Lillian, Kristy,
Geof, Kathy, and Greg

# PREFACE

This study began some years ago, during my first encounters with modern literary criticism. I was then, as
now, in some awe of its brilliance; it glistened, and it
shed a glistening light on an astonishing number of
poems, some plays, and a few works of fiction. But
glistening lights leave much dark. And not only do our
brightest critical lights glisten, they aim their beams
at different things. If I may drop the metaphor, many
of our best critics have permitted themselves to become
specialists in this or that quality. Cleanth Brooks has
spent much of a productive career doggedly searching
out ironies and paradoxes; William Empson has worried
the ambiguity out of any number of poems and, re-
fining the technique somewhat, gone on to the structure
of complex words; Yvor Winters has cast his bait for
paraphrases, and told disgruntled stories about the
ones that got away; Philip Wheelwright and Northrop
Frye have chased their separate versions of the archetype beyond the confines of literature; R. S. Crane and
his followers have circled around a notion of poetic
form that itself seems all too circular. What contemporary literary criticism and theory have produced, then,

is a bundle of approaches that seem to have little relevance to each other and that seem, because each specializes in a particular quality of poetry, to specialize in a particular type of poetry.

Not only have the various schools of critics gone their individual ways, individual critics have gone in various ways. R. P. Blackmur, for example, has two literary theories—an early, uncomfortably narrow one, and a later, wider one—and a critical practice that keeps closer to the poems than to either of his theories. T. S. Eliot adapted his critical approach to the work at hand, which would have been exemplary had he not also announced a new theory for each new approach. The Cleanth Brooks of *The Hidden God* has as little in common with the Brooks of *The Well Wrought Urn* as his work in *Literary Criticism: A Short History* has in common with his statement of the formalist position in the Winter 1951 issue of *Kenyon Review*. And it is difficult to find the neo-Aristotelian in Crane's work on Swift.

Given the constantly changing assumptions and theories of our best critics, a kind of constant inconstancy, the most interesting question is a simple inquiry into theoretical consistency. *If* the various positions our critics take were developed rigidly, what would be their limitations, their usefulness for practical criticism, their necessary assumptions, their inevitable implications? In order to find answers, I have had to amplify this or that aspect of the work of a given critic; that is, I have taken fairly common critical concepts—the value of semantic complexity in and for itself, for example—and isolated them, purified them, and traced them through the works of several critics. The result is necessarily some loss of accuracy in assessing the importance of the work of individual critics. The gain, a clearer understanding of the kinds of approaches in use, should be valuable.

I must also ask if the approaches can be reconciled. Unlike R. S. Crane, I am unwilling to admit that literary criticism is a hodge-podge of unreconcilable disciplines, for critics are all in essentially the same business. The critic's job, as Murray Krieger has wisely remarked, is to help us make sense of our responses to literature. We are, in all probability, likely to make better sense if we have an adequate critical theory to work with. To return to my opening metaphor, we do not really make sense of our responses to a poem when we illuminate merely its irony, its paradoxes, its archetypal patterns, its wise morality, or its basis in the poet's experience. We make sense of our response only when we illuminate the entire work that formed it—including all the work's patterns of sound and meaning, whatever their kind—with a steady, unflickering light.

My debts in completing this study are too numerous to mention. I owe much to undergraduate students who insisted that I tell them why we read poems and plays and novels, and to graduate students who insisted that I sharpen my answers. The debt to a long succession of teachers is unpayable. Especially, though, I wish to thank Professors Robert Faner and Robert Knoll, who gave encouragement; Professor Murray Krieger, who introduced me to the intricacies of modern criticism; and Professor Royal A. Gettmann, whose encouragement was always warm and whose advice was always wise.

# CONTENTS

# THE PARTIAL CRITICS

# I

## A SURVEY

The literary critic's chief obligation is to evaluate works of literature and to make his evaluations intelligible; all his other professional tasks are subordinate to this double duty. The importance of the facts that scholars unearth and the significance of what they publish is borrowed from the value of the works they study. But most importantly, readers read poetry (in the broad, Aristotelian sense) because it has a kind of value that ordinary writing lacks. That special kind of value should be the concern of the critic.

Practical critics and theoreticians have, however, persistently refused to develop a systematic approach to the problem of literary value. T. S. Eliot set both the temper and the basic paradox of our most influential criticism when, in *The Sacred Wood*, he moved quickly from the position that the critic "must simply elucidate" to the position that he must order his impressions into "a generalized statement of literary beauty." [1] But surely a critic cannot *simply* elucidate and still reach general conclusions about literary beauty. On the one hand, modern critics recognize that a work of art is a unique creation and that beauty is something unto itself which violates

3

rules even as it transcends them. On the other, they want to accept both the professional and the social responsibilities that force the critic to push explanation and evaluation to its utmost limits; and they have very strongly suspected that, because fine poems share something with each other, a general literary theory is possible. The result is a kind of critical schizophrenia, a radical separation of theory and practice, of professional and personal response. William Empson, for example, painstakingly analyzes "Tintern Abbey," arguing that the grammar is muddled, the thought confused, the basic idea unsatisfactory. Then, without embarrassment or explanation, he admits his admiration for the poem.[2] He has, in other words, kept his critical game apart from his personal response. That his method damns lines he likes causes him no consternation, no sense that he is not doing his job fairly. Such irresponsibility is inevitable unless the critic makes evaluation an integral part of his work.

The position taken by such critics as Mortimer Adler, D. W. Gotshalk, I. A. Richards, and Randall Jarrell [3] is better only because it is more honest. Each in his special way maintains that criticism is merely persuasive rhetoric. Jarrell hopes that he can convince his readers that the *Iliad* is superior to "Trees," but admits that he cannot prove it.[4] Richards' early distrust of value statements is notorious, and Adler and Gotshalk assume fundamental dichotomies of taste which make criticism a defense of group reactions. Much may be said for these views, but left unqualified they undermine the authority of criticism because they fail to recognize that criticism, as structured thought, reflects back upon and alters tastes. Despite the precautions they have built into their critical systems, each finally makes the critic responsible only to himself — not to the poem, not to his better sense, not to the traditions of literature, not to his reader.

4

Several broad causes may be brought forward to explain the reluctance to take evaluation seriously enough to make it an integral part of criticism; a detailed discussion of them would lead too far astray, so I shall indicate them only briefly. They include the reaction against nineteenth-century impressionistic criticism, the relativistic temper of the modern mind, current philosophical concern with description and methodology rather than with the ascertainment of order and value, the subjectivist inclination furthered by some branches of psychology, and the attempt to emulate the dispassionate objectivity of science. Any one or any combination of these might influence an individual critic, and each may lead to the conclusion that evaluation is neither meaningful nor possible.

The attempt to emulate science is possibly the most basic of these causes. Summing up the position accurately, Thomas Clark Pollock argues that literary theory should have the same relation to literature that physiology has to medicine; it "should be objective rather than evaluative," and stake out the areas where "objective knowledge" is "difficult or impossible." [5] I shall return to Pollock's theory later; here I want merely to show the easy assumption of the objectivity of science and the subjectivity of value.

The assumption is part of the now defunct logical positivism of the 1920's and 1930's which claimed that value statements are merely veiled commands.[6] In the influential but theoretically naïve *Meaning of Meaning*, C. K. Ogden and I. A. Richards echo the positivist line by asserting that a statement like "this is red" is meaningful, whereas a statement like "this is good" is simply an "emotive sign." They argue that *red* refers to a quality in the object; *good* does not.[7] Now, this is not at all true, for when a critic says "this is good" he is merely using a convenient contraction of the fuller statement "this has such and such properties." He is in precisely the same position as the physicist who sums up data about the place of a color in the spectrum by saying "this is red." The properties a critic describes as "good" may not be those that another person would find good: he may be eccentric, inept, or have read badly; if so, his evaluation is merely wrong — it is not thereby meaningless.

Objections to evaluative criticism also come from scholars, amateur classroom philosophers, technicians, and simple appreciators of literature. The scholar objects that "the value of a literary work is established only by due process of time, and the canon of literature is therefore a canon of past works. A consensus of literate readers of many generations establishes value; there are no short cuts. The most certain fact about the past is that it is gone; to understand a work, to value it properly, we must recover the past through scholarship." The argument is tenable, at least to a point. But the fact is that the conscientious literary scholar does make evaluative judgments. He quickly learns, for example, that there is too much sixteenth-century lyric poetry to cover in even a two-semester course. Does Skelton, therefore, rate more than passing notice? Should precisely the same time be given Wyatt and Surrey? Are their sonnets to be discussed in their own right or as models improved by Shakespeare and Donne? How much time can be taken away from the greats and given to Peele, Campion, Drayton, and Daniel? To answer these questions, the scholar must make value judgments. To answer blindly questions relevant to one's profession is irresponsible and foolish.

A second difficulty in the scholar's objection stems from the unfortunate tendency to accumulate fact for the sake of fact. As Northrop Frye has observed, scholarship that begins with background finds it difficult to get to the foreground. Even a Shakespeare is of interest only as a writer; a fact, no matter how interesting, which throws no light upon a literary work, is irrelevant to the student of literature as a student of literature. Briefly, the honest scholar is obliged to understand the relevance of his facts.

John Crowe Ransom brilliantly caricatures the next objector, the classroom philosopher who extracts from the poem "a nugget of wisdom, a principle that makes for righteousness and the welfare of humankind" to present to his students.[8] Although literature may at times possess such nuggets, the subject matter of literary study is the unique quality of the individual work of art, not the tags it shares with such diverse purveyors of human betterment as religion, ethics, and the social sciences. To consider literature as if it were a series of exquisitely stated lessons is to deprive it of its proper dignity. The classic notion that literature is more true than either history or philosophy may be accepted only with the addition of the all-important phrase "in its own way." The ramifications of this last give direction to literary study and a discipline to the student of literature.

I must, however, insist that I am not urging a study of techniques only. Our third group of objectors, in fact, are those chiefly interested in technique; they usually object that judgments are unscientific. But if it is true, as I believe, that no critic intentionally deals in trivia, then the decision to write about one poem rather than another is a value judgment — either of the poem or of the point to be made. Dispassionate objectivity cannot account for our spending more time with Shakespeare than with Daniel.

Even the selection of details to be treated "scientifically," moreover, requires an evaluation of the poem.

Something in the poem calls out for technical analysis by impressing the critic with its brilliance or dullness, its success or failure. A study of Hopkins' syntax, for example, is likely to turn up more interesting results than a similar study of Tennyson, which is another way of saying that the success of Hopkins' poems depends more upon syntactical variations than does that of Tennyson's poems.

Still other difficulties beset the critic of techniques. Suppose he notes the metrics of a poem. Ignoring the fact that any given line may usually be read in several meaningful ways and that the reading chosen is based upon a complex series of judgments leading to the choice of the "best" interpretation, the critic may note that a line is strict iambic pentameter. Neither he nor his readers get very far; the clause that I am writing now also begins as iambic and may be broken into a pentameter line. Or the critic may concern himself with metaphor, but even well-used metaphor is not an exclusive property of good poetry, nor is it indispensable in the finest poetry. "It is a beauteous evening, calm and free," is a truly beauteous line, despite the minimal imagery. A critic with sufficient technical vocabulary and patience might even show that some of the power of the line derives from its rich sound, but I doubt that he could explain its full effect. In short, technical criticism cannot succeed if it limits itself to dissection of poems for any given technique; it succeeds only by discussing the fusion of a sufficient number of the constituent members of the poem to account for its value. But by the time the critic has begun to discuss such fusion, he has judged the proportion and integrity of the poem; when he shows the workings of a number of strands in their interrelationships, he is really showing that the poem is beautiful or ugly. The best technical criticism does this, but to state all the premises and withhold the inevitable conclusion is an elementary rhetorical trick; it cannot be made the distinctive feature of a responsible discipline.

Our final group of objectors, the appreciators, fear that a theory might undermine the purity of their immediate responses. Helen Gardner champions the position as ably as one can:

If a critic is to be judged by his success in giving just the right amount of approval, then he, and the common reader who is to learn from him, is required to take up an attitude to works of art which is highly inimical to their proper enjoyment, whether they are works which give profound delight, or works which give lesser pleasures.[9]

This attitude commands respect only so long as one imagines the critic reading a poem by, say, Richard Wilbur, and vexing himself about whether it is 80 or 83 per cent effective, whether it rates four notches above a poem by Roethke or only two, whether Wilbur gets an "excellent" for imagery and only a "good" for metrics, and so on. Miss Gardner, fortunately for poetry, has set up a straw critic. Actually, evaluative criticism falls somewhere between rationalization and logic. The critic first reacts to the poem, and Miss Gardner rightly wants the reaction as uncluttered by preconceived critical standards as possible. But the standards are not applied while the reader is reacting; they emerge only when the critic analyzes his reaction. Evaluative criticism borders on logic for the very good reason that the critic is obliged to discuss poetry and his reaction to it in an orderly way; if he changes his standards as he moves from poem to poem, we suspect his value as a commentator. But it also borders on rationalization because the sensitive critic learns something from each successful poem and adjusts his system accordingly. Or, to cut the cake differently, response and formal evaluation are distinct activities — analogous to liking a person and writing a letter of recommendation for him. In the first the standards are loosely and probably even unconsciously applied; in the second they must be made orderly and conscious. I do not see how standards can be done away with; the only question for the critic is whether or not he and his readers know what his standards are. Despite the possibility of occasional flashes of unsystematic brilliance, better criticism is likely if the critic knows why he reacts as he does.

Kenneth Burke's aphorism that "the critic tries to explain a complexity in terms of a simplicity . . . and a simplicity is precisely what a complexity is not" [10] expresses the strongest theoretical justification of the appreciator. The logic seems clear, yet the theorist has his answers. He may reply (as Burke does) that because the response is not a mere gush but rather a response to a particular work of art, it should be possible to talk about the factors that stimulated the response. He may go on to note that critics and readers generally agree about which works merit consideration, a fact which implies that poems share characteristics that can be isolated and discussed. He may argue that although the theorist and the appreciator share the same body, duties change as function changes. Because the appreciator, the reader, has only to respond and the critic has to clarify the response, the latter needs overt standards. Our theorist could also say that the inevitable alternative to standards is prejudices, and that prejudices are erratic and uncontrollable. And he could add that criticism does not substitute for literature; it rather fosters an understanding that leads to increased responsiveness.

To sum up the argument for evaluative criticism thus far, no critic or scholar deliberately deals in trivia.

Wordsworth's sonnet "Composed upon Westminster Bridge" receives a great deal more attention than William McGonagall's lines:

Oh! mighty City of London, you are wonderful to see,
And thy beauties no doubt fills the tourist's heart
    with glee,
But during my short stay and while wandering there,
Mr. Spurgeon was the only man I heard speaking
    proper English, I do declare.

A critic setting out to analyze Wordsworth's lines rather than McGonagall's has made an act of evaluation. The quantity of writing is so great and time so dear that each of us must somewhere draw a line beyond which, as professionals, we refuse to pass. And within this area we inevitably establish orders of precedence. Even the apparently innocent act of taking an edition of Dryden from the library (if not forced by some practical need) is an unexpressed act of evaluation.

If value judgments are unavoidable, is it not wise to develop some kind of rationale to handle them? Ransom, writing of the aversion the early Eliot and Blackmur had for theory, noted that, as they examined their texts more closely, they found theoretical questions that were progressively more difficult.[11] As Eliot himself noted in his early work, perceptions do not "accumulate as a mass, but form themselves as a structure." [12] Eliot expresses here an understanding never realized in his own criticism, an understanding that intelligent appreciation must be a part of a structure, a system, if it is to be more than emotional release. To put perceptions in order is to formulate a theory; to put responses in order is to formulate an evaluative theory.

After arguing that a theory of evaluation is inevitable, I shall have to reverse myself momentarily by arguing that, in a sense, it is also impossible. The reasons are numerous and easy to come by, so I shall cite only the most telling. Literary criticism is subservient to literature, and literary criticism precedes literary theory. As one whole school of critics taught — with some justification, albeit too confidently — the function of poetry is to surprise the reader; the poem comes before the critique. I suspect that no theory will ever be complete enough to predict all the surprises poets have in store for us. Perhaps the most the theorist can do is to make room for novelty.

A theorist builds from the work of his predecessors and contemporaries. His ambition is to avoid their errors and irrelevancies while incorporating their insights. He must build systematically, but not rigidly; for to the extent that his work is unsystematic, it will be incomprehensible, and to the extent that it is rigid, it will be unusable. As he builds, he has to keep his eyes cocked upon several sets of plans, keeping in view not only the schematizations of poetry and of his own discipline, but also those of related studies.

The order is large, and in attempting to fill it I have set certain loose limits. They are, roughly, lyric poetry and contemporary criticism. Lyric poetry seems a likely place to begin a theory of literature because the individual works are relatively manageable and because the lyric raises the basic questions of literary theory. What is the relationship between form and meaning? What kind of "truth," if any, does literature possess? What is the nature of aesthetic experience? What is the relationship between the author and his work? The lyric raises these and similar questions in comparative purity. That is, there are many valid and sufficient nonliterary defenses of, say, *Macbeth* or *Crime and Punishment*; it is much harder to invent nonliterary defenses of Keats's "Ode to Autumn"

— which is to say that purely literary questions can be seen more sharply, less confused with other questions, in the lyric than in other forms.

I have started with contemporary criticism because that is what we have and because it also includes the older criticism. Although we may have no critics of the stature of Aristotle, we have critics who know what he wrote and who also know other things.

Lyric poetry and contemporary criticism should be thought of as focal points rather than as strict limits. Although I am concerned chiefly with criticism written after 1920, I cannot totally ignore Bergson nor avoid Coleridge. Lyric poetry does not provide a precise limit because no one knows what it is. It is usually described as brief, emotional, and personal, but these adjectives are meaningless. "Brevity" must stretch to include both the haiku and "Adonais." "Emotional" cannot be applied consistently to both the playful, deliberately literary, and sophisticated "Had we but world enough, and time" and to the sincere "Break, break, break." And "personal" fails since Eliot has taught us to expect impersonality in our best poetry. Moreover, I should hope that my comments about the lyric will (with some adjustments) be applicable to other forms; I have, therefore, occasionally wandered away from the lyric in order to test the general applicability of my work and to indicate its relevance to other forms.

My handling of problems more properly the subject of other disciplines has been deliberately cavalier. Discussion of critical issues leads very quickly into matters of epistemology and psychology — to name only two very near neighbors of literary theory. A theory that elevates William Carlos Williams above Wallace Stevens suggests certain assumptions about man's way of knowing reality; one that sees poems as expressions of a mythic consciousness comes very close to accepting a major philosophical position. A literary theorist soon finds himself embroiled in a number of nonliterary issues — e.g., shall he be a subjectivist or an objectivist, or shall he compromise? He must, in practice, decide whether to analyze poems as objective creations or to analyze his experience of the poem. If he rejects these extremes, as I believe he must, his honesty forces him to work out arduously some system which does justice to the fact that he knows only his own experience, and which also recognizes that ultimately his criticism must be about the objective poem.

The theorist cannot, of course, solve the problems that intrude from other disciplines; but he can recognize them, consider their implications, and borrow what he can from the specialists. If he works carefully, he is protected by the grandiose claims of philosophy and psychology — the one purports to embrace the universe, the other all the mind of man. He is protected because a philosophical or psychological system that leads to an inadequate aesthetic, and thence to an inadequate literary theory, does not meet its own requirements. The theorist need not be a metaphysician or a logician to realize that logical positivism in its more popular forms offers no very comfortable place for aesthetic experience. A philosophy or psychology that makes no room for what the critic knows to be true may be summarily rejected.

The surest way of building an evaluative theory of poetry is to discover the kinds of values that readers usually find in poems. Poems do not break into the neat little packets of value I shall suggest, but critiques of poems often suggest that they do. Critics are generally somewhat limited in what they publicly demand of poems, so that often an individual critic seems to read only to search out a particular quality. The best critics, of course, read more widely, but even our best critics are im-

14

paled on an excessively uncomfortable dilemma. To the extent that they attempt to recognize the richness of individual poems, their criticism tends to lack theoretical consistency. Yet when they try for consistency, they are often blinded to the fullness of the poems. Our best practical critics are generally our worst theoreticians; and when by chance a critic does combine subtle theory and shrewd analysis, the two often have little in common.

The positions usually taken in evaluative criticism may be schematized quite simply, although the entire output of any one critic is likely to bulge over into several categories. I believe, though, that the kind of scheme I suggest helps to clarify the variety of positions in general use. I shall not attempt to do justice to individual critics because the bibliography of works analyzing the contributions and confusions of Eliot, Ransom, Tate, Winters, Brooks, and so on, grows constantly longer; [13] I see little reason to add to it. I am interested rather in what may be done and what has been done within the most extensively used approaches to literature; consequently, the same critic may appear in several sections of this book if his approach to literature is varied, self-contradictory, or has shown development.

The basic division of this study needs little explanation. Poems are said to have value either as imitations of something else or as achieved forms. The difficult fact is that either source of value, conceived simply, excludes the other, yet any respectable theory must in some way manage to include both. *Mimetic theories* are theories that value the poem as an imitation; all other theories are *formalistic*.

*Imitation* and *mimesis* are used very broadly here. Hazlitt provided the clue when he observed that the notion of imitation need not be limited to externals — actions, events, objects, and so on — but that it could with equal propriety be applied to internal happenings — thoughts, emotions, and dreams.[14] Anything outside the poem may be said to be re-created within the poem and so to lend the poem the kind of value it possesses. Thus a poem may imitate the personality or the experience of the poet; abstract pronouncements on morality and philosophy; social mores, norms, or ideals; perceived objects; other literary works; the unconscious. The list is, I believe, exhaustive; at least I know of no major mimetic system it does not include.

Each category generates its own kind of criticism, its own principles, favored types of poetry, and weaknesses. To admire Frost's "Mending Wall" for the concreteness with which it presents an experience is far different from admiring it because of its wise moral. The critic who does either will find his work moving in a predetermined direction, stressing some qualities and ignoring others; if he tries to have the poem both ways he will, under threat of inconsistency, feel compelled to show evidence that he understands the relation between the two qualities he admires. And obviously, when he moves to other poems, he will find the approach he has chosen will determine what he can consistently approve of.

Mimetic criticism dominated literary theory until the end of the eighteenth century. Plato repudiated art as an imitation of an imitation, and Aristotle replied that imitation delights and instructs. Horace's *utile* is but the representation of moral or social ideals; St. Thomas taught that poetry mirrored the harmony of the universe; Sidney justified poetry as a counterfeit of a second or ideal nature; Rymer contended that the fanning of passion to a white heat in *Othello* was like nothing in nature and therefore inartistic. Among English critics I could cite Spenser, Jonson, Pope, Addison, Johnson, and even Wordsworth to show the extent of their dependence upon mimetic standards. Critics of the past were as aware of the differences between reality and art as critics now, but they preferred to leave the relationship unspecified. It was usually enough to assume that the passions or the mind of the poet in some way refined the crude material of his experience; anything more was — and perhaps still is — speculation. Even genre criticism is mimetic in our sense because it judges the poem by standards outside itself, by conformity to an abstract pattern.

Mimetic criticism is still with us. An amusing instance of its vigor occurs in an exchange between F. R. Leavis and René Wellek concerning the "tangled boughs" passage in "Ode to the West Wind." Leavis was unable to make sense of the passage in terms of the way clouds and leaves naturally behave; Wellek helpfully pointed out that Shelley may have been describing leaves or leaves and clouds as reflected in water.[15] Both critics are invoking rather crude and obvious mimetic standards to support their evaluations of the Ode. John Crowe Ransom, certainly one of the most influential modern critics, writes that "mimesis is as much a passion as science is" and that the proper business of art is the imitation of the individual object.[16]

My categories of mimetic criticism may be made to overlap, logically or illogically. A theory could be developed, for example, along these lines: the poem reflects the personality of the poet (personality theory), but the poet is a man gifted with an exceptionally keen ethical and religious sense (morality or edification theory) in combination with unusually acute senses (perception theory); the poem is valuable because it is the work of a man with such equipment. The reader may make his own combinations at will and feel assured that he has come up with nothing new.

Formalistic criticism, on the other hand, at its purest

denies that the poem derives any value at all from the thing imitated, and may even deny imitation entirely. Poetic value is then said to arise from the creation of forms that are interesting because they are unique, novel, immediately appealing, and so on. Pure formalistic theories are rare; they tend to transpose into mimetic theories, as I shall show, in order to avoid circularity. Most recent critics would argue that poetry succeeds to the extent that it achieves a unique form which somehow reflects back upon the real world. The glory of art, they argue correctly, is that its freedom from scientific abstraction and practical exigencies makes possible the creation of cognitive structures unrealizable in any other way, and that to give man a new structure for cognition is to give him a new view of his world.

Formalistic criticism is based upon the insight that the ugly, the evil, and even the abstract are often a source of aesthetic pleasure, coupled with the corollary that we habitually accept in art what we would not tolerate in reality. It then assumes that imitation is not the cause of all (or of any) aesthetic pleasure and that such pleasure must issue from the arrangement of the material.

The theoretical foundations of the approach were established in English criticism by Coleridge and developed largely from his notions of organic form and the imagination.[17] The metamorphoses of these twin concepts cannot be traced here, but in contemporary criticism they have come to designate a closed, or relatively closed, system in which the tight integration of each aspect of the total structure permits no disruptive element. Art is then valued for its tightness of form rather than for its significance for life in general. Jacques Maritain has noted that modern poetry is characterized by "a remarkable search for self-purification . . . for the purification of poetry itself of all extraneous or adventitious elements,

or of a search after the pure essence of poetry." [18] The critics have both followed and led the poets.

Formalistic theories fall into three categories, depending upon their purity. Theories of closed form are the most pure; the poem is considered to be autonomous, a totally unique creation related only accidentally to the rest of the world. Theories of open form admit the significance of objective pattern, attempting to correlate the subjective response of the reader with the objective pattern of the poem. Theories of symbolic form accept the conclusions of the preceding and go on to consider the poem as a unique creation which, despite its uniqueness, presents in itself and through itself a picture of the universe unavailable elsewhere.

Throughout the following pages I shall assume the validity of the symbolic form approach. I believe I can show that, unlike mimetic theories, it neither prescribes nor proscribes the kind of content we may value in poetry and that it approaches the poem as a whole, with just respect for the craft, the power, and the mystery of poetry. Unlike theories of closed form, it restores the poem to the world, seeing poetry as analogous to other modes of knowledge.

# II

## THE MIRROR OF THE MAN
### Theories of Personality and Experience

Once we feel the power of poetry, we are likely to try to find its source. The favorite hunting ground after the start of the nineteenth century was the personality of the poet and the way he used his experience. Being in love, feeling a west wind, parting, rejoicing, ageing — these are common to poet and clod, for poets live in our world and use our language. The difference, then, seems to be not in what happens to the poet, but in what happens within him. Perhaps his receptors are more sensitive than ours; perhaps a built-in amplifier makes his experiences ring while ours ping; perhaps he is wiser than we and knows what we unsurely guess. Whatever the specific reason, the source of poetry may be within the poet's personality.

At about the turn of the nineteenth century poets seemed to awaken to the seriousness of their calling. Wordsworth described the poet as a man who saw more and understood better than others, as a philosopher returned to the cave enlightened by his vision and compelled to tell it. Personality theories, so stated, are not new; yet something new had happened. *The Prelude* is both a symptom and a cause, at once part of the rise of a movement and an instrument of its creation. By direct-

ing attention to the poet as well as the poem, Wordsworth (despite his intention) emphasized the differences between the poet and the ordinary man. When, for example, George Herbert prays poetically the prayer keeps God in the foreground; the poet is simply a generalized humble sinner, as in "Discipline":

> For my heart's desire
> Unto thine is bent;
>         I aspire
> To a full consent.

Wordsworth prays like this:

> My heart leaps up when I behold
> A rainbow in the sky:
> So was it when my life began;
> So is it now I am a man;
> So be it when I shall grow old,
>    Or let me die!
> The Child is father of the Man;
> And I could wish my days to be
> Bound each to each by natural piety.

Wordsworth's poem is about neither God nor sinners, but about his own wonderful self. He implies that he has some view of life, some special receptive equipment, that enables him to feel poetically. Pope boasted that he "lisped in numbers" and was proud to have perfected his gift; Wordsworth's pride is in his ability to react properly to experience. Although this new attitude worked for Wordsworth, it did not work for his successors. Byron and Shelley had not made the all-important journey from Plato's cave and so lacked the wisdom of Wordsworth; but thanks partly to Wordsworth, they had a theory of the poet as personality, a theory they were willing to exploit. That is why Byron and Shelley are so easy to caricature — they spent much of their energy becoming characters, as Tennyson did later, as Arnold did in his youth, as do many of Browning's dramatis personae. Still later, between Swinburne and Wilde, what had been the eccentricities of individuals degenerated into cultishness. Nor was the development limited to England: the *Sturm und Drang* writers in Germany, the Baudelaire-Verlaine group in France, Pushkin and Lermontov in Russia, Poe in America — all suggested by statement or example that the man who lived an ordinary life and whose responses were ordinary could not be a poet. The poet had become the personality, the poem its expression.

And, of course, the poets were supported by the theorists. As early as 1778 Herder described the best reading as "divination into the soul of the author." Even Tolstoy and Baudelaire could agree that, in Tolstoy's words, the artist "should experience feeling," and in Baudelaire's, "the artist, . . . the poet, should only paint in accordance with what he sees and with what he feels." [1] Perhaps Eugene Veron, representing still another pole of nineteenth-century thought, sums up the theory best: "*truth* and *personality*" are the "alpha and omega of art formulas; *truth* as to facts, and the *personality* of the artist." Truth is "our personality itself." [2] Modern aestheticians as different in their general approaches to literature as Croce and Richards, Maritain and Dewey, Bergson and Bradley, have accepted some of the implications of personality theory.

Recent personality theories grow out of either the intuitionist philosophy of Henri Bergson and Benedetto Croce or the relatively more pedestrian approaches of John Dewey and I. A. Richards. The former stress the artist's intuition, the latter his communicable experience.

Although the distinction between intelligence and intuition (the distinction upon which the more mystical theory is built) is hardly new, its contemporary importance dates from Bergson. For him, intuition is a conscious and immediate vision which both resembles the object seen and extends consciousness to an affirmation of "a psychological unconsciousness." Intelligence is a mere mediator which communicates the intuition.[3] Intuition, the amalgam of the unconscious and the most conscious life of the poet, is the object of aesthetic expression or (from a different point of view) the content to be expressed.

Croce works the same terminology somewhat differently, drawing up a list of contrasting features of the two forms of knowledge. Intuitive knowledge is obtained through the imagination and is a knowledge of individual things or individual relationships; it results in images. Logical knowledge, on the other hand, is obtained through the intellect and is a knowledge of universals and of the relations between them; it results in concepts.[4] Unlike most aestheticians, Croce considers intuition the sole source of art, carefully but insistently separating it from the form-content relationship, from the useful and the moral, from pure form, from pure beauty, and from its material embodiment.[5] As Croce's theory develops, the public work of art matters less and less, the private intuition more and more, until finally the critic has only the intuition to evaluate. And because each intuition is personal and unique, evaluation is impossible. The follower of Croce, like Croce himself, becomes the purely speculative theoretician or the historian; he has not the material to become a critic.

Croce values intuition because it is the best part of man's experience; the more empirical Dewey also values the best part of man's experience as the source of art, but would hardly call it intuition. Dewey sees the source of art as an "excitement about subject matter" which activates memories of previous experiences and translates them into "emotionalized images." [6] As the artist orders this welter of material into an aesthetic pattern, a "perceptible form" emerges which then may stimulate us to "go through in our own vital processes the processes the artist went through in producing the work" so that we "perfect the power to perceive." [7] But even though such perfection of our powers heightens our moral stature, the value of art is its ability to transmit the artist's most valuable experiences.

Other major aestheticians have similarly found the source of art at least partly within the experiences of the artist. Like Dewey, Samuel Alexander sees the origin of art in a passionate excitement about the experience and about its re-creation.[8] Jacques Maritain finds it in "that intercommunication between the inner being of things and the inner being of the human Self which is a kind of divination." [9] And even Richards cannot avoid a trace of personality theory. He argues that a major value of art is its ability to transmit complex experience and that artistic genius is probably the ability to draw upon vast stores of experience.[10] This minuscule anthology is not intended to imply that the over-all theories I have looked at are identical; I want only to suggest the extent and variety of personality theory in modern aesthetics.

Before turning to specifically literary criticism, I should say a few things about personality theories in general. First, they inevitably transpose into some other kind of theory because intuition and experience are essentially private and the work of art that we value is essentially public. A second difficulty is that neither intuitions nor experiences are intrinsically valuable, and that they are not all equally valuable. Even if we could prove that a poem perfectly embodies an intuition, we should still have to show why the intuition of a Shakespeare is more important than yours or mine. When we set up criteria for judging intuitions or experiences, we go beyond personality theory.

These difficulties carry over from aesthetics to literary theory and practical criticism. In criticism, personality theories take either the intuitionist approach of Croce or the more practical approach of Dewey. The following quotations set the tone of each type:

> I believe that criticism must concern itself, not only with the work of art in itself, but also with the process of writing, and with the writer's state of mind when inspired — that is to say, criticism must concern itself, not only with the finished work of art, but also with the workman, his mental activity and his tools.[11]

And:

> *literature (L) is the linguistic process through which a psycho-physiological experience (E) of one person leads to the production of a series of symbols which in turn evoke in another person a controlled experience (E) . . . similar to, though not identical with, the experiences (E) which resulted in the production of the symbol-series.*[12]

The first is by Sir Herbert Read, the second by Thomas Clark Pollock. Read is perhaps the most vocal and perceptive of the critics who explain the value of poetry chiefly in terms of the poet's sensibility; Pollock is perhaps the most modern in temper, the most positivistic, of the critics who base evaluative criteria primarily upon the transmission of the poet's experience.

The most convenient way to arrive quickly at Read's notion of poetry is to consider his distinction between poetry and prose. After dismissing formal and technical characteristics as "mechanical," he argues that they represent two distinct forms of mental activity; poetry is "creative" or "original," prose "constructive." [13] In dismissing technical and formal considerations, Read also dismisses the most obvious symptoms of the presence of poetry. For the reader, the distinction between poetry and prose lies not in some profound psychological characteristic of the writer, but in the way words are put together; or rather, if the reader senses the psychological difference, it is because certain techniques give him clues. More positively, to dismiss technique in favor of a problematic psychological event is to suggest that the critic ultimately judges the event. And for Read, the aesthetically important psychological event is private, unique, or eccentric. His contrast between character and personality makes this clear: character "is an impersonal ideal," personality a gathering of our individual "sentiments and emotions." He concludes that all poetry, in its widest sense, originates in the personality.[14]

From this point in personality theory we can logically pursue one of two lines: either the poet expresses a common emotion somehow intensified or made viable, or he expresses a distinct kind of emotion resulting from a special faculty given only to poets. The first line, because it emphasizes communication, quickly passes into a discussion of the effects of poetry and consequently will be discussed in the next chapter.

The second is Read's line. He wants a personal emotion in poetry that is neither the aesthetic emotion resulting from the enjoyment of art nor the emotion of creativity *per se*. It is, rather, the emotion the poet tries to put into his poem. Since with this kind of theory emotion cannot get into poetry unless the poet has experienced it, the approach tends either to demonism or to mysticism. The first, mainly of historical interest, views the poet either as a Faust who subjects himself to depravity (or who so poses) in order to experience the widest possible range of human emotions, or — again like Faust — as a man superior to conventional morality. Demonism is the mask that Byron found himself wearing and making the most of, that Swinburne vainly tried to assume, and that only Baudelaire and his French followers succeeded in growing into. The poet deliberately sets out to become "*voyant*," to arrive "at the unknown by deranging all of the senses" at the cost of immense personal suffering.[15] Although the notion of the demonic poet has been important both in literature and in criticism, it survives today chiefly on the faddist fringe of "beat" literature.

Read favors the more common view — the poet as mystic. In English literature the first significant and concerted expression of this position occurs in the work of the later metaphysicals, particularly Vaughan and Herbert, but the appropriate critical theory did not form until the time of Wordsworth and Coleridge. Briefly, criticism came to admit seriously and systematically the idea of the poet as seer, as one who had learned to read the "one mighty alphabet" of nature. The poetic personality as envisaged by Wordsworth, Coleridge, or the German transcendentalists need not be examined here, for the details are largely of historical interest; in broad outline, however, Read has kept the romantic conception of the poetic personality.

If the poet is a seer, what does he see that makes him different from ordinary men? For Read, he sees the "realm of essence" in moments of vision that are short-lived but profound. These visions, an approving quotation from Rilke seems to indicate, are memories of reality which take on a special quality.[16] Or perhaps the poet feels rather than sees them, for he creates "in words an objective equivalence of his emotional experience: the words may not make sense, but they make the emotion." [17] Or perhaps the content is cognitive, for the poet "achieves a thought capable of taking on a new aspect for every new generation — he enriches humanity with a sum which is not spent at once, but goes on earning interest indefinitely." [18] For all this, we still do not know what Read means. The inspiration seems to be an emotional urge which leads to the vision, a blind stimulus to create. Although in the heat of the creative emotion images present themselves ready-made, Read admits that "a good deal of selection and rejection of images still goes on." [19] He rightly suggests that both emotion and judgment function in the creation of poetry, but this is merely a truism; for Read it is also a difficulty because he insists that judgment and vision belong to different worlds. By what principle does judgment reject inspiration? Would the judgment not reduce poetry to prose — unless the judgment itself is inspired? Read's terminology suggests that poetry expresses an "intellectual vision" achieved without the mediation of the intellect.

Read's notion of the realm of essence would seem to avoid the subjectivism (or confusion) of such a position. The interest on the capital sum with which the poet enriches humanity is earned from "the accumulation of selected perceptions . . . [from which] a general view of life may be constructed, and this general view may possess great ethical and aesthetic value." [20] Despite all the rigamarole, then, about personality, inspiration, essences, and what have you, the value of poetry is apparently its content of ideas. Yet other bits of Read's theory suggest that he does not mean this at all.

Read's essences, for example, tend to get mixed up with the Freudian unconscious mind. Using the notion that there are layers of consciousness and unconsciousness, Read argues that upheavals sometimes cause the deeper layers to erupt and expose areas known only to artists and mystics.[21] If we accept Read's belief that there are no formal differences between poetry and prose, we shall not be able to distinguish between art and dream.

Any attempt to apply Read's work to the evaluation of a poem leads quickly to a dead end; everything he offers to explain poetry — essences, emotion, conscious or unconscious knowledge — leads rapidly to the unexplained or the unexplainable. The very variety of explanations Read offers should make his work suspect. Although a poem may offer any of the values he claims, the theorist's job is not to grasp desperately for any and all possible explanations, but to show their interrelationship. The major objection to Read's theory is not that he makes the base of poetry so broad, but that he would have poetry rest on several separate bases.

What happens when Read applies his theory? He is not only a sensitive reader, but also extremely well informed and prolific, so that if his view of poetry could lead to a sound criticism, his discussions of poems should be unusually valuable.

His practical criticism centers on his notions of imagery and form. He wants poetry to be visual, and ranks poets as visualizers (Shakespeare, Shelley, and Blake) or as metaphorical poets (Dryden, Pope, and Wordsworth); the former are said to be the better poets.[22] Perhaps Read semantically connects the vision of the aesthetic theory with the visual of the critical theory, possibly because he is one of those persons whose visual sense is more highly developed than his other senses; his interest in painting and the content of his own poetry suggest as much. Yet a personal peculiarity, even though common, can hardly serve as the basis for criticizing poems. As Samuel Alexander has pointed out, the peculiar advantage of poetry is that it uses words, and words are able to go beyond their imagistic implications.

Nor is Read's notion of form usable. Although he has argued that the essential characteristic of poetry is "material" rather than "formal," he later denies much of the force of this by arguing that the only useful criticism is one that treats the form-content relationship.[23] The difficulty is that he follows Croce in failing to differentiate between intuition and expression, between form and conception. What Read cannot admit, and what would put him in the mainstream of contemporary criticism, is that language itself is creative. In the act of creation the poet may discover what is in himself, but he also discovers the relevant potentialities of the words themselves. It is the latter discovery that is important for readers and that is the legitimate interest of criticism.

Since Read's version of personality theory lacks consistency and clarity, a theory developed more scientifically, more rigorously, might make a more valuable contribution to evaluative theory. Thomas Clark Pollock attempts such a scientific explanation of literature. Where Read's approach was almost consciously mystic, Pollock's is self-consciously scientific; where the former was concerned with the more esoteric phases of psychology, the latter is concerned with semantics; where Read was chiefly interested in the private poetic experience, Pollock is chiefly interested in its public communication.

Here is Pollock's definition of literature:

the utterance of a series of symbols capable of evoking in the mind of a reader a controlled experience. This is of course a contracted definition. A somewhat fuller statement would be that it has as its purpose the expression of an experience of a writer through the utterance of a series

30

of symbols capable of evoking in the mind of a properly qualified reader a controlled experience similar to, though of course not identical with, that of the writer.[24]

Literature, including lyric poetry, is to be judged by its success in conveying an experience from the mind of the writer to the mind of the reader.

Relying heavily on Richards, Pollock distinguishes between literature and scientific writing; the symbolism of the former is "evocative," that of the latter is "referential." Referential symbolism refers chiefly to objects, but fails at least in part because it is based upon what Whitehead calls the "fallacy of misplaced concreteness." Meaning involves experiences, Pollock argues, and experiences are precisely what referential symbolism avoids.[25] *Salt,* for example, suggests not only a particular group of chemicals, but also human experiences with the material; hence the chemical formula, the purely referential symbol, is less accurate and less complete than a literary description evoking the taste and feel of salt. The formula refers only to the object, the description to the nexus of factors surrounding it. Although I cannot pause here to explain why, Pollock's argument, it seems to me, restores to literature some of the significance and dignity it lost with the rise of logical positivism, which charged that poetry (and, presumably, all literature) "does not contain knowledge." [26] The best that literature can do, then, the only kind of fact permitted it, is the record of what a given author experienced at a given moment. Thus *The Waste Land* refers to a period in the life of T. S. Eliot; it is irrelevant to our experience of the world. Pollock's answer — that as human beings knowledge of mere things is less significant to us than knowledge of how things affect us — is convincing.

Unfortunately, Pollock's distinction between referen-

tial and evocative symbolism breaks down because he
sees it as absolute, not relative, and because he insists
that poets "express and communicate their own privately
discriminable experiences." [27] Actually, literature, including lyric poetry, is both referential and evocative.
The image-laden line

Poor Soul, the center of my sinful earth

derives much of its splendor, much of its specifically literary quality, precisely because the words are used refer-
entially. "Poor" is evocative, a metaphorical description
of a subjective condition; but its referential meaning
grows increasingly important as the sonnet continues.
The correct line of argument is that words evoke to the
extent that they refer. An economist writing "poor"
would feel compelled to limit its meaning to only one
referent. The poet prefers to build upon a multiplicity of
referents. As Shakespeare uses the word, it refers to an
economic condition and to much else.

Pollock is also unable to say how much of the poet's
experience the poem actually transmits. He gives two
contradictory opinions, and the more useful runs counter
to the general direction of his theory. He suggests at one
point that literature controls the reader's experience
rather than giving him an experience because the "demand characters" of the poem manipulate his expectations and thereby control, momentarily, the direction of
his experience.[28] As Pollock indicates in a footnote, a
very productive approach to criticism could derive from
the notion of the poem as a "control device" functioning
through the organization of its "demand characters."
This, though, is not the path Pollock takes.

Instead, the tenor of his argument is that the poem
gives an experience substantially like that which inspired
the poem. He insists upon the actual communication of

the experience partly to avoid the dangers inherent in the notion of aesthetic experience — a notion dangerous because it may lead to the conclusion that the experiences evoked by literature are essentially different from other human experiences. By denying aesthetic experience, Pollock hopes to avoid the aesthetic-mystic confusion that vitiates many personality theories (including Read's), to keep the range of literary subject matter and thematic content as wide as possible, and to circumvent the task of justifying a thoroughly nonutilitarian evaluation of literature. He hopes to accomplish these by insisting upon the reality of the literary experience, both for the reader and for the writer.

Yet some kind of concept of aesthetic experience is necessary for at least four reasons. If literature tightly controls the experience of the reader, it would seem that a relatively controlled experience differs from a relatively uncontrolled one. Moreover, even assuming the perfect poem, if literature is the transmission of experience from the poet to the reader, a second-hand experience is likely to be different from a first-hand experience; reading "Tintern Abbey" is not quite like seeing it. And, still assuming the perfect poem, differences in personality between reader and writer would place identical experiences in different contexts, would make them, in short, different experiences. But most conclusively, readers are moved by words, by symbols or signs of things rather than by things themselves; radically different stimuli should produce radically different reactions.

Because he denies aesthetic experience, Pollock has great difficulty in working out an evaluative theory. After two hundred pages of highly technical jargon purporting to show precisely what literature is, he is forced to distinguish between literature, which expresses an experience actually had by the poet, and pseudo-literature, which evokes an experience not had by the poet.[29] Because pseudo-literature uses all the means of real literature, the only difference between them is the purpose of the author. Hence the *Odyssey* is, perhaps, not literature because we do not know Homer's purpose; Shakespeare's work is suspect because the poems and plays may have been means of professional advancement rather than re-creations of his experience as Cleopatra. With admirable honesty, Pollock admits that no one can *prove* whether a work is literature or pseudo-literature, although intelligent readers *know*. Nor is this all, for even if we did discover that Shakespeare did not write from his own experience the discovery would have no effect upon *Hamlet, Lear*, and *Romeo and Juliet*.[30]

If I have followed Pollock correctly, thus far the only criteria to which his scientism has led are the unknowable intention of the poet, supported by the unprovable instinct of an intelligent reader, capped with the admission that the intention is, after all, irrelevant to the value of the work.

I have, perhaps, been unfair in attempting to correlate Pollock's functional description of literature with an evaluative system, but certainly one of the criteria for evaluation is whether or not a thing functions as it should. Pollock suggests a second criterion more explicitly: *"the value of the experience* which is communicated." [31] The critic is to estimate that value "in relation to (1) his own immediate personal needs for experience, and (2) the general socio-ethical system which he really, as distinct from verbally, accepts." [32] Both of these criteria are questionable. To dispose of the second first, one can appreciate in quick succession the earnest tone of Sidney's "Leave Me, O Love," and the courtly playfulness of Marlowe's "The Passionate Shepherd to His Love." Literary experiences may reflect diametrically

34

opposed views of man's relationship with men or God, and still be enjoyed and valued by the same person. I shall not comment upon the absurdity of arguing that a reader's beliefs change as he moves from, say, Homer to Hopkins. This difficulty, it may be noted, is a direct consequence of Pollock's denial of aesthetic experience.

The problems involved in using a critic's "own immediate needs" are more formidable. Pollock may be right; a reader's evaluation of a poem may be determined by his immediate needs, needs which change from reader to reader and from moment to moment. Yet surely the literary theorist should put up more of a fight before admitting what puts him out of business. Pollock is like the physician who, realizing that he does not understand the nature of good health, diagnoses each case simply by asking the patient how he feels. Despite the doctor's honesty, the patient may feel cheated. Literary criticism, like medical diagnosis, is valuable only if it describes the condition of the poem in reasonably objective terms. Actually Pollock's retreat into subjectivism is unnecessary even within the context of his own theory. If a literary experience is a controlled experience, as Pollock claims, the poem in part determines those needs. It is not unusual, I believe, for a reader to begin by browsing (with no immediate need other than to pass a few moments) and end by finding himself trapped within the poem. The best literature, perhaps, is that which, by playing upon the narrative, thematic, and aesthetic expectations of the reader, is most likely to trap him, not once, but repeatedly.

Like other theorists who base their systems upon the communication of the poet's experience, Pollock finally has to abandon his position by claiming that the final judgment of experience is neccessarily ethical.[33] If we make the ethical judgment solely in terms of our personal ethical system, the reading of literature becomes a mere narcissistic indulgence of our private moral sensibilities. If we make the ethical judgment in other terms, if our ethical sensibility is shaped by the poem, we are beyond personality theory.

The approaches represented by Read and Pollock constitute the extremes of personality theory. Neither the sensitivity of the one nor the scientism of the other establishes criteria for the judgment of poetry. Yet personality theory is so deeply rooted that many of this century's most respected critics have evolved elaborate stratagems to avoid it. It has, after all, much to recommend it. "What can we reason but from what we know?" may be a truism, but it is nevertheless true that the poet writes only from what he perceives, knows, and feels. And unlike other mimetic theories which circumscribe the limits of poetry to more or less narrow radii, personality theories tend to admit the entire range of a poet's experience. Both considerations exert a strong common-sense appeal, and it should therefore not be surprising that Kenneth Burke, John Crowe Ransom, and T. S. Eliot — to cite merely some of the more important figures — have had to reckon with it.

Burke, for example, reverses completely Pollock's distinction between literature and pseudo-literature. Arguing that "the self-expression of the artist, *qua* artist, is not distinguished by the uttering of emotion, but by the evocation of emotion," [34] he shifts the entire basis of judgment from the experience lived by the poet to the experience formed by the poem.

T. S. Eliot's relation to personality theory is more difficult to summarize for a number of reasons. For one, Eliot was not a systematic critic, but a gifted and supremely sensitive amateur reacting to particular works and particular issues. He is provocative; his general statements are sufficiently pertinent and wise to compel thought, but cryptic and undeveloped enough to permit his would-be disciples to set out in diverse and even in opposite directions. Moreover, he has a habit of making apparently forceful statements, then qualifying all but the last drop of meaning from them. A final difficulty, and one especially important here, is his historical position. As one of the first distinctly modern critics, he wrote when neither the techniques nor the vocabulary of criticism was as advanced as now; and to accomplish his mission as a critic he was forced, even with his imperfect weapons, to do battle against the cult of personality. He is one of those who, as Murray Krieger observed, "desire to justify classicism with the theoretical tools of romanticism, yet without permitting a reconciliation between the two." [35]

The crux of Eliot's early antagonism to the cult of personality is contained in a brief passage from the very influential "Tradition and the Individual Talent." "The more perfect the artist," Eliot writes, "the more completely separate in him will be the man who suffers and the mind which creates; the more perfectly will the mind digest and transmute the passions which are its material." [36] What Eliot has done is to split the poet into man plus creator, so that there is no necessary connection between the experiences of the two halves except that the "impressions and experiences" of the one "combine in peculiar and unexpected ways." [37]

Because Eliot tried both to avoid and to challenge personality theories while using their vocabulary, his early theoretical work, despite his intention, forces us to consider the mind of the poet. But with a difference, for with Eliot it is the activity of the mind that is important — not its content. The mind is a "medium" which "works to combine" and "transmute" experiences.[38] It would seem, from the separation of man and poet Eliot makes and from his emphasis upon impersonal emotion, that he would have moved toward either a formalistic theory or a conception of aesthetic emotion; the fact is that as he grew older he turned more and more toward a personality theory.

Several things help account for the change of direction. Eliot's religious conversion is certainly important, but criticism itself had also been converted. Eliot had succeeded in fathering a school of criticism; or better, he lived to see hosts of bright young disciples galloping off in every which way armed with one or another of his precepts. Perhaps they galloped too far and too fast to suit Eliot. No matter how brilliantly a poet might write, he is not a great poet in Eliot's later view unless we feel his works "to be united by one significant, consistent, and developing personality." [39]

Still, Eliot makes a rather typical refinement in his adoption of personality theory; the poem is not an expression of personality, nor — as he had it earlier — an escape from personality, but rather a result of personality. The poem expresses "a general truth" which somehow retains "all the particularity" of the poet's experience.[40] This latest view merges with morality or edification theory, which I shall discuss in the following chapter. What is interesting here is Eliot's double relation to personality theories. After early rebellion against any kind of mimetic standard, he has come to place progressively greater emphasis upon the personality of the poet and the meaning of the poem.

John Crowe Ransom's attack on personality theories has been more direct, more consistent, and more convincing. Insisting unequivocally upon the "anonymity" of poetry,[41] he sees art either as a restraining force or as the result of restraint; either way, it is an alternative to the simple and crude grabbing of the desired object. Man desires to seize, to use, the object; art restrains him by removing "him to where he cannot hurt the object." [42] All the formal traditions of art operate to keep the poet and poem apart; as Ransom expresses it later in *The World's Body*, the poet dons a mask and costume in order to prevent his personality from showing through the work.

This is by no means a complete survey of personality theories and their opposition in contemporary criticism, but it does present the main outlines of the approach, as it applies to the judgment of poetry. Its two chief weaknesses should be apparent. The privacy of both personality and experience forces a transformation into some other kind of view because the relevant question becomes "What constitutes a valuable experience or a valuable personality?" And secondly, whether emphasis is upon the value of the experience, the uniqueness of the personality, or the maturity of the poet, the theory calls attention to the poet rather than to his poem. Biography, though helpful, is not criticism.

Moreover, within the framework of personality theories, there persists a tendency to limit the personality of the poet to emotion, feeling, sensibility, or some other single aspect of the total character of man. Eliot and others have opposed such limitations (and sometimes imposed their own), but, nevertheless, the tendency to maintain the separation of the poet and the man of knowledge, the separation of poetry and rationality, remains. Poetry is then left with mere emotional content.

To the extent that personality theories stress emotion, they generally leave a number of questions unanswered. What is the emotion expressed? Is it a personal emotion, a reaction to external reality, or simply a need to create? In other words, exactly what is the nature of the inspiration that the poem is to embody? And, if emotion is the basis of poetry, how do we distinguish the poet from the neurotic? And finally, why should a reader prefer canned emotion to fresh?

A second series of difficulties arises from the fact that readers are affected by poems, not by poets. Words, melodies, tempi, meanings, suggestions, pauses, images — these move the reader, and only through these does he know the poem and only because of these does he care about the poet. It does not take an especially perceptive critic to distinguish the letters of Keats from his poems; some arrangements of words are poetic and some are not, and either may or may not express the poet's personality. As a result, theorists who explain poetry by personality cannot account adequately for poetic form and for the way language operates to make a coherent form. If the poem expresses something that pre-exists, language must be assumed to be thoroughly passive. The critic must assume that the poet masters completely a completely pliable medium, otherwise the inspiration would be lost, altered, or distorted in the act of creation. Yet such alterations occur; language is a structure of sounds, grammatical relations, and meanings which the poet must in part respect. To violate radically the structure of language is to be totally unintelligible.

Finally, personality theories are inevitably circular. The poem is valuable to the extent that it reflects the poet's personality; his personality is known largely through the poem. I know of no critic who would argue seriously that "Sumer Is Icumen In" is not a fine lyric simply because we know nothing of its author.

Despite the difficulties, however, personality theories do provide a valuable insight into the nature and worth of poems. By focusing on the poet, they force the critic to add another dimension to his appreciation of the work — a dimension that Lionel Trilling, writing about Keats's letters, called the "virtue of potentiality." [43]

Awareness of the personality behind the poem and respect for its worth forces the critic beyond the inwardness of his own experience and into a realization of another and possibly far different world. One of the values of literature is its use as a human document. To know of Coleridge's personality is to be able to find a quality in his work that is otherwise not so readily apparent. The hardheaded denial of such material or the claim that it is not "aesthetic" is valid only within a very narrow conception of literary value. The denial is not valid if one of the tasks of criticism is to explain the total value of the poem, to explain why one work endures and another does not. The error — and this is an error common to all critical schools — is to suppose that poetry must rely upon a predetermined and single source of value.

# III

## THE MIRROR OF MORALITY
### Edification Theories

Both Pollock, who finally concluded that the judgment of poetry is an ethical judgment, and Read, who would have poetry lay up capital in some "realm of essences," had to abandon personality theory and stress the poem's "message." The difference between personality theories and what, for want of a better term, I shall call *edification theories* depends upon what the critic expects the poem to imitate. Edification theories judge the poem as a reflection of a moral or philosophical truth. To evaluate a poem wholly or in part as a statement of eternal verities, as a vehicle for maxims about the good life, as a statement about man's relation to God, the universe, or other men — to apply any of these standards is to judge the poem within the framework of edification theory. The evaluative formula of a pure edification theory is simple: the worth of a poem is directly proportionate to the validity and greatness of its content.

Despite the best efforts of the most productive critics since the 1920's, poems are still judged by their morals. We expect a writer with the interests of Alfred Kazin to ask that an author give us "a clue to the world." [1] Nor are we surprised when George Orwell finds that our reaction to a writer is always a reaction to what he says.[2] But we are surprised when Austin Warren, a major force in modern criticism, retreats into an edification theory by arguing that Edward Taylor's "Meditation Eight" is saved partly by the power of its theme.[3] And Randall Jarrell, one of our most influential younger poet-critics, summarizes his approval of Frost's "Provide, Provide" by writing that "it is full of the deepest, and most touching, moral wisdom." [4]

At least two good reasons account for the vitality of the moral view of poetry. The first is that a significant part of man's values are moral, and the expression of such a basic kind of value enriches literature. David Daiches concludes an exceptionally shrewd defense of formal analysis with the observation that forms exist to express, and the expression of aspects of "man's fate is, in fact, directly or indirectly, the sole subject of art." [5] If art is to interest, it must deal with man's interests. For the intelligent reader, man's relation to man and man's relation to his universe — morality and philosophy — are dominant interests.

The second reason for the continued vitality of edification theories is applicable to literature but not to other arts. Yvor Winters, with characteristic sharpness, argues that because rational import cannot be eliminated from words, it cannot be eliminated from literature; to admit this is to be forced to admit that the quality of thought in a poem affects the quality of the poem.[6]

Yet a third factor keeps edification theories in contention among the rival schools of criticism — the notion that the aesthetic is somehow less valuable and less fundamental than either morality or truth. Eric Gill's "look after goodness and truth, and beauty will take care of herself" [7] states this view at its most extreme. Although not even Winters, the most conservative among major literary critics, would go this far, the attitude occasionally finds its way into criticism. The usual version is that if the writer sees the truth clearly enough, effective literature results automatically.

Historically, edification theories are as old as aesthetics. Plato, sometimes considering art as morally dangerous and sometimes as inspired, and therefore irrational, set the pattern for the two basic types of edification theory. Aristotle reversed Plato by considering art as the imitation of a universal or an ideal rather than as an imitation of an imitation, but the reversal is not a new basis for literary theory since art is still an imitation and still affects us morally. Without exaggeration, the views of Plato and Aristotle's compromise set the problems and answers for literary criticism until the end of the eighteenth century.

German idealism at the turn of the nineteenth century had as revolutionary an effect on edification theories as it had had on personality theories. Describing the change that came about after Dr. Johnson, T. S. Eliot remarks that we no longer expect a poem to be intentionally didactic.[8] The quality and nature of didacticism changed as theoreticians and poets became interested in developing a precise formulation of the role of content in poetry. Addison, for example, despite all his eighteenth-century charm as a writer and his perception as a reader, could not get much beyond the notion that the aim of literature is to instruct and please. Criticism needed an epistemology that would closely link perception of particulars, emotional involvement, and intellectual apprehension. German idealism provided the epistemology.

With comparatively few exceptions, epistemology had been dominated by the assumption that reason is superior to sensation, to will, and to imagination. The result in poetics was emphasis upon truth — factual truth, universal truth, or ideal truth; pure art was merely decorative, the cherry flavoring in the bitter medicine. Because the earlier theories placed truth on a pedestal, they lost the ability to see the poem as a whole.

What happened at the end of the eighteenth century was, to use another metaphor, a change from a telescopic to a microscopic view of the universe. Alexander Pope, inviting St. John to "Expatiate free o'er all this scene of man" expressed a complete view of life. He invites St. John to stand far from what they are viewing, to note its general outlines. And there is a curious feature of distant prospects, whether they be visual or intellectual: disorder is lost sight of; reality appears as neatly patterned, so that if one looks from a mountain top he feels safe in asserting that the garden is green, the ploughed field brown, the house white. But moving closer, he finds that the garden contains patches of other colors; what had appeared to be a knowable, measurable green square is now a hodgepodge of shapes and colors. The brown field has bits of golden stubble, some grayish rocks, and flecks of green; and the house has an occasional spot of dirt and a patch or two where the original color of the wood shows through. The same thing happens with intellectual perspectives. When I was an undergraduate, life was simple, the eighteenth century classic, and the nineteenth century romantic. Now I have to account for Thomson, Young, Blake, and Landor. The point is that Pope "expatiating" and Blake seeing "a World in a Grain of Sand" depend upon two different outlooks — the former is distant and rational; nature is orderly, judgments are made about it, and literature expresses those judgments. After the eighteenth century, didactic content could not be conceived of so simply. Epistemology now put imagination on an equal, and often superior, footing with reason. Metaphor replaced direct statement as the principal carrier of literature's messages because the universe itself was conceived of metaphorically, with each part a reflection of the whole.

Thus during the reign of German idealism critics and poets were learning that literature could teach without making explicit statements — or, more generally and more accurately, the mechanism by which literature teaches was described more precisely than it had been. The themes of literature were no longer thought of as effectively stated and predigested truths, but rather as reminders of something in nature that would illuminate the infinite. The scope of serious poetry widened. If everything is a symbol with potentially profound ramifications, everything in the poem is of profound importance. But what English lyric poetry gained in high seriousness, it sacrificed in elegance and ceremonious charm.

Keats, the only likely candidate for the title of "aesthete" among the major romantic poets, repudiates the old didacticism and accepts the new in his letter to Reynolds (3 February 1818):

> We hate poetry that has a palpable design upon us — and if we do not agree, seems to put its hand in its breeches pocket. Poetry should be great and unobtrusive, a thing which enters into one's soul, and does not startle or amaze it with itself, but with its subject.

The subject, quite possibly, is philosophical or moral, for in the famous "Mansions of Many Apartments" letter (3 May 1818), Keats praises Wordsworth for exploring the "dark passages" and finding there "Philosophy, human and divine." Since the best poets of the time were philosophically ambitious and the belief that the trivial reflects the infinite was dominant, the pastoral, the light lyric, and the occasional poem — those stalwarts of earlier lyric poetry — became shallow absurdities.

Our present, relatively sophisticated attitude toward the didactic in poetry is the legacy of writers of the romantic period. They left behind the firm conviction that poetry is somehow an instrument of human betterment, and the equally firm conviction that it should not be overtly didactic. Neither conviction is in danger so long as some system of philosophical idealism prevails. As long as the world of tables and chairs and grass and stone and space and time is seen as the reflection of some richer world, imagination is more important than reason, poetry more true than science or metaphysics. When science was relatively weak and metaphysics strongly poetic, literary theories could safely maintain the opposition between poetry and science. But as science triumphed by demonstrating its control over nature, and as philosophy consequently oriented itself more toward science, the difficulties of defending literary truth increased. The heirs of romanticism found themselves fighting a rearguard action, attacked by both the new positivism and the proponents of a return to the older didacticism.

Samuel Alexander's position is a typical return to the older didacticism. Claiming the ultimate discontinuity of beauty and truth, he must argue that they require separate judgments. Subject matter and form account for greatness and beauty respectively, and greatness and beauty are the objects of the double valuation of art.[9] Double valuation, unfortunately, is probably more a theoretical fiction than a habit of readers; time and critics have a way of rejecting (or at least of pushing into the background) works that are deficient in either form or content. In practice, the judgment that a poem is profound but poorly done (or superficial but artful) is also a prophecy that it will not long endure.

The notion of multiple valuation is not, of course, peculiar to Alexander. D. W. Gotshalk saw the need for sixteen kinds of aesthetic judgment, plus innumerable other judgments ranging from the spiritual and cultural to the commercial and recreational.[10] Mortimer Adler sees truth as something added to art and separates the question of what is said from the question of how well it is said.[11] I doubt, though, that we can be certain of what is said unless it is well said; if expression is imperfect, the best we can do is to guess at meaning.

Two of the complex attempts of modern aesthetics to retain some of the features of edification theory and to avoid multiple valuation should be examined in more detail. John Dewey's work will represent the more immediately contemporary approach, and the neo-Thomistic aesthetics of Jacques Maritain will show a recent interpretation of the problems in terms of an older philosophy.

Dewey forcefully opposes any separation of form and content, finding in theories that make the division a "fundamental fallacy." His attempt to avoid the "separation of the live creature from the environment in which it lives" [12] is based on the assumption that

> expression strikes below the barriers that separate human beings from one another. Since art is the most universal form of language, since it is constituted, even apart from literature, by the common qualities of the public world, it is the most universal and freest form of communication. . . . That art weds man and nature is a familiar fact. Art also renders men aware of their union with one another in origin and destiny.[13]

Art "weds man and nature" because "underneath the rhythm of every art and of every work of art there lies, as a substratum in the depths of the subconsciousness, the basic pattern of the relations of the live creature to his environment." [14] Art, embodying "full and intense ex-

48

figure rather than a radical innovating force. Thus much of the confusion in Eliot's work results from his attempt to found his theory upon the very insights he was attacking. His conclusion that modern poetry must be complex because the poet has complex things to say about a complex world is based upon the assumption that poetry must reflect the world; like the romantics, he accepts the correspondence theory of art — that the form of the poem corresponds to the intention of the poet and thereby to the form of the world. Eliot may think his world noisier and busier than Coleridge's, but each sees poetry as the reflection of his world.

From here Eliot's criticism could move in one of two directions: he could evaluate a poem by arguing that its form is or is not appropriate to its content, or he could evaluate a poem by arguing that the content is or is not worthy of expression. He uses both standards. The former is Eliot at his best, but even at his best his technique is theoretically unsound. He can say extremely perceptive things about individual poems and even about poetry as a whole, but the suggestion of a double standard always remains in his criticism. His contention that "only good style in conjunction with permanently interesting content can preserve" [23] is typical.

It is interesting that when Eliot criticizes Milton's poetry he does so because he senses a separation of form and content. The "musical significance" (or "auditory imagination") overwhelms the other possible values of Milton's poems because, Eliot urges, Milton permits one phase of his virtuosity to develop unchecked. But this lack of integration is really symptomatic of a failure of sensibility, a failure to integrate sensory data into a meaningful experience.[24] Although "a thought to Donne was an experience," [25] to Milton, presumably, thought was thought and euphony euphony; to the extent that they are separated in the poem, the poem is flawed.

Eliot's line of reasoning here could have been made more sound theoretically had he been willing to broaden his terminology to refer to the poem rather than to the poet. He approaches the right method when he implies that poetry may express "the emotional equivalent of thought," [26] although I am not sure I know what "the emotional equivalent of thought" is because, as Eliot himself has remarked, there are no substitutes for either. I assume that Eliot, like Dewey, is arguing for the fusion of thought, emotion, and (if we include the notion of the "objective correlative" here) sensation. But rather than emphasizing now one, now another, of these elements, it seems sounder to argue that a poem transmits a complete experience. It differs from other kinds of writing not because it emphasizes one or the other element, but because it presents various elements in an experiential unity. It is not necessary to argue that the poem transmits experience without distortion; claiming that the poem transmits experience suggests only that, like real experience, a poetic experience is at once unified and multidimensional. One could then argue that to exaggerate any element — the sensory, the emotional, the intellectual — is to distract the reader and so prevent him from feeling the high degree of integration possible in fine poetry. This is the kind of theoretical position Eliot approached but never quite reached.

To move to specifics, Eliot criticizes Tennyson's line

moans round with many voices

as "too poetical" to be the highest poetry because such "overloading" distracts "us from the main issue." [27] He is right, but not precise. The line is not "too poetical," it

54

is too onomatopoeic; the auditory image distracts the reader from attending to more important things. The basic error in Eliot's critique is his division of the poem into some problematic "main issue" with "poetical" parts.

Eliot's criticism, then, tends to keep thought ("main issue") and technique (the "poetical") as separate and detachable parts, each of which he can discuss in isolation. The result is a body of practical criticism that is much too facile. I have already cited the reason for his inability to read Shelley; he could not read Milton because he disliked the theology.[28] Yet he admires Shakespeare's work even though the philosophy is weak.[29] When Eliot criticizes the poetry of Shelley and Milton because the thought is inferior, but approves of the philosophically weak Shakespeare, precisely what standards are being applied? He persists in raising the question, and persists equally hard in avoiding an answer.

Since Eliot has at times attached great importance to meaning in poetry, we should expect a working out of the problems implicit in its relation to the whole poem. He offers two solutions. One argues that in some poetry (Eliot characteristically neglects to tell us which kinds) meaning merely diverts and quiets the reader's mind, "much as the imaginary burglar is always provided with a bit of nice meat for the house-dog." [30] He accepts this view, possibly because since the 1930's he has found much poetry that he admires but cannot consent to intellectually. This also probably accounts for his second solution, which is a more serious but hardly a more satisfactory restatement of the first. It amounts to establishing a degree of credence which, in connection with his discussion of "Tintern Abbey," he calls "acceptability." [31] More generally, he is willing to substitute for truth the presentation of a "view of life" that "the reader can accept as coherent, mature, and founded on the facts of experience." [32] Although substituting the criterion of maturity for truth as the test of poetry permits Eliot to enjoy a greater variety of poems, the standard is still largely subjective. "Maturity" is as vague a concept as "truth" and just as capable of shifting definitions from person to person. Interestingly, as Eliot has become more positive in his personal beliefs, he has tended to consider truth in poetry proportionately less significant.

Other critics have analyzed the place of meaning in poetry more systematically than has Eliot, but his consideration is especially valuable because he is aware of the ramifications of the problem. He may not always come to grips with the difficulties, and he rarely solves them; but he does have an invaluable ability to throw them into sharp relief. More important, however, is the fact that Eliot has come closer — in his extremely disconnected way — to showing the full complexity of the problem of meaning than have more systematic critics. That is why Eliot's acceptance of meaning in poetry as a kind of non-irritant pacifier is important. His work shows the difficulties that beset even the most perceptive of readers when they attempt to discuss poetry without the kind of support that only an adequately developed theory can provide. The value of a theory is not that it inhibits the reader's reaction to poetry — that would be the greatest disservice it could commit — but that it forces him to consider his fleeting reactions, his moment-by-moment preoccupations, in a larger context than otherwise. If the theory is adequate and consistent, it forces him to become increasingly aware of as much of the poem as he can grasp.

Although William Empson has not, at least in his published work, discussed the problem of belief as variously as has Eliot, he has nevertheless offered a partial solution to one aspect of it. The basic problem is that men tend to think of themselves as possessing a certain quite definite set of ideas and ideals which determine their thoughts, feelings, actions, and judgments. What happens, then, when a person reads a poem which expresses ideas obviously hostile to his own, and when he finds himself still admiring the poem? Logically, one might expect a violent clash, an angry slamming shut of the book and a mental note to avoid the works of that author. This sometimes happens, but more often the reader remains quite calm. Empson accounts for our tolerance of hostile beliefs by talking of the "present state of indecision of . . . the cultured world." [33] We are accustomed to a barrage of conflicting opinions, beliefs, reports, and attitudes and to not reacting when thoughts unlike our own are expressed. Our only reservation is that what is expressed must be able to be incorporated into a rational system. This account of our tolerance of radically differing systems of thought is like Eliot's, but gets behind his and is probably more precise, especially if one discounts Empson's assertion that such tolerance is modern — Renaissance Catholics admired Homer and Puritans admired Dante. But putting aside the question of whether or not such tolerance is modern, we still have to explain how poetry can make an otherwise unacceptable point of view palatable and to account for the increased thrill we get when we encounter a poem that seems to coincide with our personal convictions.

I. A. Richards treats the problem of meaning more completely than Empson and more clearly than Eliot, but like Eliot he argues both for and against truth in poetry without reconciling his arguments. I shall look at only one of Richards' solutions here; the other — that poetry is pseudostatement and therefore without reference to the real world — will be examined in another context. In *Principles of Literary Criticism* he argues that "the arts are our storehouse of recorded values. . . . The arts, if rightly approached, supply the best data for deciding what experiences are more valuable than others." [34] This certainly gives literature the highest possible value, one inconsistent with his description of it as "emotive." The implication is that the poem can communicate, and communicate precisely, for "the artist is an expert in 'minute particulars' and *qua* artist pays little or no attention to generalisations which he finds in actual practice are too crude to discriminate between what is valuable and the reverse." [35] Now, if words in poetry are not referential, as he has often argued, when placed side by side the two parts of his theory go something like this: a poem is a group of words which avoids the referential use of words in order to create a new and total reference. With much qualification and expansion, this could be made into an effective definition of literature; as it stands it contains several half-truths. As I showed earlier in my comments on "Poor Soul, the center of my sinful earth," words in poetry are referential in a very important sense. The system which is the poem at once expands and limits the references in order to make a new and total reference — or, more correctly, the system of the poem directs the potentialities of growth of meaning which the traditions of language have put into words. Nor is the new and total reference ever communicated completely. Richards' notorious psychologism should have led him to a more sophisticated understanding of the problem, or at least prevented him from arguing that the arts permit us to compare our experiences accurately enough so that we can agree which we prefer. [36] Richards here falls into the same error as his detractors — the assumption of the perfect reader reading the perfect poem. Actually, as Richards sometimes admits, only bits and pieces of the poet's experience get into the poem, and probably only bits and pieces of the poem get to the reader.

Perhaps the most serious error in Richards' early theory is his emphasis on poetry as "emotive language" and the consequent de-emphasis of its rational or referential content. The result is a theory of poetry as language minus something. If poetry reproduces experience, or if it is to communicate an experience obtainable only in the poem, it must be remembered that experience is often partly intellectual. If it is to serve as "our storehouse of recorded values" and as a means of comparing what men have experienced, it must record the complete range of man's experience: it must be at once intellectual, emotional, and sensuous. There is ample reason for suspecting that Richards would have it so, but the theory he developed is too conscious of the poetry-science dichotomy to allow consistent development of the more adequate side of his work.

The contribution of meaning to the total value of a poem may also be analyzed in a way indicated by Read and developed most thoroughly by John Crowe Ransom. Both talk of pure or physical poetry and Platonic poetry; the former is the poetry of things, the latter the poetry of ideas. Ransom goes on to note that neither can exist unadulterated, although "all true poetry is a phase of Physical Poetry." Physical poetry will be discussed in the next chapter; the Platonic poetry is of interest here. Purely Platonic poetry is a contradiction in terms because it would be all ideas, all science, the purpose of which, according to Ransom, is to gratify *"a rational or practical impulse"* with *"the minimum of perception. Art gratifies a perceptual impulse and exhibits a minimum of reason."* [87] Read felt that a touch of reason was necessary to shield the reader from "the instantaneous expression of the image in 'the insurgent naked throb of the instant moment.' " [38] Ransom finds a better use for the content he so grudgingly admits into the poem; meaning is neither the burglar's "nice bit of meat" to quiet the dog nor the dilution of a "naked throb," but rather an essential ingredient in the poem. It is the prose core around which the poet builds a "tissue of irrelevance," a poetical part.[39] The value of the poem, for Ransom, tends to be the value of the irrelevancies; the prose core is relatively unimportant in the aesthetic judgment. This is but another variant on the notion that poetry is language minus something — this time, minus the prose core, the rational content.

Frederick A. Pottle's attack on the notion of pure poetry is effective and clear. He notes that pure poetry makes us settle for a single value, but that two values are always preferable to one. We are, therefore, likely to get more from a poem whose intellectual content seems true than from one whose doctrines seem irrelevant or foolish.[40] Unfortunately, Pottle's answer to the proponents of pure poetry does not go quite far enough, for it still leaves poetry with a double value and the critic with a double valuation system. The alternative to accepting either the limited value of pure poetry or the double value of impure poetry as an ideal is the realization that there are no "impure" kinds of value in poetry; there are only poems which, because of this or that imperfection, incite for the reader irrelevant experiences and for the theorist impure theories of evaluation.

Allen Tate's conclusion that "poetry is one test of ideas; it is ideas tested by experience, by the act of direct apprehension," [41] is one of the earliest and best statements of this position, for it requires of the poem a wholeness, a completeness, an integrity of all the components that make a full experience. After writing that Emily Dickinson "attains to a mastery over experience by facing its utmost implications" and that "we are shown our roots in Nature by examining our differences with Nature," [42] Tate makes the following analysis of "Because I could not stop for death." It is worth quoting at length because it is one of the finest things of its kind; its attention to detail is not typical of moralistic criticism:

> If the word means anything in poetry, this poem is one of the greatest in the English language; it is flawless to the last detail. The rhythm charges with movement the pattern of suspended action back of the poem. Every image is precise and, moreover, not merely beautiful, but inextricably fused with the central idea. Every image extends and intensifies every other. The third stanza especially shows Miss Dickinson's power to fuse, into a single order of perception, a heterogeneous series: the children, the grain, and the setting sun (time) have the same degree of credibility; the first subtly preparing for the last. The sharp *grazing* before *grain* instils into nature a kind of cold vitality of which the qualitative richness has infinite depth. The content of death in the poem eludes forever any explicit definition. He is a gentleman taking a lady out for a drive. But note the restraint that keeps the poet from carrying this so far that it is ludicrous and incredible; and note the subtly interfused erotic motive, which the idea of death has presented to every romantic poet, love being a symbol interchangeable with death. The terror of death is objectified through this figure of the genteel driver, who is made ironically to serve the end of Immortality. This is the heart of the poem: she has presented a typical Christian theme in all its final irresolution, without making any final statement about it. There is no solution to the problem; there can be only a statement of it in the full context of intellect and feeling. A construction of the human will, elaborated with all the abstracting

powers of the mind, is put to the concrete test of experience: the idea of immortality is confronted with the fact of physical disintegration. We are not told what to think; we are told to look at the situation.[43]

Thus are ideas presented in poetry to be tested. But despite the excellence of this as practical criticism, it raises problems that will be more apparent after looking at other aspects of Tate's theory. He obviously does not want the poem to contain thought as such, for he goes on almost immediately to observe that Emily Dickinson's inability to think improved her poetry. Tate seems to be saying that Miss Dickinson's ideas are no larger than her poems; they are such that they can be expressed with nothing left over.

On the other hand, Tate finds that Hardy's " 'philosophy' tends to go a little beyond the range of his feeling: his abstractions are thus somewhat irresponsible." [44] This comes after an analysis of Hardy's "Nature's Questioning," which Tate finds "magnificent" in parts. The judgment only appears to be based on the structure of the poem rather than on its ideas:

In the second stanza what appeared to be a simile becomes completed metaphor. We have here, in the terms of Mr. I. A. Richards, an instance of metaphor in which the "vehicle" replaces the "tenor": the natural objects (tenor) are so weakly perceived that the children (vehicle), who appear as the conveyance of their significance, cancel out the natural objects altogether; so that, as the poem proceeds to the fourth stanza, we get a group of inanimate objects as school children asking this question:

> Has some vast Imbecility,
>   Mighty to build and blend,
>   But impotent to tend,
> Framed us in jest, and left us now to hazardry?

Now Hardy is saying that the children are Nature, or would like to say, since he is a nineteenth-century monist, that they are also mechanically determined, as nature is.[45]

Tate is here certainly attempting what a critic should attempt; he is trying to account for his reaction to the poem with a minimum of external data. Nevertheless, it does seem odd that he cannot accept the personification of nature in Hardy's poem but can accept a similar personification of death as a genteel caller on an old maid. He criticizes "Nature's Questioning" because the symbols of nature are not fully realized and because the conception of God seems to shift from human (the schoolmaster) to inhuman, from personal to impersonal. But would not these "errors" be justifiable from the point of view of a nineteenth-century monist? Tate seems to have missed the magnificent irony of the poem — which is not, incidentally, the kind of irony he usually approves of. The irony is that of man and nature, since the two are similar in the eyes of the monist, still, after eons of questioning, repeating the ancient and desperately hopeful question yet once more. The acceptance of the poem, if I am correct and if Tate's otherwise high praise of it is just, depends upon the ability of the reader to see for a moment the predicament of man and nature from the monist's position. And in precisely the same way, acceptance of Miss Dickinson's poem depends upon the acceptance of the Christian belief that death is a prelude to immortality. Tate could put himself imaginatively in the position of the one, but not of the other. The result is that by his criterion (poetry as a test of ideas), Hardy's poem seems to fail and Miss Dickinson's to pass. What fails and what passes, obviously, depends upon what the what is and who is doing the testing. For this reason any critic who wants to be consistent, if not systematic, must be aware of the importance of ideas in poetry. They may not actually exist there, but they do live just under its surface, always ready to show themselves nakedly if either the poet or the reader should momentarily lose his grasp on the total poem.[46]

Tate's difficulty is that he wants to maintain two different notions, both correct but mutually contradictory without a great amount of clarification. On the one hand, Tate correctly argues that ideas as such do not appear in poems; on the other, equally correctly, that poetry affects readers as if ideas were present. The seeming paradox can be resolved only in a much larger framework than most critics provide; that framework will be discussed in the final three chapters of this study.

Perhaps theories that more straightforwardly admit the value of meaning may fare better; they are not currently fashionable, but they do have adherents. E. M. Tillyard's notion that poetry expresses "great commonplaces" is probably the most old fashioned, although he admits that the commonplaces must be "organic" to the poem and "powerfully and consistently dominant." [47] Depending upon how clearly the commonplace is expressed, poetry is "direct" or "oblique," with no poem being entirely one or the other and all poems being more one than the other.[48] If the purpose of poetry is to express great commonplaces, then the techniques of oblique poetry — paradox, ambiguity, wit, irony, and so on — are not *per se* valuable and their elevation by the new critics is unnecessary and unwise. Tillyard's view of poetry is important because it reminds us of two fundamental notions that modern critics usually prefer to ignore: that poetry of direct statement has a place and that often the best the critic can manage with the theme of

64

the poem is to state it as if it were really a great common-place.

Yet Tillyard goes too far. One should, I believe, ask for more in his theory than he can always get in his practice, which is another way of saying that a theory should force the critic to extend himself. Furthermore, what Tillyard and his kind of theory cannot explain is why, if the commonplace is what interests us, we undertake the immense labor of creating poetry and the equally huge labor of learning to read it. Also, if one posits meaning as the major value in poetry, he must then posit other values to account for the value of the "poetry" itself; again we have an unworkable double or multiple standard of evaluation.

At its simplest and worst, edification theory almost completely ignores individual poems. It begins with a set of beliefs and uses the poem as an occasion for a sermon. Irving Babbitt's statement that the only serious moral in *The Rime of the Ancient Mariner* is "perhaps a warning as to the fate of the innocent bystander; unless one hold that it is fitting that, for having sympathized with the man who shot an albatross, 'four times fifty living men' should perish in torments unspeakable" [49] is typical. As Babbitt hurries to mount his hobby horse, he forgets that the whole of Christian theology turns upon the damnation of a significant portion of mankind because one man nibbled an apple. Babbitt's critical technique is the only one possible for the literal-minded moralist; he considers his version of the truth so superior to any possible aesthetic criterion that the incorporation of an idea or a sentiment an inch beyond his notion of common sense, the least taint in the philosophy expressed in the poem, destroys the work of art.

Before looking at our last edification theory (Yvor

Winters'), I should like to consider W. K. Wimsatt's work briefly. It is a symbolic form theory rather than an edification theory, and so will be returned to later; here I want merely to show the connection between the two approaches. Wimsatt's starting point is that our pleasure in poetry arises from something more active than mere contemplation of the words in poems because "we are bound to have a point of view. . . . To evaluate the past we have to penetrate it with our own intelligence." [50] This is a much more adequate description of reading and evaluation than we have yet encountered because it acknowledges the mental activity of the reader. What the reader's intelligence penetrates to in the adequate poem is unique because of the peculiar metaphorical structure of poetry, which operates by suggesting a resemblance between two classes and which thereby posits a "more general third class." The content of the poem is unique because the third class "is apprehended only through the metaphor. It is a new conception for which there is no other expression." [51] Thus Keats's "On First Looking into Chapman's Homer" describes or metaphorically points to "a certain kind of thrill in discovering, for which there is no name and no other description." [52] The thrill, note, is not "a certain thrill," but "a certain kind of thrill." As such it is communicable, even though it is an abstraction obtainable nowhere else. The most important implication of this, the advance made over other theories we have looked at, is that it both admits the cognitive content of poetry and still — because the content of the poem is unique — makes the application of any external standard necessarily indirect. Discussion of that indirectness will have to be postponed until after a long detour through epistemology.

Yvor Winters has probably done more to defend the importance of meaning in poetry than any other critic of his generation, and it is fitting that his work should be the last to be considered here. He never tires of reiterating his basic position, sometimes almost quoting himself and always stating the problem in its sharpest terms — to the great annoyance of critics who would much rather hedge, qualify, or even contradict themselves:

> I believe that a poem . . . is a statement in words about a human experience. . . . In each work there is a content which is rationally apprehensible, and each work endeavors to communicate the emotion which is appropriate to the rational apprehension of the subject. The work is thus a judgment, rational and emotional, of the experience — that is a complete moral judgment in so far as the work is successful. I see no escape from these opinions.[53]

Quite aware of the ultimate unworkability of a double evaluative standard, Winters describes the perfect style as one befitting man's nature as a rational, emotional, and sensory animal living in a physical universe.[54] Ideally, then, poetry is a fusion of emotion and motive (the rational justification for emotion). In our age the most common kind of defective poetry is that which is unmotivated — e.g., that in which the cause of the emotion is left undescribed. His analysis of Hopkins' "No worst, there is none" may clarify the issue:

> This is not a poem about the effects of violent emotion in general; it is a poem about a particular violent emotion experienced by the poet. The nearest thing to a statement of motive occurs in the first line and a half of the sestet; but what are these mountains of the mind? One does not enquire because one holds them cheap, but because one has hung on so many oneself, so various in their respective terrors, that one is perplexed to assign a particular mo-

tive. . . . We have passed beyond the limits of generalization; we are in the realm of uncertainty; and the mind
cannot organize itself to share Hopkins' experience with
any real feeling of security.[55]

We should note that Winters does not demand a general
statement in the poem; he argues, rather, that the personal experience displayed in the poem does not get to
the reader because Hopkins has not made it particular
enough. The paradox is only apparent; Winters' point is
that unless the reader knows the particular nature of the
emotion, including its full motivation, he cannot share it.
An adequately developed poem does not offer insoluble
riddles, either about its emotions or about its ideas.
What Winters is pleading for is poetry that is full, poetry
that is rich with sensuous and rational appeal, for only in
such poetry is emotion motivated. He deprecates the new
kind of poetry dating from Verlaine and Rimbaud because it is "the old kind of poetry with half the meaning
removed. Its strangeness comes from its thinness." [56]

Contrary to the opinions of his adversaries, Winters
does not subordinate poetry to morality or philosophy,
despite his argument that, since poetry must deal justly
with human experience, poetry is always involved with
ethics.[57] The ethical, it should be remarked, is not
necessarily the didactic; poetry is ethical in Winters'
sense when it attains sufficient particularity to serve as a
basis for what he calls "generalization" — although
"communication" or "symbolization" might be preferable terms. In fact, didacticism is likely to defeat such
particularization. At his best, Winters does not judge a
poem by its message, but by its ability to present its message with experiential complexity.[58]

Winters himself, however, does not always observe the
distinction between the ethical and the didactic. At his

worst, as in the criticism of Frost's "The Bear," he can be as rashly superficial and as wrong as Babbitt. Singling out the following couplet,

> I own I never really warmed
> To the reformer or reformed,

he pedantically points out that there are good and bad reformers, and that Frost should have said which he meant, lest he obscure "the difference between St. Thomas Aquinas and Pussyfoot Johnson." [59] Winters' error, all too typical of the weaker parts of his work, is to seize upon the denotative meaning of a single word and to ignore the connotative limitations the poem places upon it. But even though this kind of error is explainable in terms of the heavily moralistic tone of his criticism, it is a deviation from his more considered and complete view. At his best, Winters understands that denotation and connotation exist in the word as a unity; their attempted separation by either poet or theorist is a mistake.[60] Because of this union of denotation-connotation, the poem does not and cannot, if it is successful, separate ornament and meaning. Because a poem is composed of aspects of words that are only logically separable, it may not be chopped up into the various functions of its members.

Winters' clearest statement of this position occurs in his attack on Ransom's dualism, in which he argues that

> The rational content of a poem is not a *core* to which irrelevancies are attached in a kind of nimbus; it is something which exists from moment to moment, in every word of the poem, just as does the feeling; and the value of the poem resides precisely in the relationship between these two elements, and not in qualities supposedly attaching to one of the partners in the relationship.[61]

This provides well enough for the unity of the poem. Language, when the poet is able to exploit its fullest potentialities, is the basis for both the integrity and the complexity of poetry. The result of this integrated complexity, this fusion of sensation, intellection, and emotion, would be the perfect poem, the "new word," a concept or — better — an experience that "may be very different from its paraphrasable, or purely logical content." [62]

If Winters were not an absolutist, his conception of the poem as a "new word" (probably something like "unique symbolic structure" would be more accurate) could lead to a theoretically consistent and practically applicable poetics. The difficulty is that no new word is possible for the strict absolutist; there can be a new expression of the absolute or a new experience of it, but by definition the absolute must remain unaffected by the poem. However Winters chooses to describe his absolute, it pre-exists the poem; and the poem that is truly a new word contradicts it. This is why Winters is led so easily into the kind of naïve criticism he made of Frost's lines and why, despite his better knowledge, he often proceeds on the assumption that poetry that is not paraphrasable is therefore defective. A more subtle epistemological context, such as that developed by Ernst Cassirer, permits the poem to be truly a new word, and thereby a unique and valuable word, because it rests upon the assumption that the final test of meaning is not rational statement alone; rather, rational statement, like poetic statement, is but a way of meaning.

It should be clear by now that the majority of contemporary aestheticians and critics have been unable to explain successfully either how poetry edifies or the value of meaning in poetry. Whether they see the poem as pseudoreferential, contextualistic, pure, multivalued —

but why extend the list? — they invariably are unable to account for the unity of poems and for the great value men find in them. Those who deny the relevance of meaning to the full effect of poetry cannot explain the significance that men have for generations attributed to poetry. The outright seekers after wisdom come to poetry with standards that are not hers; rather than affirming the value of poetry, they attach value to it by attaching it to something else. The something else — a moral or philosophical system — always tends to loom over the poetry and eventually to invalidate the work of even the most able of moralist-critics.

I have shown the difficulties that arise when one misjudges the extent of the contribution made by the edifying in poetry. What, then, is the proper value of truth and morality — or, in a word, of wisdom — in a poem? René Wellek has argued that such content "seems to enhance artistic value because it corroborates several important artistic values: those of complexity and coherence." [63] "Complexity and coherence" suggest that Wellek is familiar with the aesthetic theory of Alfred North Whitehead. Although Whitehead's analysis of beauty will form the basis for the final chapter of this study, this is the proper place to sketch his view of the relation between wisdom and aesthetic value. I shall have to state briefly what will be explained more fully later; I am attempting to deduce from Whitehead's aesthetic theory, which is stated on an unusually high level of generality, certain notions that will clarify the kind of value wisdom has for poetry.

First, a work of art has two modes of being — it is an artifact, an object which can be touched, dropped, torn, and so on; and it is also a certain relation between the artifact and the mind of an apprehending subject — in the case of poetry, the reader or listener. This second mode, for reasons I cannot discuss now, is the only meaningful existence the work has; markings on paper are not yet art. The value of a poem results from a transaction between the mind of the reader and the artifact, in which the latter gives to the former a focus for attention, a definite direction of interests, and enough moment-by-moment titillation of the senses and expectations to keep the reader turning pages; in turn, the mind provides a context for the poem, a soil in which the words may grow and bear fruit. Although most critics and literary scholars would insist that such a view leads directly to subjectivism, the whole business of literary study consists largely of preparing the mind to be a receptacle capable of holding the work without damaging it, or, more accurately, to be a co-creator capable of remaking the work so that it retains and exhibits most of its potentialities. To recognize that the poem is primarily an experience of the reader, and to recognize that the poem is nurtured by the *controlled* flow of the reader's thoughts, feelings, memories, and what have you, is to take the first important step in assigning the correct place to meaning in poetry. (I should stress here that I am interested in problems of evaluation, not of ontology; for the purposes of evaluation, the only legitimate consideration is what the reader experiences from the poem.) Two general qualities account for the peculiar nature of poetic experience; Whitehead frequently uses the terms complexity and intensity, but at this point terminology is not especially important — such classic pairs as harmony and multeity, uniformity and variety, or unity and complexity will do as well.

Three questions are of concern here: What contribution does wisdom make to the complexity of the poem? What contribution does it make to the intensity? How important is it that the wisdom of the poem agree with the wisdom of the reader?

The first may be answered quite simply. As a rule of thumb, works of greater complexity tend to be valued more than works of lesser, other things being equal. This quantitative factor might best be illustrated with the novel. The reason that Tolstoy's *War and Peace* is a great novel and Forster's *Howards End* only a very good one is that in the former a huge cast moves through a world seemingly as complex as the real world; the characters in *War and Peace* are immersed in their world in the novel, and that world is related to ours in a rich and tangled way. The characters live in a world with historical, emotional, psychological, physical, economic, and social similarities to the world in which real men and women move. The characters in *Howards End* seem to have just what they need to function in the novel, and the world in the novel is just large enough to accommodate them. All this is merely to say that the degree of complexity in a given work of art is directly proportionate to the number of aspects of reality which the artist will entrust to his talent. This knowledge of men and their universe that I have called wisdom is one such aspect; it is one factor in what might be termed the internal complexity of the poem, and it is a major factor.

Perhaps the function of wisdom in promoting intensity is not quite so important; its most obvious use is to provide a frame from which to hang the poem in the sense that all of the poem is "about" the same thing. Intensity of experience is impossible unless the experience has coherence, for without coherence the effect is dissipated. The easiest source of coherence is an intellectual burden, either a thread of rational argument or implicit meaning, carried throughout the entire course of the work. Such coherence can, however, be achieved in other ways.

The third question is the most important. The notion of the poem as a transaction between reader and artifact is crucial here. Let us imagine a reader in three stages of his life reading Meredith's "Lucifer in Starlight." The first time may result only in a minimal understanding; only the fine rhetoric and the colossal images attract our reader. Then, later, may come a realization that the poem is part of a coherent and mature system of ideas, though as yet the ideological content is unacceptable. The poem immediately takes on additional complexity, for the reader has become aware of new elements that fit into its pattern; it probably seems a better poem. The more the reader learns about Lucifer, chaos, celestial harmony, Victorian beliefs about physical and moral law, the sonnet form, and so on, the greater the number of links forged between poem and reader. Each fact that the reader can relate to the poem increases the complexity to be valued. Nevertheless, such appreciation is limited; to the extent that the reader has reservations about the "truth" of the poem, the range of complexity he is able to value in it is lessened; the falseness he finds simply does not permit it to relate to the most significant areas of his experience. But suppose that the reader comes to accept the world view carried by the poem. Instead of a relatively closed system, instead of a dead-end meaning, he now finds that the poem has been transformed into a system with innumerable ramifications, each of which represents an element in its total complexity. On a sheerly quantitative level, acceptance of the content as true adds greatly to the complexity. Of course, poetry that one accepts as "true" may be excruciatingly bad (the sonnets or free verse most of us wrote at sixteen), but here we are interested only in the positive value that "truth" adds to the poem.

"Truth" furthers complexity by enabling the poem to relate to a quantitatively and perhaps qualitatively large portion of the reader's experience; it also promotes intensity. Negatively, content that can be accepted permits the poem to be read with a minimum of distraction. We worry over what we think untrue and imagine other possibilities; such distraction is largely absent when content is acceptable. Positively, meaning that is true for the reader permits him to read the poem as a unified creation; he does not have to break it down into the basic categories of the true and the false, the morally good and the morally pernicious. As Whitehead wrote:

> The general importance of Truth for the promotion of Beauty is overwhelming. After all has been said, yet the truth-relation remains the simple, direct mode of realizing Harmony. Other ways are indirect, and indirectness is at the mercy of the environment.[64]

One thing more should be said about the importance of the edifying in poetry: our values are probably not as simple as we would have others and ourselves believe. Men seem to have very few principles that they hold inviolable, and within a given culture they agree to differ within a permissible range. A reader may accept or reject the quietistic theme of "Ozymandias," but either way he will find much company and more tolerance. And even further, to return to Empson's point, people believe less wholeheartedly than they would want the world to realize. Our institutionalized, codified beliefs rarely coincide with the code by which we really live. There is a bit of the Socialist in every member of the National Association of Manufacturers who hopes for a federal subsidy, just as there is a bit of the pagan in each Irish Catholic who carries a four-leaf clover. It is not surprising, then, that we are able to respond favorably to a great variety of poetic content.

# IV

## MISCELLANEOUS MIRRORS
Social, Tradition, Psychological,
and Perception Theories

In this chapter I shall discuss several mimetic theories which, for one reason or another, can be treated relatively briefly. Some of the theories are not sufficiently popular at present to merit lengthy discussion, others are but special developments of personality or edification theories and have already been discussed in part. These theories judge the poem by its social relevance, its relation to literary tradition, its use of either of two distinct kinds of psychology, or its verbal reproduction of an object.

SOCIAL THEORIES

Social theories and edification theories are basically alike in that both judge the poem by the value of its content. Edification theories, however, assume that the content somehow reflects something constant or universal in human nature. Social theories see the poem as a reflection of a given age and a given society. To use an obvious example, "The Passionate Shepherd to His Love" contains a moral relevant to man in any age and place. It also belongs definitely to a specific society; it can be valued as an expression of certain aspects of the Elizabethan period both in terms of the emphasis it gives the *carpe diem* theme and in terms of its unique mode of expressing that theme. Obviously, social theories are valid to the extent that the worth of a poem depends upon the representation of social values.

The two broad types of social theory may be called the dogmatic and the general. The dogmatic assumes a standard of social norms or ideals and judges the poem as the reflection of that standard; the general is not concerned with the incorporation of a specific social view, but rather with the value added to a poem by its reflection of society as such.

I shall limit discussion of the dogmatic theories of social criticism to the Marxist because it is the most fully developed of such views. Anatole V. Lunacharsky, the first Soviet Commissar of Education, illustrates the typical dilemma Marxist literary critics face. On the one hand, Lunacharsky was bound by Marxist dogma; on the other, he seems to have been relatively sensitive to the claims of art. The artist "has the right to create freely, in accord with his ideal, no matter what it is"; yet, Lunacharsky continues, quoting Lenin, " 'we are Communists. We must not stand by with empty hands and permit chaos to develop as it will.' " [1] This suggests the art-and-prudence split judgment found in most edification theories, with the disproportionate emphasis on the prudence.

In order to make the prudential judgment, Lunacharsky reduces all literary problems to specifically social problems. Even genius, for example, is subordinate because to understand the literary artist we "must begin with social relationships, since only this investigation gives a clue to the real understanding of personality." He again quotes Lenin: " 'Down with the literary superman! Literary material must become an affair of the entire proletariat!' " [2] Like genius, morality and philosophy are subservient to Marxism, for man becomes a moral being only when he escapes the "blind necessity" of his natural condition, and the only salvation is through knowledge of the laws of dialectical materialism. The chief purpose of literature is to help us to know those laws.[3]

The task of the Marxist critic, therefore, is to "try to give a complete picture of the entire social development of an epoch" since "literary work always reflects the conscious or unconscious psychology of that class which the given writer expresses." [4] With this as the first task of the Marxist critic, problems of form and technique are relatively unimportant. The literary genius is not a craftsman but the possessor of an ideology; his originality consists not in the way he writes but in the fact that "he is more normal than other people" and so can "pass his insight on to his readers. In short, a genius is simply a man who is ideologically ahead of his time." [5]

Yet it would be unfair to say that Marxist critics are blind to the problems of form. Although content is primary, "any given content exists only to the extent that it has optimum form." [6] This, incidentally, is the closest Lunacharsky could bring himself to a modern theory of organic form. When a Marxist practical critic such as Pavel Antokolsky considers such technical matters as linkages of imagery, symbolic presentation of a theme, and so forth, the overriding criterion is still the presence of a Marxist — or at least, a patriotic — theme.[7]

A detailed critique of the approach is hardly necessary; it has all the faults of extreme edification theories. It restricts the range of literature too narrowly and fails to explain why poetry exerts the kind of appeal that sociology does not. Even Lunacharsky is aware that orthodoxy is not sufficient for literature; he criticizes a dogmatically correct volume of poetry called *The Tractor Farmer* be-

78

cause its poems are "boring; you read one after another and find nothing." [8] Yet he immediately proceeds to attack less orthodox and far better Russian poets — notably Pasternak and Tikhon — even more vigorously. The only solution Lunacharsky can offer is a rather desperate plea "that the Communist heart throb in a purely artistic way" and that writers sing brilliantly "in Communist." [9] He cannot face the fact that the claims of art and the claims of Marxism might not be identical.

Before leaving Marxist criticism, an example of its American branch should be cited. I have chosen Granville Hicks on Emily Dickinson because the treatment is typical; after a paragraph describing Miss Dickinson's family background, Hicks writes:

> In such an environment Emily naturally occupied her young mind with religion, and her early letters bear much testimony to the seriousness of her affirmations and her doubts. . . . Certainly thoughts of religion did not darken her life; she could be gay and even giddy. She engaged in such social life as Amherst afforded, and even the most intuitive of her friends must have believed that she would, in due season, marry some minister, lawyer, or teacher, and settle down in conventional domesticity.
>
> By some event, still a mystery, that path was closed to her. In one sense what happened does not matter. Reading the letters we can see that, as Colonel Higginson observed, "the mystic and bizarre Emily is born at once between two pages," and that is enough to confirm the tradition that somehow love was aroused and frustrated. How Emily would have adjusted herself to domesticity we cannot surmise; it may have been well both for her and for poetry that the adjustment did not have to be made. As it was, she turned to solitude. There were inner resources for her to rely upon, fortunately for us, for other-

wise she would have been one more New England old maid, of the kind Mrs. Freeman so often described, instead of the most distinguished poet of her generation.

For a person of Emily Dickinson's intensity no compromise was possible: either she accepted the active life of the average women of her day, or she lived in and for herself. For her as a poet, solitude was imperative. The spirit of her age, of those momentous years between 1850 and 1880, could only have interfered with such an imagination as hers. In other ages, perhaps even in the period of Emerson, she could have found some nourishment in the life about her, but by the time her poetic powers were ripe, that was impossible. Presumably, after her love had proven fruitless, she wanted to live as she did live and write as she did write; it is, however, worth observing that, whether she knew it or not, she had no choice.[10]

I have quoted this entire passage with only one omission (a description — three sentences — of her intellectual life and spiritual doubts) because it is all Hicks's Marxist theory permitted him to say about Emily Dickinson and her poetry. He does not explain why it is "fortunate for us" that she could turn to inner resources; there is neither a single title nor the quotation of a single line. The criticism is nothing but a cursory biography ending in a cliché. This is precisely the kind of criticism Lunacharsky asked for; it is hardly literary criticism.

Hicks, like others who emphasize content, assumes that technical criticism can be ignored because it is done automatically — that because Emily Dickinson is an acclaimed poetess, her art is therefore sound. And for the critic who relies upon a set of ideas — be they political, moral, philosophical, or social — the only proper evaluative criterion is the immediate effect of the work of art upon the social health of the people. Such a critic may never ask why a work is popular; he must deal solely with its effects. The consequence is not literary criticism, but its avoidance.

Perhaps the surest indication of the failure of literary theories advocating specific causes is the failure of literary works advocating them. Anyone who has worked with the ephemerae of a period knows that few things are as dead as literature based on contemporary issues. At worst, an overabundance of social content inhibits appreciation; at best, it plays no positive part in the judgment of a work.

There are, of course, more indirect ways in which literature may be said to be beneficial or harmful to a society. It may express a moral tone, but then edification theory is involved. Or it may provide an emotional outlet, a way of vicariously working off the excess emotional energy of the people, but this assumes only a negative, not a positive, carry-over from art to life. It also unduly stresses the value of popular art.

General social theories see the poem not as the bearer of specific dogma, but as the bearer of the assumptions by which people really live, the assumptions which most truly and most powerfully shape the culture. Not much critical acuity is needed to realize that Yeats and Frost, Whitman and Wyatt, came from different worlds. We know so not because their works reflect different formal systems, but rather because each assumes sets of questions and answers characteristic of his own milieu and unimportant to others. Erich Auerbach in *Mimesis* noted that the contrasting styles of the *Odyssey* and the Book of Job bespeak entirely different worlds. To summarize briefly, the narrative style of the Greek text assumes a world in which externals — objects and situations, definite times and places — are in a "perceptual foreground." The Hebrew presents only those externals absolutely necessary for the narrative; time, place, objective action are frequently omitted in the Book of Job, so that it is "permeated with the most unrelieved suspense and directed towards a single goal. . . . [It] remains mysterious and 'fraught with background.'" [11] The contrasting styles result from the contrasting world views of the two cultures.

Kenneth Burke achieves a more complex version of the approach by noting that

> any particular cluster of conditions will involve the recurrent emotions (fear, tenderness, delight, etc.), and fundamental attitudes (belief, cynicism, skepticism, expansiveness, reclusion, etc.); but the particularities of the cluster will require the stressing of some and the slighting of others.[12]

The ingredients of art and life are ever the same, but the proportions in which they are mixed varies from society to society. Burke's refinement is important because it accounts for both the temporary and the permanent aspects of content, for that which reflects a given age and that which reflects what seems to endure in man.

Assuming, then, that such general social content exists in poetry, what is its value? Or, to put the question negatively, if the social content of a poem is markedly different from the social experience of the reader, to what extent does it inhibit appreciation of the poem? There is certainly some inhibition; we are annoyed by the prudishness of the Victorian novel, the tidiness of the world view of Augustan poetry, the optimism of the romantics, and so on. The answer is probably that the inhibition is slight if a work has what Burke calls "recurrent emotions" and "fundamental attitudes" in sufficient quantity to attract the reader and to impel him, through scholarship and development of the proper mental resources, to become a naturalized citizen of an alien time and land.

Thus we grant Donne certain concessions in both attitude and technique that we would not grant a modern poet. We do not so much condescend to Donne's work as admit that we have entered a culture with laws and habits different from our own.

Positively, social content increases our appreciation of literature in at least two ways. The first, the novelty of an alien culture, can be handled briefly. The imaginative and emotional capacities of readers are seldom exhausted by their own environments. A glimpse of the courtly elegance of a world in which Lyly could write "Cupid and my Campaspe played / At cards for kisses" is stimulating; the delight may not be purely aesthetic, but the feeling is quite likely to be a factor in the total appreciation of the poem.

Secondly, alien social content increases aesthetic distance. Although such distance may be achieved in other ways, remoteness in time or place (or even in social class) is the most certain and obvious means of attaining a mixture of involvement and detachment. By playing out familiar ideas and emotions against an unfamiliar background, poetry may force a reader to see those ideas and emotions more plainly than before — without petty involvements in politics, national prejudices, current cultural mores, etc. And whether the poet builds the unfamiliar background into his poem (as the Coleridge of the ballads did) or not (as Wordsworth did not), the effect is there for those who come after him. It is probably, in most poems, a minor effect, but it is nevertheless part of the total value structure of poetry.

What does social content in itself — alien or not — contribute? It adds two factors that make the poem proportionately more valuable: it gives an additional element in its total complexity; and, by providing a locus in time-space, it promotes for the reader a feeling of both complexity and harmony. Insofar as it reflects a real, or at least a possible world, the poem points at events, ideas, and objects outside itself to which the reader may refer and which thereby enrich the poem. Unless a poem has such a locus, the reader is likely to be unable to supply the kind of exact and detailed context poems need for completeness. Much of the difficulty with Poe's work, for example, is that his poems often "hang"; they float airily, supported by nothing significant that we know about his world or ours. Moreover, social content is so difficult to avoid that the most the poet can do is refuse to place his work in a specific time and place. Although social content may not be a major strand in the fabric that the poet and his reader weave as they make the poem, it does nevertheless contribute positively to its total structure and to its total value.

### TRADITION THEORIES

Theories that attempt to judge poems from standards derived from what a critic believes to be the central tradition of literature or a literary genre will be called, naturally enough, tradition theories. The usual procedure is to posit, either implicitly or overtly, a "great tradition" against which individual works are measured. The method has two outstanding virtues: it cuts across all other evaluative standards because it can define tradition in terms of any kind of content or form, and it also usually stays fairly close to the literary qualities of literature. The approach is based upon the assumption that we must always judge against a background, and the most appropriate background for judging literary works is one composed of other literary works.

The best-known exponent of this method is T. S. Eliot, although the establishment of a great tradition is

84

common critical practice. Allen Tate's great tradition "unites Shakespeare and Donne, includes Milton and much of Dryden, but passes over the eighteenth century until the year 1798." [13] Blackmur criticized Hardy for ignoring the tradition of poetry; [14] F. R. Leavis attempted a "revaluation" of the literary tradition; Cleanth Brooks tried to force his own view of the tradition on to criticism; and the conservative Gilbert Murray fought for his conception of a far different great tradition. [15] Only Eliot, however, seems to have made evaluation by tradition a critical principle.

As Ransom has observed, Eliot's usual critical procedure is to set the poem against its literary background to determine the appropriate kind of criticism for it. [16] A valid work of art has to be traditional, Eliot argues, not because of the intrinsic value of the tradition, but because "its fitting in is a test of its value." [17] I assume Eliot is saying that unless a work shares certain qualities with other works, it simply is not art. Empirically, we do judge works of art — whether we want to or not — by comparing them with others. We feel more comfortable, especially with a difficult poet, when we can classify him; and, from another perspective, we are likely to be thoroughly satisfied with *Astrophel and Stella* only if we have not read Shakespeare's sonnet sequence.

But despite the empirical validity of comparison — I should say its inevitability; it seems a mental habit — the approach does pose some difficulties, the most important being the precise definition of the tradition. Eliot, for example, wants to consider it as both an absolute and a changing order. At one moment it is what it is, yet it changes with the addition of any truly original work: What makes up the tradition at any given moment? If we include the body of known poetry, the answer is meaningless because it includes so many disparate kinds of poems. What kind of a tradition could we make of Stephen Duck and John Donne, Felicia Hemans and Robert Herrick, Joyce Kilmer and T. S. Eliot? Surely they are not all in the same tradition, and all are certainly not in the tradition Eliot prefers. How, then, do we limit the tradition? Eliot wants Donne in and Shelley mostly out; Gilbert Murray, on the other hand, makes a good case for centering the tradition around Shelley's kind of poetry. Whose tradition is *the* tradition?

The notion of tradition is usable so long as we do not assume that the tradition is both a knowable and an absolute order; although it is probably most effective for the critic to admit the possibility of an absolute order, the content of which he does not know precisely but which he attempts to approximate by making an intelligent and diligent effort to reconcile his own prejudices with what is and has been accepted by his peers. But the critic who claims to know for certain the absolute order of the tradition is almost certainly defining it as "those works I like."

The basic difficulty is that the use of tradition and comparison is at best a technique for the aid of judgment. To be a value in poetry, tradition would have to be defined as a nexus of conditions potentially present in whole or in part in poems; it would have to serve as a shorthand term for a specific group of qualities. A critic basing his judgment on tradition should be able to say, "because the poem has these characteristics, it is itself great." Cleanth Brooks is the only critic who has carefully defined his notion of the tradition, but since it is formalistic, it will be considered later. Unless the critic does define his tradition, his placing a poem in it is little more than a circumlocution expressing admiration for something which he is either unwilling or unable to specify.

86

Despite the number of schools of psychology, only two headings are necessary for the discussion of their relation to mimetic criticism. The first, stimulus theory, derives chiefly from applications of diluted physiology and neurology to literary theory; the second, psychoanalytic theories, derive from Freud and Jung. Stimulus theories see the poem as a stimulus providing the reader with the opportunity for certain incipient physical actions; psychoanalytic theories see it as an expression of man's unconscious.

Stimulus theories may take three forms, two of which are of little value to criticism; the third may be useful. The first, the one developed by the early I. A. Richards, is largely inapplicable to practical criticism. I must apologize for dissecting Richards' work anew — that has been one of the easiest and most pursued hobbies of theorists — but it is necessary because his work has too frequently been damned for its virtues and imitated in its errors. For Richards, a poem is primarily a stimulus; the real poem happens in the mind, which in reality is a part of the activity of the nervous system. When a poem is read, the eye picks up visual sensations of the printed words; images closely associated with the words appear, followed by a free flow of images; finally the images stimulate thoughts, followed by emotions and "affective-volitional attitudes." [18] Although Richards' description of the process may be insufficiently technical for the psychologist, it is probably accurate as an outline.

Generally, then, all stimuli create their appropriate physiological and, consequently, their appropriate affective-volitional responses — whether the stimulus be a lyric, an auto appearing suddenly in the wrong lane, or a tastefully prepared dinner. The organism responds by adjusting to the stimulus. But stimuli given through art have two advantages that other stimuli lack. The first simply is that art is not reality. An object referred to in a poem ("marble," for example, in Shakespeare's "Not marble, nor the gilded monuments") appears in a strange context, a context which is often unusual for the object and even for the word; because of the strangeness of its setting, it forces an awareness of itself. The second advantage of art, and the cause of the first, comes from its organization. The whole poem is a single stimulus composed of carefully selected stimuli. The rhythm, for example, of ordinary conversation is usually so disorganized that individual rhythmic units are confused and ignored; but in poetry, rhythm is a "texture of expectations, satisfactions, disappointments, surprisals." [19] Richards' most important contribution here is that he sees rhythm (like the other elements of poetry) as an event in the experiencing mind.

These two advantages of art — the creation of a new context for a familiar word and the organization of the stimuli — make possible "balanced poise," "a general characteristic of all the most valuable experiences of the arts." [20] Here Richards provides a psychological basis for the notion that the poem is a closed system, relatively disconnected from life. Although he apparently feels that the concept of balanced poise is necessary to account for the fact that we do not react to art as directly as to immediate experience, the notion is nevertheless too simple. It explains, for example, that the playgoer does not leap upon the stage to warn Hamlet that the sword is poisoned because his concern for Hamlet is balanced by his wonder at the beauty of the spectacle and the language. But it makes explanation of an equally important fact impossible: given the obvious artificiality of art, why is concern for Hamlet felt often and strongly enough to be a critical problem?

Richards' chief contribution to literary criticism is his insistence that the poem is a stimulus, that it is something which produces a state or complex of states in the reader. Practical criticism is largely a matter of finding out what in the poem stimulated a particular response — of explaining the critic's reaction in terms of the stimulus. And in fairness to Richards, he insists that the reader re-acts to the poem rather than merely acts. There must be something specific in the line "When I have fears that I may cease to be" that shapes the reader's response; Richards' view forces attention to the details of the poem. It encourages the reader to think about Keats's line in terms something like these: "this passage induces a feeling of pensiveness; what in it causes that mood? Just the thought, 'When I get worried about dying' does not evoke it, so I have to look more closely. The regular iambic pentameter suggests a quiet, conversational tone; the rhythm is slow because of the long vowels and the absence of stops — with the exception of *that*, which is so high pitched and short that it forces a brief pause, as if in fear . . ." I could go on, and such an exercise would be as valuable as grandiose comment about the content of the sonnet. If the purpose of criticism is to help the reader make sense of his own responses to an object, the technique is surely sound.

This modification of Richards' position leads to the second kind of stimulus theory. The difference between the two is that Richards sees the stimuli as canceling out one another (the balanced poise); this considers the stimuli as cumulative. At its extreme, this second approach considers all symbolization as an objectification of what would have been for primitive man both private and physical. The approach is based upon the Vernon

Lee theory of the origin of language, which claims that use of a word like *rise* evokes a barely perceptible sensation of rising.[21] A poem, then, is simply a container of incipient sensations. The theory is largely inapplicable because language has developed so far that a study of poetry based on its origin misses much and because it cannot account for strictly poetic value.

The third type of stimulus theory is not so much a theory as a technique — actually, it amounts to taking what is most usable from the other varieties of the theory and combining it with other approaches. F. R. Leavis' discussion of "Strange Fits of Passion Have I Known" illustrates the method:

> The poem opens with a promise of a dramatic surprise. The surprise is that, after half a dozen stanzas of preparation, we are given a bathos — bathos except "in the Lover's ear alone." Actually the success of the poem depends on our getting both that surprise and the Lover's surprise, for Wordsworth induces in us enough of the appropriate "ear." As the Lover trots steadily on, his mind on Lucy and his eye on the moon, we share something of his blissful state of hypnosis.
>
> > My horse moved on; hoof after hoof
> > He raised, and never stopped
>
> — that suggests the uninspired matter-of-factness parodied in *Rejected Addresses:* . . . It has, of course, an essential function: to complete the setting up of that background of routine sensation against which the sudden awakening surprise is to stand out. . . . Then dramatically, to the Lover and to us, the unconscious identifying trick of his mind is revealed.[22]

Leavis' analysis suggests that he has felt the stimulation of the words and their arrangements rather than merely their bare meanings — e.g., that the success of the poem depends directly upon a physiological reaction from the reader. He could have gone on to suggest the effects of the double alliteration in the first line, the regularity of the rhythm, and so on. Leavis was probably correct in not paying much attention to these minor techniques; what is important is the effect they produce. It is the *functional* monotony that makes Wordsworth's lines art.

Psychoanalytic theories have been much more prominent in literary criticism than stimulus theories because they have more to offer. Most critics would claim to find something in poetry that transcends the everyday rules of logic and grammar, and technique alone probably does not explain the transcendence. We generally recognize that the total significance of a poem is greater than the total effect of its units. Moreover, since Coleridge distinguished between reason and imagination, the analysis of the differences between science and art, discourse and dreams, poetry and prose has become part of the job of every literary theorist. Even critics of such diverse sensibilities as Ransom and Read argue that true poetry is that which bears least resemblance to prose. Psychoanalytic theory is one explanation of the alogical, the nonprose, in poetry.

Technical discussion of the differences between the ideas of Freud and of Jung is not necessary here. The work of each has three uses in contemporary criticism: to explain the genesis of individual poems or of poetry in general, to interpret the work, and to evaluate it. Freud's theories are usually invoked for the first and second of these, Jung's for the second and third. Briefly, Freud finds the origin of art in neurosis; the artist is a neurotic who is able to "elaborate his day-dreams, so that they lose the personal note" and may be enjoyed by others; the artist thereby wins "through his phantasy — what before he could only win in phantasy: honor, power, and the love of women." [23] Although Wellek and Warren try to refute the notion of the artist as neurotic by urging that the poet "is engaged in an act of externalization and of adjustment to society," they actually only restate Freud.[24] Susanne K. Langer's dismissal of this part of Freud's work is more to the point; she observes that Freud "makes no distinction between good and bad art." [25]

Rather than attributing art to neurosis, Jung emphasizes a welling up of "great 'primordial images'" — "potentialities of human representation of things as they have always been, inherited through the brain structure from one generation to the next." Such images "are the deepest, the most ancient, and the most universal thoughts of humanity. They are as much feelings as thoughts, and have indeed an individual, independent, existence." [26]

In assessing the value of psychoanalytic theory for evaluative criticism, Freud and Jung may be discussed together because the intellectual climate they created is vastly more important than the differences over which their disciples quarrel. As Trilling notes (in relation to Freud), analytic psychology "makes poetry indigenous to the very constitution of the mind." [27] Instead of the wild babblings of a primitive witch doctor or the decadent mutterings of an over-civilized poet, poetry is here recognized as the central function of man's mind. Reason, not imagination, is the interloper, and poetry no longer has to be defended against logic. Not only that, but for good or ill a whole new realm of content opens up for literature — a realm not new because it had neither appeared nor been known before, but new as a recently independent nation is new. As long as reason was monarch, poetry had to strain to be reasonable; Freud confirmed the insight of the romantics that the alogical has both its own laws and its own vitality.

Equally important for our purposes is Jung's observation that psychic phenomena "consist not only of *meaning* but of *value*." [28] The "primordial images," if I read Jung correctly, release emotional forces which are readily translatable as feelings of value or disvalue. Moreover, because the primordial images are subconscious rather than conscious, their presence in a poem has a paradoxical effect — because they are subconscious their conscious use is surprising, and because they are primordial they are common to all men, so that response to them is at once easy and powerful. The poet does not discover new psychological content; his task is to bring the experience to the surface and to embody it in such a way that the reader will recognize, understand, and value experiences that are part of him but that have been hidden from him.

One of the best applications of psychoanalytic theory is still Maud Bodkin's *Archetypal Patterns in Poetry*. In writing of *The Rime of the Ancient Mariner*, she describes her method:

> Particular words and images, such as those of wind, of storm-cloud, of slime, of red colour, have been examined for their emotional symbolism, but mainly with reference to their capacity to enter into an emotional sequence. Within the image-sequences examined the pattern appears of a movement, downward, or inward toward the earth's centre, or a cessation of movement — a change which, as we urge metaphor closer to the impalpable forces of life and soul, appears also as a transition toward severed relation with the outer world, and, it may be, toward disintegration and death. The element in the pattern is balanced by a movement upward and outward — an

expansion or outburst of activity, a transition toward red-integration and life-renewal.

To the pattern thus indicated in extreme generality we may give the name of the Rebirth archetype.[29]

The force of *The Rime of the Ancient Mariner* certainly cannot be explained by either logical or common-sense interpretation of the images; nor can logic or common sense account for the coherence of parts we recognize in the poem. The archetypal theory, as Miss Bodkin uses it, does both. Within the words of a successful poem, so the argument runs, is leashed a certain fury which cannot be understood solely in terms of technique or of "prose" meaning. It is difficult to quarrel with this view.

Neither proper psychological definition of *archetype* nor the relative soundness of Freud's and Jung's views of the content of the unconscious need concern the literary critic directly. The only significant fact is that elements do get into poetry which can best be explained by psychoanalytic theory. It should make very little difference to the practical critic whether color symbolism, for example, be accepted as the manifestation of "primordial images" or as a literary convention — that is a matter of genetics. What is important is that it is used and that somehow it generates an emotional response. Readers tend to feel a sense of disappointment or dramatic change (depending upon the author's talent) if a heroine all in white suddenly seizes her lover and begins passionately making love — passion is for ladies in red. For the theorist, the notion of archetypes may explain the particular items that get into literary traditions and account for their emotional force.

The approach, though, has two difficulties — one accidental to it and the other inherent in it. The accidental is the over-use of psychoanalytic concepts. Critics are eager to pounce upon any hero whose first name begins with a *J* or to make the most of any description of concave, convex, or flat surfaces — without explaining how an author can avoid all three possibilities. The method must be used carefully; primordial images, archetypes, latent contents — whatever vocabulary the critic uses — refer to the lowest common denominator of humanity. They do not refer to the entire content of human experience, nor even to all that is significant in human experience. Even assuming that Freud is correct, mankind has come far since the sons slew the father and devoured him. Poetry reflects not only the primitive and subconscious, but also the civilized and the conscious. Its criticism, therefore, must go beyond whatever traces of the primitive it contains.

The inherent difficulty is that psychoanalysis is necessarily concerned with fantasy or "psychic reality" rather than with art. Without going beyond itself, it cannot distinguish between the fantasy of a madman and the lyric embodying the same psychic content. But the question for the literary theorist is precisely the question of that difference. Why do I frequently re-read *The Rime of the Ancient Mariner*, but avoid my neighbor with the neurotic glittering in his eye? Analytic theory provides no answer because it lacks the means to discuss the work in terms of form and technique.

PERCEPTION THEORY

Perception theory is superficially the simplest of all mimetic theories. It sees the poem as a linguistic representation of a thing that has been perceived; in some way the poem is the equivalent of an object, and its value depends upon how accurately it represents that object. Its strongest point is that one can easily move back and forth from it to other kinds of theories. A critic chiefly interested in personality may argue that the unique characteristic of the poet is his ability to observe; the poem is the record and proof of his observation. A critic wanting moral values in poetry but trying to avoid overt didacticism may claim that "A poem must not mean, but be" and that by its very being it edifies. Proponents of perception theory usually accept the division between poetry and rational or abstract knowledge; abstract knowledge enables man to deal with generalities, but poetry is said to be his most effective way of apprehending particulars and his only sure way of knowing them. Since reason may not properly know the particular, its standards are not applicable to poetry. The only two kinds of criteria relevant for perception theory are the faithfulness of the poem to the individual object, or the integration of the material in the poem into a complete perceptual unit. Since the latter is a formalist standard, it will be considered in the next chapter. Most often, though, critics use both sets of criteria, John Crowe Ransom, for example, writes like the narrowest of imitationists while building his theory, but like a formalist when he discusses individual poems.

Perception theories are founded on the insight that sense perception is the most common source of both feeling and thought, if not the only source. Although the insight was old, the English romantic poets — especially Coleridge and Keats — seemed to be the first to appreciate the value of objects as a means of attaining knowledge of the universal. One branch of English romanticism is characterized by its emphasis upon the particular, the individual.

From the realization of experience of the individual object as an embodiment of the infinite and so worthy of accurate reproduction to the acceptance of accurate reproduction as an end in itself was a logical step. It was also inevitable after the intellectual upheavals of the last half of the nineteenth century had created a terrain on which one's stand on social, moral, or intellectual issues was likely to be precarious. When an age loses faith in universals, art and aesthetics take up particulars.

Much of modern poetry, in fact, has followed Marianne Moore's dictum, "Be abstract / and you'll wish you'd been specific" — a dictum only occasionally taken seriously before the twentieth century, before the contrast between fact and abstraction was so sharply drawn. The physical poetry of such writers as Miss Moore, Wallace Stevens, and William Carlos Williams asks to be judged from what seem to be purely aesthetic standards. Stevens' "Study of Two Pears," for example, apparently offers only the formed imitation of a perception. Its aesthetic judgment would seem uncomplicated by extraneous factors.

Pure perception theories treat language as transparent, or at least potentially transparent. In the classic statement of the extreme form of the theory, T. E. Hulme distinguishes between prose and poetic language; the former is a "counter language," the latter "a visual concrete one." The whole point of poetry's attempt at originality and freshness is to make the reader see the object; its purpose is "to arrest you, and to make you continuously see a physical thing, to prevent you from gliding through an abstract process." [30] Hulme, in other words, assumes that poetry is the perfect verbal equivalent of objects. Because ordinary language registers as language rather than as thing, the business of the poet is to fulfill the "passionate desire for accuracy" [31] of poet and reader. Although "accurate, precise and definite description" [32] is not unattainable in poetry, the importance Hulme attaches to it and his literalness about it severely limit his poetics. In the first place, the kind of description he wants is impossible unless the object itself is "precise and definite." But certain important areas of human feeling, human knowledge, and even human perception cannot be so characterized. Does "precise," with its connotations of "finely chiseled, sharp, clearly delineated," describe "Dover Beach"? Or Shakespeare's sonnets? — Such poetry penetrates too deeply and in too many directions to be "precise." A theory that does not account for many of our best poems argues strongly against itself.

The second limitation of Hulme's poetics is his denial of the creativity of the poet as a user of language. "The mind," he writes, "cannot *create* form, it can only *edit* it." [33] If Hulme is correct, then (as most modern theorists would quickly point out) a poem is merely a substitute for something else. Actually, however, the mind does create form, or at least participate in its creation, with every sense perception. A wall, for example, with a mirror, a shelf, and a clock hanging on it changes form as we are interested in adjusting our tie, finding a pencil, or knowing the time. In addition to this elementary and constant mental creativity, language is itself creative. Words in proper combinations explode, scattering bits of their influence throughout the entire poem. Ordinary language is not dead, as Hulme suggests; it is filled with infinite, but buried, possibilities, possibilities which are resurrected in poetry. Its potentialities of description exist side by side with potentialities of meaning and feeling. The best poetry makes words work together to realize all that is in them.

John Crowe Ransom is the most respected of the critics who rely on perception theory. We value art because it is an imitation, and "we value an imitation because it gives us pleasure." [34] And even when he changes from an Aristotelian to a Kantian terminology — "Poetry is the representation of natural beauty" [35] — the idea does not change. Unfortunately, when Ransom is thinking as a pure imitationist he rarely either discusses technique or analyzes specific poems; but since we can judge poetic imitation only by the way language is used — in terms of technique — this part of his work is unsatisfactory.

Ransom does admit one important difference between an imitation (a poem) and its original. The "imitation is better than its original in one thing only: not being actual it cannot be used, it can only be known." [36] There are three good reasons for quarreling with this. First, the material of poetry differs from the material of the objects it imitates; poems and skylarks exist on entirely different levels. The "barred clouds" of Keats's "Ode to Autumn" are neither real clouds nor even well-pictured clouds; they are merely functions in the larger structure of the Ode.

Or, granting that the poem is an imitation in Ransom's sense, why is it better because its only function is cognitive? What we get in poetry that attempts to be pure is most frequently a purification of the object — a change in it — so that the knowledge it offers is no longer precisely knowledge of the object. An analysis of a seemingly pure poem, Wallace Stevens' "God Is Good. It Is a Beautiful Night" will show what I mean.

> Look round, brown moon, brown bird, as you rise to fly,
> Look round at the head and zither
> On the ground.
>
> Look round you as you start to rise, brown moon,
> At the book and shoe, the rotted rose
> At the door.

This was the place to which you came last night,
Flew close to, flew to without rising away.
Now, again,

In your light, the head is speaking. It reads the book.
It becomes the scholar again, seeking celestial
Rendezvous.

Picking thin music on the rustiest of string,
Squeezing the reddest fragrance from the stump
Of summer.

The venerable song falls from your fiery wings.
The song of the great space of your age pierces
The fresh night.

Is this poem only an imitation of a certain night, seen by
a certain man, under specific conditions? Or is it not,
rather, a selection and a creation? Stevens' picture of the
night in the opening lines — the purest part of the poem
— is incomplete, although the slightest amount of imagination could fill in the details. If there is a moon,
there are probably stars, and there may or may not be a
breeze. A house certainly stands behind the door, the
book has pages and a cover of some color and size, and
the song has melody and rhythm. But none of this is in
the poem; it is not needed because the poet is doing
something more than imitating nature; he is creating a
perception of nature (and a mood) by selecting a few details from a much larger store.

The third reason for refusing to accept Ransom's perception theory may also be shown by an analysis of a
poem — this time Stevens' "Study of Two Pears."

I

Opusculum paedagogum.
The pears are not viols,

Nudes or bottles.
They resemble nothing else.

## II

They are yellow forms
Composed of curves
Bulging toward the base.
They are touched with red.

## III

They are not flat surfaces
Having curved outlines.
They are round
Tapering toward the top.

## IV

In the way they are modelled
There are bits of blue.
A hard dry leaf hangs
From the stem.

## V

The yellow glistens.
It glistens with various yellows,
Citrons, oranges and greens
Flowering over the skin.

## VI

The shadows of the pears
Are blobs on the green cloth.
The pears are not seen
As the observer wills.

The last two lines are especially interesting because they
are totally unnecessary for the description; the insistence

upon what the pears are not has already made the point. Nevertheless, Stevens' poem would have been much thinner without the final predication. By relating the description of the pears to an abstract idea, a whole new area of complexity emerges from the poem. Even though the effect does not last, the poem is momentarily enriched because of the interpenetration of the physical and conceptual worlds. Perception theory fails to admit such enrichment.

The new realm of complexity introduced in the final two lines does not last because, as the poem itself proves, the pears are seen as the observer wills. They are seen by Stevens as objects to be described and cherished, and possibly as props for an idea; if he were hungry he would probably pay less attention to the look of the pears and more to their aroma, their probable succulence, and their texture. I am suggesting that a poem is likely to be both more and less than a rendering of a perception; a part of the original physical reality is left out, and a part of the world of ideas put in.

When Ransom attempts to apply his version of perception theory the result is usually a criticism of imagery, such as this:

> Tennyson in his boldest lyric sings:
>
> > Come into the garden, Maud,
> > For the black bat, night, has flown,
>
> and leaves us unpersuaded of the bat. The predication would be complete without the bat. . . . later in the same poem he writes:
>
> > The red rose cries, "She is near, she is near";
> >     And the white rose weeps, "She is late";
> > The larkspur listens, "I hear, I hear";
> >     And the lily whispers, "I wait."

and this is a technical conceit. But it is too complicated
for its author, having a plurality of images which do not
sustain themselves individually.[37]

"Black bat," Ransom is saying, is a gratuitous detail, nor
is there any precise reason for assigning a particular line
to a particular flower. The die-hard Tennysonian might
point out that the cry of the red rose is a passionate cry
and the weeping of the white rose more innocent, but
the suggestions in the color symbolism are too tenuous to
be thoroughly convincing. The result, if the lines are read
critically, is a slight mental reservation which might inhibit the reader's appreciation of the poem.

T. S. Eliot's version of a similar approach illustrates, I
believe, a more legitimate use of it:

> This guest of summer,
> The temple-haunting martlet, does approve
> By his loved mansionry that the heaven's breath
> Smells wooingly here: no jutty, frieze,
> Buttress, nor coign of vantage, but this bird
> Hath made his pendent bed and procreant cradle:
> Where they most breed and haunt, I have observed
> The air is delicate.

It may be observed that such an image, . . . not only
offer[s] something to the eye, but, so to speak, to the common sense. I mean that . . . [it] convey[s] the feeling of
being in a particular place at a particular time.[38]

This precision of detail, which may be valued for its own
sake, also helps the reader accept the theme of the passage. Eliot is merely recognizing that Shakespeare wrote
about the real universe, so that if Shakespeare does offer
more than description, the reader may feel, "Yes, he and
I live in the same world; what this man says may be

worthwhile." But here the criticism passes beyond evaluation in terms of perceptual content.

The final approach to be considered here is the most impure of perception theories. Wallace Stevens has given it its best expression; he is writing about a poem by Marianne Moore — the bird is an ostrich:

> Somehow, there is a difference between Miss Moore's bird and the bird of the *Encyclopedia*. This difference grows when she describes her bird as
>
> > *The friend*
> > *of hippotigers and wild*
> > *asses, it is as*
> > *though schooled by them he was*
> > *the best of the unflying*
> > *pegasi.*

The difference signalizes a transition from one reality to another. It is the reality of Miss Moore that is the individual reality. That of the *Encyclopedia* is the reality of isolated fact. Miss Moore's reality is significant. An aesthetic integration is a reality.

Nowhere in the poem does she speak directly of the subject of the poem by its name. She calls it "the camel-sparrow" and "the large sparrow Xenophon saw walking by a stream," "the bird," "quadruped-like bird" and

> *alert gargantuan*
> *little-winged, magnificently*
> *speedy running-bird.*

This, too, marks a difference. To confront fact in its total bleakness is for any poet a completely baffling experience. Reality is not the thing but the aspect of the thing. At first reading, this poem has an extraordinarily factual appearance. But it is, after all, an abstraction.[39]

And, on a more theoretical level:

> We have not been studying images, but, however crudely, analogies, of which images are merely a part. Analogies are much the larger subject. . . . Poetry becomes and is a transcendent analogue composed of the particulars of reality, created by the poet's sense of the world, that is to say, his attitude, as he intervenes and interposes the appearances of that sense.[40]

This position is very like the one to be developed at the end of this study. Stevens' special advance is his realization that all views are analogies, that any apprehension of reality — be it conceptual, emotional, or perceptual — is formed both by the object and by the subject of the experience. He suggests that the object must be a particular, but the particularity of the object is not essential to his view. A general idea, for example, is not an unchangeable entity deposited without modification in the human mind; on the contrary, like a particular, it is modified by the entire fiber of each person who entertains it. As a consequence, the distinction between a general idea and a particular object may be irrelevant for purposes of poetic expression; each event in the mind is a particular realization. And this is true not only for ideas and perceptions, but also for emotions. What matters, then, is not the object to be imitated, but the presentation of an experience with sufficient depth and richness that it can be felt as unique. This approach allows the broadest possible basis for poetry and also accounts for the world-poet-poem relationship.

It also helps account for the fourth factor necessary in a theory of poetry — language. Stevens' general view of poetry implies no limitation for language. Because the object may be any kind of object, any kind of language may be used in its realization. The only qualification is that the words make "a world that transcends the world." [41] Despite the vague terminology, the view is meaningful in context. Stevens does not, however, adequately explain the role played by poetic technique.

In summary, the purer forms of perception theory, by concentrating upon the uniqueness and objectivity of poetry, avoid some of the difficulties of other theories. In particular, the whole question of poetic belief can be evaded and, since the object of imitation is a segment of physical reality, the difficulty of purely private poetry is often obviated. But such gains are made at the cost of an impermissible limitation upon the range of poetry and a weakness in analyzing the role of technique. As perception theories manage to avoid these weaknesses, they tend to pass over into other kinds of approach. The positive value of perception theory, like that of any mimetic theory, is that it admits into the spectrum of literary theory its own special kind of value, the value lent to poetry by its inclusion of the description of physical reality.

# V

## THE POEM AS CLOSED FORM

Because mimetic theories do not provide an adequate basis for literary evaluation, recent critics and aestheticians have developed a number of antimimetic approaches. The constant danger of mimetic theories is the temptation to forget about literature and to lose oneself in the world of politics, or ethics, or philosophy, or psychology, or flowers, or whatever the poem is supposed to imitate. The most popular way of avoiding getting lost has been to consider the poem as a closed form, an autonomous system. The approach comes with a great number of trims, but generally the poem is said to be a form so tightly woven that it shuts out the rest of the world. The poem is isolated from other experiences because, it is said, it completely fills the reader's attention. Murray Krieger, using the terminology of Eliseo Vivas, describes the poetic experience as one of "intransitive, rapt attention" upon the poem, so that whatever functions, functions "reflexively." The aesthetic experience is shattered, so the argument runs, if the material in the poem leads "back into the world," thereby diverting attention "from the self-sufficient system constituted by these symbols" which make up the poem.[1]

The advantages of arguing that poetic form is closed are numerous and obvious. Among the most important is that the approach checks the reader's imagination, insisting upon adherence to the text. It likewise forces attention to the detailed relationships within the poem — again keeping the critic at his proper job, the criticism of the poem as poem. These advantages are not to be rejected lightly.

Yet the approach leads to excesses, and these in turn lead to contradictions, the most serious and common of which is the double claim made for art — that it both ennobles man in some mysterious way and also is unsmudged with any utilitarian benefits. Croce wants to keep the intuition pure and unique; Bergson bravely contends that the sole purpose of art is to "brush aside the utilitarian symbols" so that we may see reality better, but he does not explain how we can see reality except through the foggy glasses of utilitarian symbols; Bernard Berenson assumes that the world is a messy and unpleasant place from which we flee to art; Ortega y Gasset fears that if a bit of the world creeps into a poem, his sensitive nose will "smell the Philistine." [2] Later I shall show why theories that isolate art cannot also glorify it; for now I want merely to call attention to the large, respected, and respectable body of criticism that urges the complete isolation of the work of art.

Our desire to glorify art by removing utilitarian dross is only one of the factors contributing to the influence of closed-form theories. Exploration of the unconscious had led to the exploitation of irrationality in art generally and, especially, in poetry and painting. Elizabeth Sewell — who, I believe, is one of the more convincing advocates of this line — posits the utilitarian worlds of science and practical activity on the one side, worlds of dream and nightmare on the other. Poetry avoids the former by following the structural principles of the latter. The result, as she applies her method, is exceptionally close reading for the illogicalities of poetry and an equally exceptional blindness to common-sense interpretations.[3]

Another factor, diametrically opposed to Miss Sewell's kind of interest but with similar effects, is the vogue of logical positivism and its notion that poetry (and, presumably, even philosophy) cannot make valid statements. It too has contributed to the assumption that the only test of a poem's value is its internal coherence, its form-as-removed-from-everything-else.

I shall not make a detailed critique of theories of closed form before looking at the approach more closely, but I should like to make clear my bias. On the credit side, theories of closed form lead to much and good practical criticism; they require an attention to detail which makes for better understanding and better appreciation of the poem than is possible with mimetic theories. On the debit side, however, they lead to insurmountable difficulties. Poems are made of words, and, whether we like it or not, words are worldly things. They bring their references with them despite our theories, and their references are to the outside world. Once inside the poem, they may point only indirectly to the world outside, but they do point. "The Love Song of J. Alfred Prufrock," for example, seems to refer to no person, to have no specific setting, and to deal in purely imaginary thoughts and feelings. But this is not entirely true. Much of the value of the poem comes from our recognition that Prufrock represents a class of persons, that he has much the same status as the "economic man" or the irrational number. The "Prufrock man" is a fiction which somehow increases our understanding of certain aspects of modern culture. The poem is valuable precisely because it refuses to close itself to the world; it is valuable because it opens onto a relatively broad and significant segment of reality.

Theories of closed form also find great difficulty in accounting for what the reader brings to the poem. Probably no critic has argued more diligently or persuasively for the necessity of remaining within the poem than has Cleanth Brooks, yet he has to admit that "we *start* outside the poem" and also that "we are forced to go *outside the poem*" if we are to understand its tensions and reconciliations.[4] (This admission, I should note, is tucked safely away in a footnote; Brooks makes no attempt to follow it to its conclusion.) If the theorist argues that we do not start outside the poem, if it does not open to normal experience, he must posit some innate mass of sensitivity which, buried somewhere in man, miraculously throbs in the presence of poetry. But our experience tells us that the sensitivity is not innate; it must be cultivated with care, either easily through suitable environment or painfully through formal education. Because the sensitivity is acquired, it is of different kinds and of different degrees.

This leads to the last difficulty I shall mention here. "Closed" form and its synonyms suggest an absolute for what is actually relative. If the form is not partly closed, it will likely seduce the reader's imagination into a riot of revery. But if the form does not partly open, if there is no chink in its armor, its impregnability gives the imagination nothing with which to work. Shelley's notorious line, "I die, I faint, I fail," is about as open a statement as poetry is capable of. Critics usually dispose of it by noting that it is overly personal and anticlimactic, but that does not explain its badness. It is too open, it incites too many irrelevant associations. The very fact that the reader is invited to exclaim, "Aha, an anticlimax!" distracts from what the line should be doing. But still further, it introduces a whole series of irrelevant questions — at what did Shelley fail, how can he fail after death, if he can fail after death, will he perhaps not recover? The questions are impertinent but not inappropriate; Shelley asks for them by being too open. Still, the line is in a sense closed; the reader neither calls the coroner nor wonders how a dead poet finished the poem. Although all of this should be elementary, it must be denied by any critic who accepts the notion of closed form. Some word that admits of degrees — integrity, density, intensity, control — would generate sounder theory and sounder criticism.

Language is the chief source of the problems arising from closed-form theories; the approach presupposes that language can shed its normal functions. Speculation about poetic language within closed-form theories branches off in three directions: poetic language may be said to resemble ordinary language, to have no relation to it, or to form a special kind of structure within the poem.

Since Coleridge, critics have usually divided language neatly into its scientific (including practical and rational) and poetic uses. Because the approach has been seen before and will be discussed again, we shall treat it only briefly here. Questioning which symbol — $H_2O$ or *wet* — better describes water, Max Eastman rightly concluded that the poet and his readers should hold out for the latter because, even though it cannot be put into a formula with a specific reference, it does refer to what one should know about water.[5] The scientist might want to argue that "wet" tells nothing about the saturation properties of the liquid, its molecular structure, or the physical laws which control it; he would, in agreement with some aestheticians, say that "wet" is not precise. Yet the question for the literary theorist is not whether words are imprecise outside the poem, but whether they are meaningful inside it. "Wet," or a more available example, "chill" is admittedly unspecific when used alone. "Chill" connotes both "chilly" (moderately or pleasantly cold) and "chilled" (painfully cold). But when the word is given a poetic context? In "St. Agnes' Eve — Ah, bitter chill it was!" the word is at once specific and rich. The sound of the line, the emphatic structure, the qualifying "bitter" — all combine to make the term more precise than "St. Agnes' Eve — minus 23° Fahrenheit it was." The poetic term is more accurate because the thermometer temperature is irrelevant; the relevant fact is that it was an unpleasant night on which to be outdoors.

I am suggesting that science and poetry have different kinds of precision, and therefore different techniques. In scientific discourse the meanings are delimited as accurately as possible before entering into a context, but in poetic discourse meanings are stabilized only as the context develops. The poetic word steps out of language and pulls all its references with it. As the word enters the poem it has not one referent (as has "minus 23° Fahrenheit"), but a general range of referents, some of which are made to work and some of which are excluded. Poetry can achieve this control largely because of the complexity of its material. Psychologists tell us that the greater the relevant complexity of a stimulus, the more control it will have over the direction of the response. A red blob may excite any number of reactions. Add another factor by making it round, and one either admires the sunset or puts on the brakes; put it at the top of a pole with yellow and green lights, and the reaction is relatively predictable. Poetry attains its precision because of the richness of the world brought into the poem through the word. In a well-wrought poem the result is a kind of specification alien to science but no less meaningful.[6]

The relationship between poetic language and common language is more complicated. Does the provision which a closed system must make for a special aesthetic use of language require that it view poetic and common language as radically different? Is poetry simply the invigorated common language of an age, the common language with its potentialities fully realized? Or must poetic language break the bonds of ordinary language?

T. S. Eliot has been the most impressive champion of the closeness of poetic and common language, although he modifies his position to include its opposite. Specifically, Eliot faced the problem of reconciling his preference for "the common style" with his notion of the music of poetry. Although most of Eliot's discussion of both parts of the problem appears in *On Poets and Poetry*, he characteristically neglects to relate the parts, preferring to hint at the solution but refusing to describe it. The source of Eliot's respect for the common language is his belief that "emotion and feeling, then are best expressed in the common language of the people — that is, in the language common to all classes: the structure, the rhythm, the sound, the idiom of a language express the personality of the people which speaks it." [7] "Common to all classes" is especially important because it qualifies the notion of "common language." It elevates that language by purifying it; elsewhere Eliot suggests that we ought to attend more to "the good or bad breeding of our poets." [8] His quarrel with Milton's influence on this score is not so much that Milton's language is ineffective, but that "it is not the elevation of a *common* style." [9]

The common language is for Eliot the ground bass over which poetry plays its tunes. The musical conventions of poetry rigidify, forcing poetic language to become constantly less flexible, constantly more reliant upon orthodox patterns of form and diction. Only the common language of speech and prose, vast and ever-changing yet ever preserving its identity, gives poetry the firm substructure it needs to rise above decayed poetic conventions. Looked at differently, common language is the language from which poetry must vary, but the variation must never be too great. Eliot's view is based upon the conviction (typical of each new cycle of poetry and criticism) that only by plunging deeply into the general language of his people can the poet emerge with linguistic material sufficiently rich and flexible for the achievement of a distinct style.

Eliot posits a faculty, the auditory imagination, to sense and regulate the permissible variation from ordinary language. The auditory imagination "is the feeling for syllable and rhythm which, sinking into the primitive, always brings something back." [10] Strangely enough, it includes meanings in some way that Eliot does not make quite clear. This faculty, which distinguishes the poet from the common man, enables its possessor to rid the common language of its barnacles. Thus a chief task of poetry is its contribution to language; the chief task of the poet is "his direct duty . . . to his *language,* first to preserve, and second to extend and improve." [11] The auditory imagination, by changing the manner of expression, changes feeling by making it more conscious. For Eliot, then, the common language is the basis of poetry, but poetry — through the mediation of the auditory imagination — reacts upon language, making it a finer medium of expression and insight.

The relation Eliot finds between common language and poetry is probably correct, but it is not generally applicable to poetry. (It is worth remembering that Eliot himself used it to dismiss Milton.) I can understand, for example, how the standard might be applied to a poem like Francis Douglas Davidson's "Bought":

> Fine rays of praise my asking rings from her
> rose and the dying warrior can do no more
> at night on frosty plains
> to satisfy the heart's desire
> creation's bloom on dying things admire
> the fire down empty corridors the black night makes
> incarnate in the strength that sleeps it
> so dies like days in emblems pressed
> on mortal thoughts and fears which follow them
> if pity finds a heart and fills the hunger.
> Her nature drawn in smiles
> not merely wished or guessed
> miles after hours I strove to hold the essence frozen
> only she dismissed and gave my gaze to remember
> empty hands on the counter fold, unfold
> in thoughts' weave rest unrest.

Eliot's notion of "common style" is applicable to this kind of poetry, although we do not have to follow quite the same path he might take. Davidson's poem is an attempt to create a music of words, that resonance of linguistic factors and reverberations of functions of words one with another that Eliot demands of poetry. Musically, the first line is regular iambic pentameter, with the metric and semantic accents coinciding. But Davidson controls the tone of the reading, demanding a kind of angry irony. In four of the five accented beats an $r$ sound occurs, emphasized once by alliterative use, again by figuring prominently in an internal rhyme ("rays of praise"), and by being part of the rhyming syllable. Even the word order ("Fine thing it was . . .") is typical ironic inversion. There is also a certain fine play of the music of meaning and imagery in the "rays . . . rings" combination. So much for the music; the line is still faulty. The ironic inversion is trite; it is unnecessarily (and in the context of this poem, inappropriately) colloquial. But more important, the gaudiness of the sound, emphasized by the internal rhyme, might be an instance of what Eliot called "bad breeding."

As the line stands, however, it could be the start of a satisfactory poem. Quickly, though, something happens. The music of the *r*'s continues, again repeated in four of five stressed syllables, but the ironic tone has dissipated with the introduction of low-pitched vowels and the sudden, unprepared for, and unsuccessful sounding of a note of pathos. Significantly, the failure to sustain the tone occurs simultaneously with the failure to preserve conventional semantic and grammatical relations. Is "rose" a noun or a verb? It should be a verb, governed by "rays"; but the elision of the *r*'s and the grammatical ambiguity of "her" tempt the reader to follow the easier course and accept it as the object of "from." Language here has not been stretched — that would be proper poetic technique; it has been broken. In other words, the poet has chosen a form in which certain elements (the acoustical) are augmented, but in which other values demanded by the nature of language are diminished.

The analysis of "Bought" could be continued, but it has gone far enough to show how the common language can be invoked as a standard in evaluative analysis. To stray too far from the common language tends to break the many functions of words into sound plus meaning plus syntax plus symbol, rather than to create a harmony of function within the individual word and a reverberation from word to word, function to function, throughout the poem. A poet uses "fragmented words" at his own risk — the risk of creating not poetry, but nonprose;

not language used poetically, but language minus something.

Eliot's notion of the common style may also be used in connection with an excessively flat poem, like Sandburg's "Fog":

> The fog comes
> on little cat feet.
> It sits looking
> over harbor and city
> on silent haunches
> and then moves on.

Here the language, including the grammatical and referential structure, is almost too normal. The effect of the poem — and it is not without a minor effectiveness — results from the tension generated by the originality of the image and its commonplace presentation. The effect is one of cleverness, of thinness. To put this in Eliot's terms, the "verbal music" is not a rich enough accompaniment for the semantic music.

Although these quick analyses go somewhat beyond Eliot's conception of music and common language in poetry, they remain within its implications. The difficulty with Eliot's view is that it is not nearly specific enough. His vagueness about precisely what the common language is and his silence about the detailed structure of poetic music limits its applicability to the most obvious and extreme cases. The approach provides a way of talking about poems without giving the vocabulary necessary for saying much about first-rate poems. Another way of making the same observation is to note that Eliot's linguistic standard is purely negative; it can damn, but it cannot praise intelligibly. Perhaps theories based on the uniqueness of poetic language might prove more usable. Despite the work of Max Eastman and Owen Barfield,[12] the notion of a special vocabulary for poetry is largely dead. Modern poetics follows Coleridge by extending the concept of language to include not only diction, but also grammar, word order, and so on. Thus romantic and modern theories of poetic language are generally theories about form as developed through the realization of the fullest potentialities of words. Hazlitt, for example, said much the same thing Eliot said about music in poetry, but he stressed the separation from normal speech. Poetry, for Hazlitt, was "invented" in order "to supply the inherent defect of harmony in the customary mechanism of language, to make the sound an echo to the sense, when the sense becomes a sort of echo to itself . . . in short, to take language of the imagination from off the ground, and enable it to spread its wings where it may indulge its own impulses." [13] Except for the fanciful wording, only the failure to recognize that formal elements are means of attaining aesthetic distance rather than of expressing emotion keeps this from being in accord with the currently dominant poetics. Contemporary theories about the special language of poetry usually assert that poetic language transforms "real" emotion into art emotion. René Wellek, for example, praises Coleridge's theory of meter because it implies that form "removes us from ordinary emotion." [14] Perhaps the most basic similarity between the view of Coleridge and that of such speculative contemporary critics as John Crowe Ransom is the latter's recognition of a strong but essentially commonplace current running throughout the poem alongside such deliberately formalistic elements as meter, genre pattern, developing metaphor, and so forth.

The differences between the views, however, are crucial. Briefly, they are these: Coleridge, more mystic than the moderns, thought of poetic language as the elevation of normal language to a higher but no less real level; Ransom considers poetic language as an inhibition of ordinary language, a guardian against crude and direct action. Coleridge, admitting the logical distinctions between form and content, still repeatedly insists upon the organic unity of the poem; Ransom's work depends upon the separation of "structure" from "texture" or "tissue of irrelevance." [15] Finally, Coleridge refers the poem to the poet; Ransom relieves the poet of complete responsibility for his creation by introducing his theory of "determinate" and "indeterminate" factors.[16]

It is difficult to say whether Ransom's theory of poetic language derives from his theory of poetic structure, or vice versa. His work, then, provides a useful bridge between theories of poetic language and theories of poetic structure. For Ransom, poetry is a special kind of language which "distinguishes itself by an act of will from prose." [17] The "act of will" is a deliberate inhibition of direct action so that creation might occur. What is inhibited is what the poet would like to say, or do, about the object. What inhibits? Texture, tissue of irrelevancies, the requirements of form — all these combine to inhibit the poet.[18]

The result is a duality between the core of the poem and its trappings, a duality that Ransom insists upon. Thus he writes that "the independent character of the detail is the texture of the poem, and it 'depends' from the logical argument in a sense, *though not closely determined by it.*" [19] I have italicized the last phrase because it completely denies the unity of the poem. Ransom's willingness to take the consequences of this denial separates him from the majority of contemporary critics.

Ransom sees the poem as developing from a determination of the poet, who knows what he wants to say or how he wants the poem to sound, or both, before writing the poem. The poet starts, then, with a determinate meaning, a determinate sound, or both. But language cannot be mastered so completely; the meaning will not fit into the emergent verse pattern, so it changes until it becomes something the poet did not foresee — indeterminate meaning. Nor will the language bear both the sound and the meaning the poet wanted, so indeterminate sound enters. Here, incidentally, Ransom's theory is far superior to most others we have examined. What happens, Ransom urges, is that the medium in which the poet works is obstinate; it forces him to admit effects of sound and sense which he did not intend and for which he is not entirely responsible. Hence, presumably, arises the "tissue of irrelevance" which Ransom considers the peculiar property of poetry.

But despite this insight, Ransom's work does present theoretical problems. Splitting the poem into structure and texture, determinate and indeterminate meanings, and so on, is a useful technique; the distinctions make criticism a finer tool than it would otherwise be. The difficulty, however, is that Ransom avoids the form-content problem merely by changing the vocabulary; he does not solve it. Is the technical abracadabra of structure, texture, tissue of irrelevance, determinate meaning, determinate sound, etc. really a theoretical advance over, say, Santayana's distinction between useful form and beauty of ornament? Either way, the critic is left with the old and unapplicable bifurcated judgment of form and content.

The second major difficulty in Ransom's system concerns the notions that surround indeterminate meaning, notions which also in practice lead to a divorce between form and content. Although the theory of indeterminate meaning contains much truth, it is overdeveloped. The issue at stake is the creativity of the poet. Ransom

claims that the poet is frustrated by language into producing good work; I should rather argue that as the poet
works with language new (not "in-") determinate meanings emerge. Like many contemporary critics, Ransom
sets up a machinery entirely too ponderous for the simplicity of the concept upon which it rests. This is more
than a quarrel with the way Ransom expresses his ideas;
it is an observation that the machinery is clumsy, that because of its ponderosity it is partly self-determining. In
other words, perhaps Ransom's discussion of indeterminate meanings itself provides a firsthand illustration of
what he is describing; this time the critic — not the
poet — has been forced by his language to continue a
concept further than he intended.

Robert Frost's statement about indeterminate meaning is not polysyllabic, erects no critical machinery, and
manages to express the idea without positing a radical
breach in poetry. "Suppose," Frost writes, the poet

> to have written down "When in disgrace with Fortune
> and men's eyes." He has uttered about as much as he has
> to live up to in the theme as in the form. . . . He has
> given out that he will descend into Hades, but he has
> confided in no one how far before he will turn back, or
> whether he will turn back at all, and by what jutting
> points of rock he will pick his way. He may proceed as in
> blank verse. Two lines more, however, and he has let
> himself in for rhyme, three more and he has set himself a
> stanza. Up to this point the discipline has been self-
> discipline. . . . The harsher discipline from without is
> now well begun. He who knows not both knows neither.
> His worldly commitments are now three or four deep.[20]

This is a simple, unpretentious, and wise statement of
the idea of determinate and indeterminate factors. It
stresses the double discipline, the double creativity, of

the poet. Words come into the poem through the poet, bringing with them his private usages. (I do not deny that meanings beyond the ken of the poet slip into the poem; I want here to emphasize the poet's control of emotional and intellectual tone.) A Poe or a Swinburne, to use obvious examples, will select his words for one kind of reason, a Donne or a Herrick for another. Although poets draw from the same stock of words, their choices differ, and it is these choices and the deep-reaching reasons behind them that give the poet his style and the poem its impetus. Yet, after this initial impetus, the poet is committed; his language and the form he has selected force alterations which he may prefer not to make. But the poet is always free to stop work on the poem or to rewrite it anew. This is the double creativity of the poet — the power to filter language for the right combination of sound and meaning and feeling, and the ability to judge what he has wrought.

The part of Ransom's theory I have been considering provides a way of breaking up the poem, but no way of putting it back together. Nevertheless, in such essays as "The Concrete Universal," "A Note on Ontology," and "Wanted: An Ontological Critic," he has argued, at times, for the unity of satisfactory poetry. In this phase of his work, he finds the content of poetry to be not a special structure, but "an order of existence, a grade of objectivity," [21] which cannot be treated in any other form. Ransom's view, with his cogent and persuasive statement of it, makes it no longer practical for a critic to consider the poem as *exactly* like anything else; but Ransom offers no means, no set of applicable concepts, with which to discuss the unique ontology of poems.

Ransom's interest in poetic devices is more pertinent to the evaluation of poems, but even here there is a debilitating lack of development. Rarely, for example, is the interest in special techniques brought together with broader theoretical issues. When a connection is made, the devices which distinguish poetry from prose are generally placed on the side of the irrelevancies. The poet, Ransom writes,

> knows that his practical interests will reduce this living object to a mere utility, and that his sciences will disintegrate it for their convenience. . . . The poet wishes to defend his object's existence against its enemies, and the critic wishes to know what he is doing, and how.[22]

As a critic, then, Ransom is interested not so much in what is preserved as in the means of preservation; hence his approach here is not purely mimetic.

Ransom finds three chief types of preservative: meter, fiction, and tropes combine to create an "increased volume of percipienda or sensibilia." [23] The augmentation of this volume (dependent apparently on some such faculty as Eliot's auditory imagination) results ultimately in the "concrete universal," e.g., the poem. Thus poetic devices are both causes of the uniqueness of the poem and symptoms of it. Fiction and tropes are of little concern here because they are shared with nonpoetic writing and, to be of major importance in evaluative criticism, would have to be defined so as to make their significance clear. Ransom's theory of the poet's mask is perhaps his attempt to come to grips with such definitions, but it amounts to little more than a graciously stated reminder that aesthetic distance is as necessary for the creator as it is for the reader.

The bulk of Ransom's studies of technique, which offer little to evaluative criticism, are concerned with meter. Like many prosodists, Ransom insists upon meter as the *sine qua non* of poetry and treats rhythm as a variation of the metrical pattern. The two functions of meter are to undetermine meaning and to prevent the creator from crudely seizing the object.[24] Just as importantly, when meters are "activated, as they are when the metaphysicals use them, [they] seem at first to be restrictive, and obstructive, upon the flow of the language, but actually they are what makes the phrases shine." "Meters activated" are meters used boldly, which, to paraphrase Ransom, jangle but not jingle. He gives this example, "All whom the flood did, and fire shall, o'erthrow," and comments:

> It has the musical quality of counterpoint; there is conflict between the powerful though irregular rhythms of the phrases and the metronome beat of the meter; it proves to be of advantage to both sides, for the phrase-rhythms refused to be muffled, yet the meter goes marching on.[25]

But is the line Ransom quotes poetry or prose? It could be prose of a very high order, the kind of prose Donne's age produced lavishly. The following, from Donne's sermons, will illustrate:

> How cheape was *Land* at first, how cheape were we?

and

> Death raises every man alike, so far,

and

> The dead heare not Thunder, nor feele they an Earthquake.

Are these lines poetry? They meet the metrical test Ransom proposes.

Possibly the distinction between poetry and prose is not the most useful distinction we can make; perhaps the basic distinction, both theoretically and practically, is between poetic and prosaic uses of language, with poetry a special instance of the former. Some prose approaches the condition of poetry, just as some poetry approaches the condition of prose; rather than a hard and fast distinction, therefore, a differentiation recognizing a wide degree of overlap may be more true to experience. It could then be argued that the *density* with which the resources of language are used determines whether a piece of writing is chiefly poetic or prosaic, and that a poem has as its special quality an above-normal density preserved throughout. Although the level of density is not kept constant in long poems, an "illusion" of density is. Such an illusion is created when devices are present which elsewhere in the poem (or in other poems) have contributed to real density. The devices are such elements as rhyme, line length, stanza form, sound effects, and so on. Poetry can be distinguished from verse — in the pejorative sense — because the latter achieves only the illusion of density, and that only temporarily. More often than not in verse the illusion depends upon a superabundance of technical tricks, as in Walter de la Mare's "The Listeners":

> And his horse in the silence champed the grasses
> Of the forest's ferny floor.

It sounds, until one is experienced enough to spot this kind of thing immediately, very poetic. But "The Listeners" is not a poem to live with long. "Champed," for example, creates a temporary density by suggesting balladry and knights; but the sound of the word, along with its connotations of vigor and force, destroys the silence. And why did the poet work so hard to call attention to "the forest's ferny floor"? There is nothing there — except the alliteration. The rest of the poem could be analyzed with substantially the same results.

The distinctions I have just made have the great advantage of recognizing that poetry is dependent upon no special device or set of devices; it is rather the result of density, or richness, or complexity. In the Donne poem from which Ransom quoted, the phonetic and semantic density were maintained throughout; the density could not, and should not, have been so maintained throughout the sermons.

Ransom discussed density at least once, but his conclusion seems applicable only in special cases — if it is not altogether unsound. Ransom suggests that "an almost quantitative rule might be formulated, as one that is suggestive if not binding: the more difficult the final structure, the less rich should be the distraction of the texture; and the richer the texture as we proceed toward the structure, the more generalized and simple may be the structure in the end." [26] At best this is a rule-of-thumb for evaluating poetry of only minor value. Ransom is saying that poetry must exhibit to some degree what I call density, but that the relation between density of structure and density of texture is inversely proportional. This is true of some good minor poems. Dylan Thomas's "If I were tickled by the rub of love" has frail structure and rich texture; Frost's "The Cow in Apple Time" has rich but not necessarily profound structure and a relatively simple texture. The examples are not important; if the reader quarrels with these, he may easily supply his own. What is important is that other poems of greater merit offer a direct proportion between their two phases. Briefly, then, Ransom's theory does not help to explain certain very important kinds of poetry. His practical poetics, with his theory of prosody, would be much more applicable if it were related to his notion of the concrete universal, if it were based upon his understanding of the richness of poetry.

Ransom's set of terms, structure and tissue of irrelevance, is simply one of many sets upon which recent critics have built theories. I shall now examine some other vocabularies that have become influential in literary criticism and attempt to express the idea that words in poems are vehicles uniting a complexity of meaning and feeling.

The development of Allen Tate's term "tension" is instructive because it illustrates a process typical of much contemporary criticism:

> Many poems that we ordinarily think of as good poetry — and some, besides, that we neglect — have certain common features that will allow us to invent, for their sharper apprehension, the name of a single quality. I shall call that quality tension. In abstract language, a poetic work has distinct quality as the ultimate effect of the whole, and that whole is the "result" of a configuration of meaning which it is the duty of the critic to examine and evaluate. . .

> Towards the end of this essay I shall cite examples of "tension," but I shall not say that they exemplify tension only, or that other qualities must be ignored. There are all kinds of poetry, as many as there are good poets, as many even as there are good poems, for poets may be expected to write more than one kind of poetry; and no single critical insight may impute an exclusive validity to any one kind.[27]

Thus far Tate's modesty is exemplary, but let us see what happens.

Tate proceeds by criticizing two extremes of poetry, exemplified by Edna St. Vincent Millay's "Justice Denied in Massachusetts" (in which the denotations of words are said to be ignored) and Cowley's "Hymn: To Light" (in which connotation fails). Denotation and connotation are the intension and extension of logic, which in the best poetry merge into the single quality, tension. As Tate uses the term, it includes meaning, sound, imagery, etc. insofar as these help emotion and content to emerge. Thus far there is still no objection to Tate's theory, although with some slight modifications Winters' motive and emotion and Ransom's structure and texture lead to much the same kind of analysis. The main advantage of Tate's terminology is that it does not automatically force slicing the poem into parts, as the others often do. "Tension" is merely an honorific term indicating that the poem has a suitable mixture of denotative and connotative meaning, of rational structure and suggestion.

Yet there is a danger in Tate's terminology, or at least in the way he uses it. The danger arises because Tate is not willing to describe tension fully; he shows its operation in three quick examples, provides several touchstones, but does no more. If he wants to argue that too much intension is bad and too much extension is bad, he should specify the happy medium; otherwise the standard is all but meaningless. Tate admits as much when he writes that his touchstones "imply the personal bias from which this inquiry has grown." [28] The modesty is disarming and confusing. If the disclaimer is intended seriously, Tate denies his responsibility to establish the validity of his standard, for he also writes that the touchstones are his "documentation." But if the reader is free to supply his own examples, as Tate suggests, the operative meaning of tension changes with each new set of examples.

Here is Tate's example of an inferior poem, and his criticism of it:

*What from the splendid dead*
*We have inherited —*

*Furrows sweet to the grain, and the weed subdued —*
*See now the slug and the mildew plunder.*
*Evil does overwhelm*
*The larkspur and the corn;*
*We have seen them go under.*

From this stanza by Miss Millay we infer that her splendid ancestors made the earth a good place that has somehow gone bad — and you get the reason for the title: "Justice Denied in Massachusetts." How Massachusetts could cause a general dessication, why (as we are told in a foot-note to the poem) the execution of Sacco and Vanzetti should have anything to do with the rotting of the crops, it is never made clear. These lines are mass language: they arouse an affective state in one set of terms, and suddenly an object quite unrelated to those terms gets the benefit of it; and this effect, which is usually achieved, as I think it is here, without conscious effort, is sentimentality.[29]

Had Miss Millay's poem been properly attacked, it would not be worth defending. But surely the idea of evil causing a blight upon the land is not mere sentimentality; it is not scientific, and it is as old as the Oedipus legend. Does Tate really want to establish scientific accuracy and novelty as criteria for poetry? Nor is the substitution of one affective state for another necessarily bad; much metaphor and most wit is based upon such substitution. The real weakness of Tate's method may be shown by applying his standard to a passage he lists as a touchstone of good poetry:

Beauty is but a flower
Which wrinkles will devour;
Brightness falls from the air,
Queens have died young and fair,

Dust hath closed Helen's eye.
I am sick, I must die.
    Lord, have mercy upon us!

Using Tate's technique, we might ask what relation the flower has to wrinkles, why brightness falls from the air, and whether it is legitimate to transfer the affective state aroused by these to the narrator. I agree with Tate that these lines are far superior to Miss Millay's; the point is that his method does not permit him to show why one passage rises to poetry and the other teeters just above the brink of propaganda.

I earlier noted Tate's apparent modesty in offering "tension" as a critical tool. He suggested that he was merely supplying a term to help explain one of the many effects of poetry; but by the time he gets to the first example, tension has become the sole standard of evaluation. His use of the term suggests that if a poem has tension, it is good; if not, it is bad. The implication, despite Tate's avowals to the contrary, is that other aspects of poetry are much less important. His scanty development of the concept does not earn him the right to imply so much.

William Empson's standard of ambiguity, like Tate's tension, is difficult to deal with because I cannot decide how inclusive the term is supposed to be. Once again there is the description of the term, the modest disclaimer that perhaps it is not of universal importance, and then the treatment of it as the prime characteristic of poetry. Empson's basic assumption, which is both valid and of major importance, is that the effects of a poem cannot be explained in terms of its large-scale meaning, that there are in the words of the poem, besides the obvious meanings, hints that the critic must take in order to discuss the poem's full effect. A poem, then, is something like a movie, with the words as individual still-frames packed with a variety of observable content. When a movie is seen, emotion is generated and progress felt, although none of the frames is seen long enough to permit complete conscious apprehension of its content. Thus in a movie, as in a poem, details that account for the effect are recognized consciously only after repeated experiences or only by slowing down the action. Empson's method is to study the word as a still-shot, as a detachable entity. Herein lies the strength and the weakness of his approach.

The strength of the approach may be indicated briefly. Stopping the progress of a poem and teasing a word to yield up its meanings often delivers important results. It is better than the gross and only partly accurate readings usually made of poems, and quite often when the reader returns to the poem after such analysis he finds it beautifully enriched. Yet the method is not entirely satisfactory, for too much hinges upon the simple notion of ambiguity. A system that attempts to sum up poetry in a word or a phrase is doomed. Either the requirements of the narrow terminology demand that the poem be unduly forced, or the requirements of the poem demand that the meaning of the terms be overextended.

Perhaps the most famous of Empson's analyses is his study of "Bare ruined choirs, where late the sweet birds sang."

> The comparison holds for many reasons; because ruined monastery choirs are places in which to sing, because they involve sitting in a row, because they are made of wood, are carved into knots and so forth, because they used to be surrounded by a sheltering building crystallised out of the likeness of a forest, and coloured with stained glass and painting like flowers and leaves, because they are now

abandoned by all but the grey walls coloured like the skies of winter, because the cold and Narcissistic charm suggested by choir-boys suits well with Shakespeare's feeling for the object of the Sonnets, and for various sociological and historical reasons . . . these reasons, and many more relating the simile to its place in the Sonnet, must all combine to give the line its beauty, and there is a sort of ambiguity in not knowing which of them to hold most clearly in mind. Clearly this is involved in all such richness and heightening of effect, and the machinations of ambiguity are among the very roots of poetry.[30]

Here the poetry is sacrificed to the theory; Empson does not go astray because (as Ransom suggests) he heeds the ambiguities and lets the reader lose track of more significant matters. In fact, Empson wisely suggests that the reader not attend to the ambiguities while he reads; they are there whether he notes them or not, like the pianissimo of a violin when the entire orchestra is playing.[31] If in a symphony, for example, the parts that are not intended to be heard distinctly are cut from the score, the result is something like the original composition but greatly cheapened. Ambiguities have the same purpose in poetry that indistinctly heard parts have in music. Yet Empson does go astray because (as Ransom suggests) "in overdeveloping the local occasions of his problem he is behind his readers in his sense of responsibility for the logical structure of poetry as a whole." [32] The ambiguities should in some way cohere — if not to each other then to the core (whatever that is) of the poem. Empson, apparently pleased with the bare idea of ambiguity, is content simply to extract a word or phrase from the poem, let associations develop freely, and present as part of the poem whatever comes to his active mind. Indeed,

Empson seems willing to accept any possible meaning of a word as relevant. In writing of Shakespeare's lines,

> I am sick at heart . . . this push
> Will cheere me ever, or dis-eate me now

the question is whether the reading of "cheere" should be "chair" or "cheere," and whether "dis-eate" should be "disseat," "disease," "disseizes," or "defeat." Empson sees no problem; he simply accepts all the readings, unafraid that, by piling up so many disparate versions on the poem, he may break it.[33]

Sometimes, however, instead of mistreating the poem, Empson has to force his key word, ambiguity, too far. The result at its worst is a willful silliness, a blind determination to overlook the obvious. His interpretation of "Song for St. Cecilia's Day" is not among his worst:

> *The* trumpet's *loud clangour*
>   *Invites us to arms*
> *With shrill notes of anger*
>   *And mortal alarms.*
> *The double double double beat*
>   *Of the thundering* drum
>   *Cries, heark the Foes come;*
> *Charge, charge, 'tis too late to retreat.*

It is curious on the face of it that one should represent, in a mood of such heroic simplicity, a reckless excitement . . . by saying . . . that we can't get out of the battle now and must go through with it as best we can. . . . Evidently the thought that it is no good running away is an important ingredient of military enthusiasm; at any rate, in the form of consciousness of unity with comrades, who ought to be encouraged not to retreat. . . .[34]

Even assuming that this is correct, it merely gives the kind of explication that critics usually sketch in behind the lines of a poem; it has nothing to do with ambiguity. But is Empson correct? Is the attempt to work in ambiguity by arguing that the soldiers' emotions are mixed plausible? The stanza is not, as Empson suggests, about the heroism of men; it is about the part martial music plays in the transformation of ordinary men into battle-ready soldiers. The music obviously does two things: it prepares and maintains the emotions of the men who are entering combat, and it announces the start of the battle. If one accepts this, there is no ambiguity. The difficulty with narrowly conceived theories is that they cannot be applied to the wide variety of poetry. It is an axiom of criticism that whatever a critic seeks, he shall find — whether it is there or not.

R. P. Blackmur's work partly corrects the excesses of Empson, although Blackmur has acknowledged a heavy debt to the English critic. Blackmur's term is "gesture," e.g., "the outward and dramatic play of inward and imagined meaning . . . gesture is that meaningfulness which is moving, in every sense of that word: what moves the words and what moves us." [35] Empson was often content to reproduce chunks of the *Oxford English Dictionary* or batches of miscellaneous textual emendations to explain the effects of a word; Blackmur promises that he will be interested in how words go together, despite the fact that he chooses "to emphasize the created or dead-end symbol." [36] Blackmur here pushes his theory too far; if the symbol, the word, is a dead end, the meaning of the word is controlled only by its context. Thus he can logically write that Macbeth's "Tomorrow and tomorrow and tomorrow" could be replaced by "Today and today and today," and Lear's "Never never never never never" by "Always always always always always," "and much the same effect transpire in either case. It is not at all the meaning the words *had* that counts, but the meaning that repetition, in a given situation, makes them take on." [37]

This is as extreme a position as can be taken. Let us consider the following passage:

> She should have died hereafter,
> There would have been a time for such a word,
> Tomorrow, and tomorrow, and tomorrow
> Creeps in this petty pace from day to day,
> To the last syllable of recorded time,
> And all our yesterdays have lighted fools
> The way to dusty death. Out, out, brief candle!
> Life's but a walking shadow, a poor player
> That struts and frets his hour upon the stage
> And then is heard no more. It is a tale
> Told by an idiot, full of sound and fury,
> Signifying nothing.

Could "Today, and today, and today" (or "In, in, brief candle!") have had the same effect? "Tomorrow" is a much slower word than "today" and so helps dramatize the dragging of time for a man who awaits his doom; the whole passage, moreover, is built on a time contrast. In the preceding speech Macbeth has recalled the past, when he was truly alive; at the beginning of this speech he looks hopelessly to the future. The present looms starkly as the queen dies. The past is gone, the present unbearable; Macbeth must turn to the future, only to find no solace there. By the end of the passage Macbeth is once more in his barren present. The structure (and thereby the meaning) of this passage would have been ruined by the intrusion of a series of "today's."

Blackmur's argument is even weaker in relation to Lear's lines:

135

And my poor fool is hanged! No, no, no life!
Why should a dog, a horse, a rat have life
And thou no breath at all? Thou'lt come no more,
Never, never, never, never, never!

Shakespeare has carefully prepared a tone of negation; to end positively would have destroyed the effect. Perhaps Blackmur best shows the inapplicability of his method by his refusal to tinker with the first line — "Yes, yes, yes life!"

Blackmur's theory, roughly, is this: the poet, by varied preparation, builds up to a climactic moment, but, once reached, it makes no difference what words he uses. Fortunately, before twenty pages have passed, Blackmur has his theory safely tucked away and once more shows himself to be among the best of our practical critics. Despite his reneging on his special theory, he holds on to the notion of closed form somewhat longer. His comments on Emily Dickinson's "Renunciation" are worth quoting at length because they show the problems practical criticism meets when it depends upon unsound theory.

> Renunciation
> Is a piercing virtue,
> The letting go
> A presence for an expectation —
> Not now.

There is no forensic here, nor eloquence, nor justness; it is a bare statement amounting to a vision — vision being a kind of observation of the ideal. It has nothing to do with wisdom, there is no thinking in it; and there is no ordinary observation in it — in the sense that there is no relation between an observer and a thing observed. The lines do not prove themselves, or anything else; they make a statement. Yet it is not a naive statement — it is not directly

136

itself — however much it may seem to be. It rises rather out of a whole way of life — the protestant, puritan way, felt suddenly at what can be called nothing less than a supremely sophisticated level. The feeling is in the sophistication.

.  .  .  .  .  .  .  .  .

Let us provisionally inquire what it is in the words that makes poetry of the statement about renunciation. Let us treat the machinery, not as what we may or may not know it to be intellectually, but as an example of words in operation; and let us look at the image — what is imagined — as the emergent fact of the words in operation, indeed, as the operation itself. That is how our best reading takes poetry in its stride; here we arrest the stride or make slow motion of it. The words are all simple words, parts of our stock vocabulary. Only one, *renunciation*, belongs to a special department of experience or contains in itself the focus of a particular attitude, a department and an attitude we condition ourselves to keep mostly in abeyance. We know what renunciation is; we know it turns up as heroism or hypocrisy or sentimentality; and we do as little as possible about it. Only one word, *piercing*, is directly physical; something that if it happens cannot be ignored but always shocks us into reaction. It is the shock of this word that transforms the phrase from a mere grammatical tautology into a metaphorical tautology which establishes as well as asserts identity. Some function of the word *pierce* precipitates a living intrinsic relation between renunciation and virtue; it is what makes the phrase incandesce. . . . The piercing quality of renunciation is precisely, but not altogether, that it is a continuing process, takes time, it may be infinite time, before the renounced presence transpires in expectation in the "Not now." It is — if we may provisionally risk saying so — the physical elements in the word *pierce* and the participial phrase *letting go* that, by acting upon them, make the other words available to feeling, and it is the word *renunciation* that, so enlightened, focuses the feeling as actuality. That operation is almost enough to make the statement poetry; we have only pseudo-names for whatever else it is that it takes.[38]

This is an excellent analysis of the effect of "renunciation," but it violates Blackmur's notion of gesture by stressing what the words import into the poem. There are parts, however, which are incomprehensible. The poem offers a definition of renunciation which arouses a feeling of the word "as actuality." Is it not perverse to contend that a statement combining definition, emotional realization, and actuality "has nothing to do with reality"? Despite Blackmur's attempt to separate the poem (and poetry generally) from other forms of knowledge, he finds it necessary to open the form to get the effect into the poem, and to open it again to get it to the reader.

Blackmur partly repudiates the stand taken in the early pages of *Language as Gesture* in an essay entitled "A Burden for Critics," in which he attempts to enlarge formal criticism "to go with the enlargement of aesthetic experience." His later view is that criticism should be chiefly concerned not with "superficial and mechanical executive techniques," but with their "relation to the ulterior techniques of conceptual form and symbolic form." Conceptual forms are what "the artist does with his dominant convictions, or obsessions, or insights, or visions, and how they are translated into major stresses of human relations"; symbolic forms are *"what gets into the arts —* that makes them relatively inexhaustible." [39] This is far from Blackmur's earlier preference for the dead-end symbol.

Cleanth Brooks's work is significant not only because it is extremely influential, but also because it has, until recently,[40] persistently advanced a single, coherent theory despite the author's awareness of its limitations. Much literary criticism since the 1920's has been theoretically irresponsible; it has tossed out theories and terminologies, then immediately denied or ignored them. Brooks's work, on the other hand, illustrates the virtues and vices of theoretical consistency. Most of his criticism develops from three sets of terms: irony (and its near equivalents, paradox and wit), drama, and metaphor (or one of its variants). Irony creates unity in variety and helps to establish aesthetic distance; drama achieves both variety and distance; metaphor fuses meanings and removes the object from reality. Brooks has, then, two criteria for aesthetic value — structure (the combination of unity and complexity) and aesthetic distance. His varied but related critical machines are built to show that if a poem has a certain kind of complex structure and achieves a certain distance, it is a good poem.

In the following I shall use *irony* as a blanket term to cover what Brooks means by wit, paradox, and irony, because each of the terms is subject to the same kind of attack and defense; I shall, however, quote the distinction Brooks makes among the three terms. Brooks sees

> (1) wit, as an awareness of the multiplicity of possible attitudes to be taken toward a given situation; . . . (2) paradox, as a device for contrasting the conventional view of a situation, or the limited and special view of it taken in practical or scientific discourse, with a more inclusive view; . . . (3) irony, as a device for definition of attitudes by qualification.[41]

Brooks's irony, much more than Empson's ambiguity, is a structural concept suggesting the combination of diverse attitudes or meanings into a unified experience. This diversity of attitudes or meanings is the source of "the lyric quality," which

> if it be genuine, is not the result of some transparent and "simple" redaction of a theme or a situation which is somehow poetic in itself; it is, rather, the result of an imaginative grasp of diverse materials — but an imaginative grasp so sure that it may show itself to the reader as unstudied and unpredictable without for a moment relaxing its hold on the intricate and complex stuff which it carries.[42]

In fairness to Brooks, it must be remembered that his theory is designed to account for the unity of the individual poem and that his critical vocabulary is deliberately selected to show how the multiplicity of data offered by the poem is experienced as an integrated whole. The intention is satisfactory; the performance is not. Whether we like it or not, words used in a theory tend to develop a life of their own; once used loosely and metaphorically to indicate a quality frequent in poetry which the critic admires, their narrower and literal meaning is likely to intrude.

To show that Brooks's method works well with metaphysical poems is hardly necessary; the test is what it does with other kinds of poems. Committed to the notion that irony is, with its variants, the distinguishing feature of poetry and sensitive enough to know that Wordsworth must be accounted for, Brooks bravely attacks the sonnet "Composed upon Westminster Bridge."

> It is one of Wordsworth's most successful poems; yet most students have the greatest difficulty in accounting for its goodness. The attempt to account for it on the grounds of nobility of sentiment soon breaks down. On

this level, the poem merely says: that the city in the morning light presents a picture which is majestic and touching to all but the most dull of soul; but the poem says very little more about the sight; the city is beautiful in the morning light and it is awfully still. The attempt to make a case for the poem in terms of the brilliance of its images also quickly breaks down: the student searches for graphic details in vain; there are next to no realistic touches. In fact, the poet simply huddles the details together: . . . We get a blurred impression — points of roofs and pinnacles along the skyline, all twinkling in the morning light. More than that, the sonnet as a whole contains some very flat writing and some well-worn comparisons.

The reader may ask: Where, then, does the poem get its power? It gets it, it seems to me, from the paradoxical situation out of which the poem arises. The speaker is honestly surprised, and he manages to get some sense of awed surprise into the poem. It is odd that the city should be able to "wear the beauty of the morning" at all. Mount Snowden, Skiddaw, Mont Blanc — these wear it by natural right, but surely not grimy, feverish London. This is the point of the almost shocked exclamation:

> Never did sun more beautifully steep
> In his first splendour, valley, rock, or hill.[43]

Except for the praise, this is about as inaccurate as criticism can be. If the poem is to be explained by "the grounds of the nobility of its sentiment," those grounds do not break quite so soon as Brooks implies. As he well knows, the paraphrase he offers comes nowhere near expressing the sentiment of the poem; its nobility is not merely in the scene and the general quality of the reaction toward it, it is also in the reaction as expressed by the tone of the poem. Moreover, why should anyone "attempt to make a case for the poem in terms of the brilliance of its images" if the images are admittedly not brilliant? The proper technique is not to impose the theory upon the poem, but to use the theory to find what the poem has to offer and then, if necessary, to adjust the theory. Only a prefabricated critical theory could find "some very flat writing and some well-worn comparisons" in just fourteen lines — fourteen lines admitted to be unusually fine.

Because the sonnet does not readily meet his usual criteria and because he knows it is a good poem, Brooks — confined by his system — must work diligently to apply one of his key terms. He argues that the poem is paradoxical because Wordsworth was surprised to find the city beautiful. The implication is that people who are not thus surprised cannot admire the poem. Brooks offers no analysis of the surprise of which he speaks, none of that fine precision of explanation and profusion of example that makes his work on the metaphysicals convincing. Instead of showing that the surprise is in the poem, he argues that he feels the surprise because he knows that Wordsworth was surprised. He supports his paradoxical interpretation by citing two lines; I have added the next:

Never did sun more beautifully steep
In his first splendour, *valley, rock,* or *hill;*
Ne'er saw I, never felt, a calm so deep!

If these lines are to convey shock, they are hopelessly bad. Shock does not register itself in three-line units with multiple pauses and call itself "calm." The correct explanation is not shock, but Wordsworth's own "emotion recollected in tranquility." But what, precisely, is the emotion? First, the lines are unusually slow, as is the entire poem; it begins:

Earth has not anything to show more fair.

This has the sound of considered statement, the voice of a man who has re-collected his thoughts and emotions and who wants to state them as simply and as powerfully as he can. If there is surprise in the poem, it is not the surprise of paradox, but the surprise of fulfillment. "Realization," in fact, is a much better word here than "surprise." Wordsworth's preference for mountain scenery is not contrasted with his admiration for the city at that moment; the point of the poem is that the poet has come to realize that the two are complementary. He shows forcefully and subtly that they are:

> The river glideth at his own sweet will:
> Dear God! the very houses seem asleep;
> And all that mighty heart is lying still!

Wordsworth's personification of the river is not unusual, but his personification of London is; the city at this time and from this vantage point is a part of nature. If one likes, Wordsworth's original emotion was satisfaction at having found that man and his works are not outside the poet's usual world view. This accounts for the tone of the poem, which is not that of a man confronted by a shocking contradiction of his previous beliefs, but that of a man who has found that the earlier belief has been confirmed, fulfilled by a new and appropriate and rewarding experience.

Although this "intentional" interpretation is tenable, it probably should not be pressed, especially within the framework of Brooks's theory and of this chapter. Brooks could have argued that the suppressed side of the paradox (the preference for natural scenery) adds an element of complexity to the structure of the poem, an element that makes it more true to the complexity of actual experience. But why, if this line is taken, bring in paradox at all? Brooks, indulging in a typically modern fallacy, assumes that the only valid complexity is through contrast of one kind or another because no one attitude is likely to be correct. I doubt that the assumption is supportable. To give just one example, Dante's *Divine Comedy* is based solidly upon a single world view; it attains its complexity not by carrying within it its own self-criticism, but by seeing its world view deeply and honestly. I am suggesting that complexity may be achieved either by contrast or by depth, so that given a view of life, the poet may do one of two things: he may examine it ironically and suggest its value by showing its ability to withstand criticism, or he may ignore the criticism and strive to make the view into an experience that will profoundly move the reader. But either way, the success of the poem depends upon the technique. In the one case success depends upon the ability of the poet to maintain unity in diversity; in the second it depends upon his ability to reach in some way the deepest emotions and convictions of generations of readers.

Irony and its near synonyms, then, are too narrow to account for the effects of poetry. For example, in writing of Keats's

> Thou, silent form! dost tease us out of thought
> As doth eternity

Brooks is willing to accept only one meaning of tease — "an attitude of mischievous mockery on the part of the urn." [44] Although this meaning fits quite well with Brooks's general interpretation of the "Ode on a Grecian Urn," "tease" (as Empson would have noted) has other meanings — to lure, or in an older sense, to untangle. The three meanings can be reconciled within the context of the Ode, but the reconciliation leads away from Brooks's interpretation. The triple signification would imply that the urn is not paradoxical, but rather that it is

144

a symbol which mocks, lures, and untangles so that Keats is led finally to a realm in which the concluding statement of the Ode is unparadoxically true.

Brooks encounters the same kind of trouble when he takes up Tennyson's "Break, break, break" and singles out "stately" to illustrate the poem's thinness, concluding that "this observation is idle and finally irrelevant. What relation has their [the ships'] stateliness to the experience of grief?" [45] Let us forget, for a moment, what Brooks actually wrote and consider what his theory should have impelled him to write. We get something like this: " 'Stately' is ironic; the main theme of the poem is the personal expression of grief, but Tennyson manages to save the poem from maudlin sentimentality by neatly and briefly working into it an alternate attitude. The poet grieves, but the rest of the world goes on, calm and dignified, about its business. But this is not the height of the irony, for the impersonal and inanimate ships have a haven and man has not." I do not think much of this line of defense of Tennyson's poem, but it is the kind of thing that Brooks's system should lead to. I would prefer to argue that, beginning in the first stanza and continuing through the third, the poet contrasts other conditions with his own. His mood is thus contrasted with those of the fisherman boy and the sailor lad. This seems obvious enough, if one is not struggling to illustrate a theory.

Brooks's other favorite terms, metaphor and drama, may be disposed of more briefly. Brooks believes that poetry is metaphorical,[46] which is harmless enough and true if he means only that the content of poetry is not immediately applicable to everyday life, or that metaphors and symbols are especially frequent poetic devices. At first, Brooks admits these limitations to his approach;[47] what happens in practice is interesting to watch. His belief that poems are symbolic becomes in practice a conviction that poems must have symbols; thus he attacks Frost's "Two Tramps in Mud-Time" because "the poetry is diluted and diffuse. A significant symptom of the diffuseness is the absence of metaphor. The very minimum of imagery is used." [48] Thus far Brooks is right (in theory) if he means either or both of two things: that the poem, other things remaining constant, would be better if it offered the added excitement of imagery, or (stressing "symptom") that metaphor is a convenient device for concisely knotting the strands of a poem. Both of these would be at once consonant with Brooks's theory and credible; somewhat later, however, he says the following about the poem: "It may not be invidious therefore to point out that it is made finally in the mode of prose rather than in terms of symbol." [49] Here the implication is that poems must have symbols, for the alternative is "the mode of prose." Brooks ignores, at this point in his criticism, all other devices available to poetry; any theory which prescribes or proscribes the use of a particular technique will fail in its treatment of the richness that is fine poetry.

Brooks develops the notion of the dramatic less fully than his other key terms. Most importantly, it serves to illustrate the tendency of Brooks (and of many other critics) to pounce dramatically upon a term, usually a term used metaphorically, and then to use it indiscriminately. Here is Brooks on the "Ode on a Grecian Urn"; Lear's line,

> "Ripeness is all" is a statement put in the mouth of a dramatic character and a statement which is governed and qualified by the whole context of the play. It does not directly challenge an examination into its truth be-

cause its relevance is pointed up and modified by the dramatic context.

Now, suppose that one could show that Keats's lines, *in quite the same way*, constitute a speech, a consciously riddling paradox, put in the mouth of a particular character, and modified by the total context of the poem. If we could demonstrate that the speech was "in character," was dramatically appropriate, was properly prepared for — then would not the lines have all the justification of "Ripeness is all"? [50]

A few pages later, he continues:

First, the urn itself can tell a story, can give a history. Then, the various figures depicted upon the urn play music or speak or sing. If we have been alive to these items, we shall not, perhaps, be too much surprised to have the urn speak once more, . . . to have it speak on a higher level, to have it make a commentary on its own nature. If the urn has been properly dramatized, if we have followed the development of the metaphors, if we have been alive to the paradoxes that work throughout the poem, perhaps then, we shall be prepared for the enigmatic final paradox which the "silent form" utters.[51]

Had Keats anticipated this analysis, he could hardly have done more to refute it; in fact, the poem exists precisely because the urn does not tell a story. The poet expects a story, at first, and even predicts confidently that the urn will tell a tale "more sweetly than our rhyme." Then Keats asks a series of narrative questions, questions about the story he expects. Who are the persons, what is happening, why the excitement? But, and Keats underlines this in every way possible to poetry, the urn does not fill out the narrative; it forces Keats to imagine the answers.

The figures do not play, the melodies are unheard but imagined, the lover can never kiss, and so on. In fact, so far is any one or any thing from speaking that "not a soul" can "tell / Why thou art desolate." It is difficult to conceive of a scene more undramatic than this. Fortunately, the explanation of "Beauty is truth, truth beauty" does not depend upon the dramatic aspects of the Ode. Brooks suggests at one point that the explanation of the lyric in terms of drama is only a "helpful analogy by which to suggest the structure of poetry . . . and . . . the least confusing way in which to approach a poem." [52]

Once again, the modest disclaimer — the all-too-confident application; the observation that poems may have or may be thought to have such and such a property — the rash insistence that they must. If, so the reasoning goes, it simplifies interpretation to think of lyrics as dramatic, the critic had better find dramatis personae in the poem. This approach might work with the "Ode on a Grecian Urn" if we assume that the dramatic hero of the Ode is not the urn, but the poet, and that the action is relatively passive meditation. Let us see what happens when the Ode is interpreted in this way.

Since not even romantic poets speak to urns and expect answers, we may assume that the opening stanza is largely an interior monologue with the poet thinking to himself. In stanzas two and three the urn does not answer, but the poet imagines. Another group of questions in stanza four is left unanswered, this time not only by the urn but also by the imagination of the poet. In stanza five Keats tells us why he did not bother to answer the final set of questions: the urn "dost tease us out of thought"; it is so exceedingly beautiful that the usual narrative questions are no longer important. Moreover, the urn "dost tease us out of thought / As doth eternity," and the comparison is especially apt. Where eter-

148

nity is concerned, the narrative questions are meaningless; only thoughts on the highest level of abstraction are
appropriate. The Ode, then, builds up to the transcendental proposition "Beauty is truth" as the meditation of the poet moves from historical to philosophical
interests. The proposition itself, I should add, need not
be true philosophically; it is enough that a highly abstract
idea has been prepared for carefully, and that its two separate aspects, its two operative terms (beauty and truth),
are made concrete by the subject matter of the Ode.
Beauty, roughly, is the urn; truth, the questioning after
ultimate reality. If this reading is correct, the drama
metaphor works best when applied loosely — so loosely
that it might as well be ignored and the poem treated
simply as a meditation.

The brilliance of Brooks as a critic is due far more to
his sharply developed intelligence than to his system.
The practical criticism fails only to the extent that he attempts to schematize his insights. In an interesting comment admitting that Shakespeare is a greater poet than
Donne, Brooks writes:

> In general, we may say, Shakespeare has made it relatively
> easy for his admirers to choose what they like and neglect
> what they like. What he gives on one or another level is
> usually so magnificent that the reader finds it easy to
> ignore other levels.[53]

It is rather vexing that Brooks, who is usually anxious to
comment at length upon the details of poems, is willing
to write only generally about a major problem of evaluative theory. Inferior poetry — not mere twaddle or gush
— offers itself on a "take it or leave it" basis because it
specializes in a single quality. This is why single-term
theories can handle the less serious of the metaphysical
poems, for example, quite well. I am oversimplifying

149

somewhat, but if one prefers metaphysical poetry to romantic poetry, he can work out a handy set of terms or a single term to account for his preference; he will have great difficulty, however, when he tries to account for certain "nonmetaphysical" effects of metaphysical poems, and when he turns to other types of poetry. That is why Shakespeare is harder for modern critics to write about than is Donne. There is irony in Shakespeare, and ambiguity, and tension, and language as gesture, and all the favored qualities of the new criticism — but there is also much more. There is depth to balance the irony, structural unity to balance the ambiguity, varieties of meaning enough to make any description of tension applicable, and maturity of content enough to make the words more than dead-end symbols.

Within formalistic theories at least two other ways remain to account for the best poetry — insofar as it can be accounted for. In later chapters I shall argue that the basic terms of the critical system should be as broad as possible. A term like "complexity" is more useful than terms like "ambiguity," "tension," or "irony" (and similar narrow terms) for two reasons. The use of the general term makes for greater precision in dealing with poetry because the critic is not obliged to find ambiguity, tension, or whatever, buried in unlikely places, although he may use the more specific terms whenever they are appropriate. With a system based on general terms, the critic is free to look into the poem to see what is there, rather than into his theory to see what should be there. Secondly, and this is just as important, general terms do not have ready-made directions of meaning, as "irony," for example, has. Despite his best intentions, if a critic is faithful to the poem, he has to force his narrow critical terms to meanings they do not ordinarily have.

The remaining formalistic approach is R. S. Crane's.

Crane, concerned with the ever-increasing number of literary theories that do only one thing well, suggests that literary criticism "is not, and never has been, a single discipline, . . . but rather a collection of distinct and more or less incommensurable 'frameworks' or 'languages.'" [54] The pluralistic critic, Crane writes, will "look upon critical principles, whether his own or others', not as sectarian dogmas to be defended on metaphysical grounds, but as instruments of research and appreciation, any set of which is necessarily limited in relation both to the aspects of poetry it brings into view and to the kinds of conclusions it permits the critic to reach." [55] This is excellent, but it would have had more force if it had not come from a critic whose work as an author and editor of polemics far outweighs his published practical criticism. The principle Crane urges has, in fact, been insisted upon throughout this study: what a critic may legitimately do with a poem depends largely upon the kind of premises he accepts and the terminology he chooses.

Unfortunately, after describing the advantages of critical pluralism, Crane attempts to enforce his own brand of monism. It is not quite so limited as other theories I have discussed, but neither is it so satisfactory a tool for practical criticism. Crane is rightly concerned that much contemporary criticism fails to differentiate among the various literary forms, treating lyrics as dramas, dramas as narratives, and so on. The problem for the neo-Aristotelian is to develop a definition of form (or of forms) that will be effective but not prescriptive. In other words, within the framework of the system, it ought to be possible to deduce that some poems are well formed and others badly formed; yet the definition or definitions must be applicable to works of literature and kinds of literature as yet unimagined.

Crane, concerned with evaluation, has written that "if

our hypothesis concerning the shaping principle of any work is adequate, it will give us a basis for saying with some precision . . . what are the necessities which such a form imposes on any artist whose aim is its successful realization in his materials." [56] I believe that by "such a form" Crane means roughly what Croce would call an intuition, although Crane prefers to emphasize the thing made rather than its origin. In making a poem (or, more generally, an imitation) the poet's problem in working out the poem's "*dynamis*" is actually a problem of specifying "the moral qualities and actions of the characters," the "imagined object," and the words and techniques that best reveal the object, in terms of the "internal idea" that motivates the work and gives it its unity.[57]

> Here then — in the artist's intuition of a form capable of directing whatever he does with his materials in a particular work — is an essential cause of poetic structure, the most decisive, indeed, of all the causes of structure in poetry because it controls in an immediate way the act of construction itself. Without it, no poetic whole; with it, a poetic whole of a certain kind and emotional quality, which will be excellent in proportion to the intrinsic possibilities of the form the poet has conceived and to his success in doing with his material in his medium all that it requires or permits him to do if its full possibilities, as a form of a certain kind, are to be realized.[58]

Crane then argues that this "shaping cause" is not only the first principle of writers, but also the "first principle in the practical criticism of their works." Here he creates difficulties he cannot work out. He must show how the critic can use the intuition of the artist in judging the work. With his usual shrewdness, he avoids falling into the intentionalist fallacy by stating that the object of critical interest is not the actual process of writing the poem, but "the actual rationale of the poem's construction in terms of the poetic problems the writer faced and the reasons which determined his solutions." [59]

Probably the clearest indication Crane has given of his notion of form occurs in his comments on Ransom's criticism of "To His Coy Mistress." He notes that Ransom's division of the poem into "irrelevant texture" and "structure" is possible only because Ransom's paraphrase is incomplete.[60] If one says that the argument of the poem is merely a plea from a lover to his beloved to hurry up, then much of the poem is indeed irrelevant. But, Crane says, suppose that in the paraphrase the lover is qualified as impatient and witty, and the mistress as coy — then many of the irrelevancies quickly disappear. The more accurate and full the paraphrase, the less irrelevancy and the more unity the poem discloses. The critic apparently discovers the "actual rationale of the poem's construction" by working backwards in this way.

Nevertheless, does it help to discover the rationale? The technique is descriptive, offering but a full paraphrase, and description is but a prelude to evaluation. Winters' comments on Crane's criticism of the "Elegy Written in a Country Churchyard" sum up the problem:

> He asks us to regard the *Elegy* as an "imitative lyric of moral choice rather than of action or of mood, representing a situation in which a virtuous, sensitive, and ambitious young man of undistinguished birth confronts the possibility of his death," and so on. Yet if I understand this account of the poem, we would have in Crane's terms a kind of dramatic monologue appropriate to the speaker and his peculiar combination of talent, education, defects, and the like; and we would know what kind of young man

he was solely from the poem; and the poem would therefore be inescapably a perfect achievement, and criticism
would be forestalled at the outset.[61]

Precisely: there is no way within the framework of
Crane's theory that any poem can be judged as imperfect. All the critic is permitted to know is the poem; he
must accept what it has to offer in good and simple faith.
Any element that for another critic might be a blemish
must, for Crane, be but a qualification of the plot.

The inability to deal with imperfection is not accidental to Crane's system. Following Aristotle, he contends that "the excellence of anything . . . is the max-
imum actualization, within the necessary limits of its
matter, of what its nature is capable of." [62] Now, although this is true ontologically, it is not true axiologically. There is a sense in which the being of anything follows its own nature and is a perfection of that nature;
hence, one may speak of an excellent murder — that is, a
murder in which the requirements of murder are met in
exemplary fashion. Joyce Kilmer's "Trees" similarly follows the laws of its nature. But what is the meaning of
"its nature"? Does, in Crane's system, the "its" refer to
the particular or to the species? If to the latter, then external criteria would have to be applied to individual
poems. The prescribed procedure would be to set up a
definition of the lyric, for example, and then to find out
how far the poem goes in meeting the requirements of
the definition. Crane seems to be doing something of the
sort when he writes that "lyrics . . . do not have plots,
but any successful lyric obviously has something analogous to a plot in the sense of a specific form which
synthesizes into a definite emotional whole." He then
gives, with another example, the plot of the "Ode to a
Nightingale," as "a man in an evolving state of passion

154

interpreted for him by his thoughts." [63] Logically, it should be possible to develop still further, saying that a poem with such a plot must contain more or less definite elements in its plot analogue. Crane does not want to do this, and avoids it by recourse to the concept of intuition. On the other hand, if "its nature" refers to the nature of individual poems, criticism is prevented because a poem can do nothing but conform to its own nature — good or bad, beautiful or ugly.

This leads to the point that Crane and the neo-Aristotelians do not want to admit, that judgment requires two distinct sets of data. It requires material for judgment, and also some kind of standard by which the judgment can be made. Wimsatt's comment on McKeon applies to the position generally, "what [is] a 'literal' theory as prescribed by McKeon . . . if not a circularity. What can the predicate of a definition of poetry be if it does not contain terms drawn from the rest of human experience?" [64]

In some way or other, criticism must be able to relate the poem to general human values and then to find its standards. The preceding analyses of formalist positions have shown that the standards cannot be narrow; they must be able to deal with whatever poems have and will have to offer. In the remaining chapters alternatives to mimetic and closed-form theories will be considered, and — it is hoped — the groundwork will be laid for a theory that is at once wide and potentially consistent.

# VI

## THE POEM AS OPEN FORM

Thus far three different notions of form have been examined and found wanting. Mimetic theories see form either as the imitation of the form of something outside the poem or as the pleasant addition of "art" to content. Either way, literary criticism is quickly led away from the individual poem. Closed-form theories see the form as the total sum of relationships prevailing inside the poem; they cannot get out of the individual poem. A fourth possibility is to argue that the form of a poem is something that comes into being as a result of the interaction of the poem and the consciousness of the reader. I shall call the idea of form derived from this view *open form*. Although most critics reject the notion of open form because of its initial difficulties, it is the only tenable basis for literary criticism.

There are numerous good reasons for denying that the poem is essentially an interaction between text and mind. That a poem is composed of the internal relationships among its patterns and subpatterns, as closed-form theories suppose, is undeniable; just as certainly, elements of these major and minor patterns may be lifted from the poem, displayed, analyzed, and valued. Moreover, extensive agreement about which works should be

To each they offer gifts after his will,
Bread, kingdoms, stars, and sky that holds them all.
I, in my pleachéd garden, watched the pomp,
Forgot my morning wishes, hastily
Took a few herbs and apples, and the Day
Turned and departed silent. I, too late,
Under her solemn fillet saw the scorn.

Although the paraphrasable content here would seem to be important, the symbol offering it is incoherent — which is another way of saying that there are at least two possible paraphrases, each of which contradicts the other. If we stress the first lines, the days are hypocritical, and man is cheated by them; if we stress the last lines, man cheats himself. Moreover, a reader has a right to expect that "daughters" will be female, yet Emerson develops them as if they were male. They march, and here one would expect a military development. But instead of marching like soldiers (or Amazons), they march like dervishes, members of a sect noted for, according to the *New World Dictionary*, "whirling, howling, etc." And if the days offer each man "gifts after his will," in what sense are they hypocritical? No matter how much one likes whichever of the two messages Emerson is trying to communicate (man as cheated or man as cheating himself) it is difficult to like the poem after a close reading. Because the symbol structure is garbled, the references made to reality and to experience are both garbled. The poem demonstrates nothing.

Other poems could be analyzed, but the results would be to repeat what should be already apparent. In the value of either a poem or an experience the basic terms of analysis are complexity and integrity; evaluative criticism is the assertion of an experience of a certain wholeness and richness, or a hypothetical statement that a certain degree of wholeness and richness should be experienced through a given object. As such, it is nonobjective. The only thing that one can say about the aesthetic experience itself is that it occurred, and then one may attempt to describe it. Thus while the critic must always begin with his experience, he may not remain with it long; he must soon get behind it to the thing that shaped it and gave it content. It is at this point that evaluation becomes objective — or better, corrigible. On the simplest level, it is possible to note that certain elements in a poem clash, that there is no conceivable way of making the piece coherent; it is also possible to show that, if a reader praises or condemns an element overly much, he is going beyond the poem. Thus the danger of moralistic criticism, as I have shown, is that it too often leads the reader to unravel a single strand from the poem and to follow it to some imaginary end, when in fact criticism should intertwine the strand with all others present in the work. A satisfactory evaluation is an evaluation of an experience referred to the full data of the object. More than this is effusion; less is partial criticism.

A complete lexicon of evaluative critical terminology would therefore need to offer concepts capable of treating any of the innumerable qualities words take on when used in combination. Probably such a lexicon is already available to critics, at least in large part, for it would consist of the kind of discriminations they usually make. Unfortunately, critics usually make their personal lexicons too brief, so that they are often obliged to admit having experienced only those parts of the poem which their vocabularies permit them to write about. I believe that in years hence students who read some of the best criticism of Empson, Brooks, and others will ask, "Did they ever read aloud the poems they discuss?" For all the talk about meaning, the "Ode on a Grecian Urn" remains a fine-sounding poem; contemporary critical vocabularies usually lack words for talking about the musical effects of the Ode. I am suggesting, in fact, that the need is for a criticism that is both versatile and complete, for critics who can deal with whatever a poem has to offer — whether it be sound, meaning, suggestion of an attitude, or these and more. To build up such a lexicon would be impracticable because it would be too cumbersome to use; the only workable alternative is to keep the basic vocabulary of criticism simple and general. In no other way can criticism avoid both inconsistency and partiality.

To say this another way, no poem long endures because of a single quality. A poem endures because it offers a peculiar combination of qualities available nowhere else. The greater the number of such qualities, the more individual strands, the greater the possible success of the poem. The central insight of orthodox contemporary criticism has been the exploration and classification of certain kinds of strands. Paradox, irony, ambiguity, tension, and all similar terms suggest the compacting of various strands of meaning and attitude. For this reason such devices are frequent in the best poetry, but they are not the only such devices, they are not peculiar to poetry, and poems may satisfy a sensitive reader without any appreciable amount of any of them. They point to but do not exhaust the possibilities of complexity and integrity. A poem endures because it is full enough to capture and fill the attention while it is being read, and because it is integrated enough to direct attention along a single course.

But some poems do more than endure. Certain poems, the ones critics write about most often, in some way seem important to mankind. The usual way of dealing with these is to make two judgments, an aesthetic or formal judgment and a moral judgment. As I have tried to show, such a procedure is faulty because only one object is involved and, strictly speaking, only one experience. The only satisfactory solution is to consider the poem as a symbol, differing from other symbols not so much by its function as by what it offers as relevant. As a symbol the poem opens out into the world, either to a relatively small or insignificant portion of it, or to a relatively major part. In this respect poems are like scientific formulae: some have a wide range of applicability, some a narrow. But a judgment as to the range of applicability — that is, to the significance and variety of the experience — is essentially a judgment of what is in the poem and of the manner in which that content is formed. The integrity of the symbol provides for the control, the direction along which the experiences are to travel; the complexity of the symbol accounts for the range that the experience includes. Both are objective in that they are in the object. A complete aesthetic judgment, therefore, may and should deal with the relevant implications of the symbol. Form is filled only by content. The formal evaluation, if one considers all aspects of form rather than certain select phases, is the same as an evaluation of content. A pattern coheres because it is made up of elements drawn from experience which cohere in that arrangement; because they are drawn from experience they are also congruent with human experience.

In the light of all this theory, how does one judge a poem? By this time the careful reader should realize that there is no formula, there are only cautions for thoroughness and modesty. There can be no formula because there is no way to predict what any given poem will offer first to experience. It may be a beauty of sound, a profundity of meaning, or an attitude; it may be an excess of alliteration, a clumsy handling of rhyme, a failure to observe the implications of words, and so on. It may be a disparity be-

Herbert feels his belief needs no proof. Romantic and postromantic poetry, on the other hand, tends to offer its metaphors as proofs.

Murray Krieger's discussion of Donne's "The Canonization" shows the quality of preromantic poetry that most appeals to modern critics, perhaps because it helps furnish an easy solution to the problem of truth in poetry. Krieger points out that the reader takes the central metaphor of "The Canonization" seriously until he realizes "that he has been taken in and that the case is not proved at all, except that poetically — that is, in terms of the language-context of the poem — it has." [21] Most postromantic poetry, on the other hand, insists on bulging out of its context, either because it does not make complete sense internally or because it seems to attach itself to some extraneous idea. Either way, the poem requires judgment by something outside itself.

T. S. Eliot has argued much and forcefully that the judgment of the poem does require something beyond the poem — and that it does not. Of the *Divine Comedy* he writes that "the end of the enjoyment of poetry is a pure contemplation from which all the accidents of personal emotion are removed." But when he turns to Shelley, he writes that "some of Shelley's views I positively dislike, and that hampers my enjoyment of the poems in which they occur." [22] What has happened, of course, is that Eliot's own ideas intrude into Shelley's poems because weaknesses in the poems permit, and the strength of Eliot's intellectual and moral convictions encourages, the intrusion.

In the preceding chapter I mentioned that Eliot faced the problem of developing a new criticism with an old vocabulary, which is another way of saying that — both in his criticism and in his poetry — he is a transitional cause of things" is to admit that the poem is art plus something else. And when that something else is truth or goodness, the natural and correct tendency of most persons is to place art second, or third. However, if art, as most of the aestheticians we have glanced at here would claim in their various terminologies, originates in the "center of the soul," it contains from the moment of its inception both truth and goodness. They are not in the poem "by way of addition"; they are essentially there.

The poet, as Coleridge knew, is the man who can penetrate to the center of his soul; and the center of the soul cannot be parcelled out in neat lots labeled beauty, truth, and goodness. The poem is an organic form that stands or falls as a whole. The line of reasoning that revolutionized critical theory ran something like this: if all that exists symbolizes the infinite, if the salvation or at least the happiness of man depends upon such knowledge, and if poetry is to be taken seriously, it must present a symbolism as valid and coherent as that found either in nature or in such other conceptual modes as metaphysics, science, and myth.

The change is noticeable in poetry and in criticism. Of course, poems written before 1798 did combine meaning and form, and serious lyrics were written before then. But, with Milton as perhaps the only major exception, the serious lyric was largely a semi-private affair; it seemed usually to be an address by man to his God, or at least an address to a confidant who understood and respected the pseudoprivacy of the poet's outpourings. After about 1800, the bulk of poetry begs to be judged as a public contribution to thought or goodness. Only an injudicious critic would quarrel with Herbert about the central metaphor of "The Pulley" because it is merely an analogy designed to support a belief rather than to prove it;

perience, keeps alive the power to experience the world in its fullness." [15] As an embodiment of "full and intense experience," it is also an embodiment of idealized experience.

The idealization is unlike both Ortega y Gasset's empty, contentless formalization and Herbert Read's retreat into essences. It is a complete experience, more complete than ordinary experience, including rather than excluding, and "marked by a greater inclusiveness of all psychological factors than occurs in ordinary experiences" and by a refusal to subordinate any one factor to any other. [16] Perhaps the most important concept in Dewey's discussion of aesthetic experience is *potentiality*. Ordinary experience seizes only a single potentiality, or at best a narrow range of potentialities; aesthetic experience explores its material fully, realizing all that is in it. The richness of the aesthetic experience is as much a matter of form as of content; or better, it is a matter of formed content. The artist, unlike the less gifted and venturesome, cultivates "moments of resistance and tension . . . not for their own sake but because of their potentialities, bringing to living consciousness an experience that is unified and total." [17] Form, then, is but organized experience, valuable because it both reflects the tensions of the world, thereby mirroring its contradictory possibilities, and also gives them unity and totality.

By considering an art work as an experience, Dewey resolves the form-content dichotomy (or at least shoves it into the background) and accounts for the moral and cognitive force of literature. Nevertheless, his work has a major weakness. The denial of aesthetic experience as a peculiar kind of experience tends to make all relatively complete experiences aesthetic. If complete experiences differ not in kind but only in content, then there is no essential difference between a mathematician's reaction to a "beautiful" equation and a reader's reaction to a beautiful poem. It follows that there can be no difference in the method of judging such experiences.

The neo-Thomism of Jacques Maritain borders quite closely on personality theory, seeming at times to be an attempt to match the Crocean concept of intuition with the older and richer Thomism. Poetry, by which Maritain means creative activity in general, originates "in this root life where the powers of the soul are active in common" and so implies totality or integrity. The knowledge it embodies, like intuitive knowledge, is nondiscursive, nondidactic, ineffable knowledge expressed through "life-bearing signs." [18] This sounds almost like Croce or Read but for the fact that Maritain carefully distinguishes between the genetics of poetry and the poem; it is the latter we judge. Unfortunately, Maritain seems unable to say precisely how we judge. Since he admits that poetry has no preset form,[19] the specific problem is how to keep the judgment from becoming circular — the only pattern we can judge by is the pattern embodied in the poem we are judging. Even if such a circular judgment were worthwhile, only a reader whose sensibilities and standards were completely unformed could make it; such a reader is probably not the best qualified judge.

But aesthetic judgment is not the only relevant judgment, for true poetry reflects "that Intelligence which is the cause of things" even though truth is related to beauty only "by way of addition." [20] On the level of the absolute, truth, beauty, and goodness are compatible, even correlative; but below that level they are inevitably distinct and so require distinct judgments. The difficulty here is inherent in all edification theories. To admit that the poem should reflect "that Intelligence which is the

all the sensa his line offers are relevant. An aesthetic
experience, then, is an integrated experience, and the
only object that can produce such an experience is one
with an unusually high degree of integrity.

In practice, the reader must accept a certain amount of
unused sensa. The look of a poem meant to be read
aloud and function words are the most common of these
— which brings up the problem of the degree of integrity
and the amount of complexity necessary for a satisfactory
aesthetic experience. Naturally, there is no easy solution,
but the general principle that an aesthetic experience fills
the attention is a satisfactory starting point. I would thus
have to admit that a very susceptible person may have an
aesthetic experience of a very poor poem, but it seems
wiser to argue that he should not have had the experience
than to argue that he did not. The minimal requirement
for aesthetic experience, then, is the filling of the attention with the data the object offers. Leo Stein defines a
"complete picture" as "a space presentation, in which
the space is [so] completely filled with rhythmic resonances, that there is no room for anything else." [13] A
poem could be similarly defined as a temporal presentation in which the time is so completely filled with verbal
resonances that there is no room for anything else. Anything more is noticed only after the experience and as an
effect of it. "After" is the key word, for it distinguishes
this view from simple mimetic positions. A poem means
(or imitates) only after all of its elements have been experienced in the complete context of the poem.

The notion of filling the attention is difficult to illustrate. The following, however, might help:

> Whenas in silks my Julia goes
> Then, then (methinks) how sweetly flows
> That liquefaction of her clothes.

Next, when I cast mine eyes and see
That brave vibration each way free;
O how that glittering taketh me!

And:

A sweet disorder in the dress
Kindles in clothes a wantonness:
A lawn about the shoulders thrown
Into a fine distraction,
An erring lace, which here and there
Enthralls the crimson stomacher,
A cuff neglectful, and thereby,
Ribbands to flow confusedly,
A winning wave (deserving note)
In the tempestuous petticoat,
A careless shoe-string, in whose tie
I see a wild civility,
Do more bewitch me, than when art
Is too precise in every part.

I certainly would not suggest that "Whenas in Silks" is better than "Delight in Disorder" merely because it is shorter. In reading the latter, though, for the $n$th time, I do feel my attention lag, not so seriously that I dislike the poem but seriously enough that midway through I am ready to turn to something else. Both poems are slight, but the first fills the attention for its brief duration; it keeps the mind busy until the quickly reached end. "Delight in Disorder" does not end quite quickly enough. If I verify my reaction — that is, do the critic's job — by looking more closely at the two poems, I find that the sweets are more compacted in the former, hence the greater fullness of attention. Ignoring the tonal qualities of the poems, the chief differences seem to be that the catalog of the second becomes mere reiteration without a corresponding increase in scope (what Whitehead called "excess of identification"), and that the items in the catalog have no focus, the clothes have no Julia on which to display their wantonness ("lack of coordination in the factors of the datum," [14] as Whitehead would have it).

Nevertheless, "Whenas in Silks" is a slight poem. It delights, it presents an experience, it fills the attention, but yet it hardly shows the most that language is capable of. Let it be further admitted that it is true to empirical reality, that it is congruent with the reader's experience of other relevant data. Yet it remains slight because the experience it creates (that of a formalized wolf whistle) does not overflow into the most significant areas of man's understanding and feeling. It is, in other words, neither complex nor powerful; it touches reality at only one point, the pleasant but inconsequential point of ceremonious flirtation. A poem like Daniel's "Care-charmer sleep," on the other hand, manages to leave more with the reader:

> Care-charmer sleep, son of the sable night,
>     Brother to death, in silent darkness born,
>     Relieve my languish and restore the light;
>     With dark forgetting of my care, return.
> And let the day be time enough to mourn
>     The shipwreck of my ill-adventured youth;
>     Let waking eyes suffice to wail their scorn
>     Without the torment of the night's untruth.
> Cease, dreams, th' images of day-desires;
>     To model forth the passions of the morrow;
>     Never let rising sun approve you liars,
>     To add more grief to aggravate my sorrow.
> Still let me sleep, embracing clouds in vain,
> And never wake to feel the day's disdain.

I do not want to claim too much for this poem, but it has an importance lacking in either of Herrick's pieces. The more orthodox of contemporary critics would contend that the importance of the experience is irrelevant aesthetically. But if a poem is valuable in proportion to the complexity of the experience it generates and controls, then it should be apparent that Daniel's poem is more valuable than either of Herrick's. (I am here assuming what I could not if I were formally evaluating the poem rather than illustrating a point, that is, that each of the poems has the complexity and integrity necessary for the minimal aesthetic experience.) Each of the poems is a re-creation of the experience of a certain feeling, but the Daniel poem adds an element of complexity which is relevant at once to the poem and to the human condition — an anguish so great and so hopeless that even death becomes a boon. Philosophical, religious, and aesthetic experiences are bound up in Daniel's poem and released in the experience of it. It should not be thought for a moment that Daniel's poem is the best of the three because of the importance of its theme; that would be contrary to the approach I am attempting to illustrate. The poem is better because it is likely to result in a more complex experience than are the other two: it has many of the values shown by the slighter poems, but it also has something more.

I want to emphasize that no one thing makes a poem superior. Emerson's "Days," for example, is a more serious poem, one apparently more directly connected with the most important aspects of human life, than "Carecharmer sleep." Yet it fails in comparison, and it fails because the clumsy handling of its imagery makes it incoherent. Here is the poem:

Daughters of Time, the hypocritic Days,
Muffled and dumb like barefoot dervishes,
And marching single in an endless file,
Bring diadems and fagots in their hands.

discussed argues against the intervention of anything so capricious as the human mind in the determination of form. And finally, the argument that has impressed critics most: if form is not objective, then perhaps nothing of any importance may be said about poetry; the critic may leave himself with nothing to do but describe the personal raptures and agonies of his reading.

Although the problem of subjectivity appears most crucially in mimetic theories, I have postponed discussing it until now because it prepares the way for consideration of the poem as a symbolic form. Moreover, the subjective response to form is subtle and, perhaps, more narrowly literary than the subjective response to content. Marxism versus Christianity is, after all, more likely to excite controversy than trimeter versus tetrameter. We usually entertain rather mild convictions about sonnets, trochees, patterns of sound, and in general all the elements that make up the superficial form of a poem. A reader's expectations about form are usually general and amenable to surprise; we are more likely to be frequently and consciously aware of our reaction to what a poem says than we are to the way it says it. Yet, in a very subtle way, both the perception of form and the response to it depend upon the predilections of the reader.

Often the response to form is not so much a matter of what the reader does or does not believe as it is of simple preference for one reading over another. As Monroe C. Beardsley points out, the line, "So if I dreame I have you, I have you," from Donne's "Elegy X," may be read stressing "I" and "you" (suggesting "I have *you*"), or stressing the "have" (emphasizing the possession), or with equal stress on all three words (to keep the ambiguity).[1] Whatever decision we make is also a decision about the form — about both the rhythmic pattern and the pattern of meaning.

Of the three objections to this view — that a good poem makes such decisions for the reader, that such decisions are not actually about form, and that they leave form at the mercy of the individual reader — the last is the most weighty and will be considered throughout this chapter. The first may be answered by remarking that the perfect poem probably does not exist, and that even if it did the critic would still have to spend most of his time with imperfect poems that permit alternate readings. The second objection is valid only if form is defined mechanically or generally. A reader does not decide that a poem is to be a sonnet, in iambics, and so on; those are decisions of the poet. But if form is something unique to the poem, not merely a type but rather a set of variations peculiar to that poem, then changes of intonation, stress, selection of this rather than that element for emphasis, flat readings — all of these change the form. Although there is no clear line between good and bad readings, we do distinguish the extremes. Open-form theories will have to explain the mechanism by which we distinguish adequate readings or interpretations from inadequate.

Although the most feared bogeys of contemporary criticism are the subjectivism and psychologism twins (and their look-alike, relativism), any evaluative theory has to face them squarely. They can be temporarily avoided by positing an ideal reader (as Brooks does; Brooks also denies his ideal reader[2]), but eventually their place must be acknowledged. Brooks, for example, is correct in maintaining that a critic cannot do his job unless he assumes that he has read the poem well, which is sound enough as a stratagem of presentation but, unless explained, weak theory. An understanding of how the poem gets to the critic in a relatively unaltered state is essential to the theory, but not to the discussion of the poem. Moreover, Brooks's approach does not permit him to criticize his own preferences; he can demonstrate that "The Canonization" is brimful of irony, but not that the irony improves the poem — at least, not if he remains consistent. A more psychological approach may not convince a reader that he must admire the irony, but it can at least attempt to show why it is valuable. When Brooks does make the attempt, his embarrassment over seeming to endorse a subjective approach forces him simply to repeat the naïve psychology of I. A. Richards with neither the extent nor the shallow depth of Richards' technical argument.[3]

Eliseo Vivas and Murray Krieger have made perhaps the best attacks against psychologism. Evaluation, they argue, is corrigible in relation to the norm given by the object. They see the aesthetic experience as a composite of "anchored" values (as contrasted with "unanchored" values). Anchored values are referable directly and completely to the poem. Unanchored values, although stimulated by the poem, are the reader's addition to the poetic experience; they are part of the experiential structure rather than part of the poetic structure.[4] Although the anchoring metaphor is useful, it cannot be applied as absolutely as Vivas and Krieger would have us believe, for analysis of structure is merely analysis of structure, it is not explanation of value. At some point the theorist must explain the kind of structure he considers valuable and the reason he considers it so. More practically, though, anchoring is a matter of more or less rather than an absolute. Some values are completely anchored, others completely unanchored; but probably most of the important values we find in poetry fall somewhere in between. Robert Frost's "Come In" will help clarify the point:

As I came to the edge of the woods,
Thrush music — hark!
Now if it was dusk outside,
Inside it was dark.

Too dark in the woods for a bird
By sleight of wing
To better its perch for the night,
Though it still could sing.

The last of the light of the sun
That had died in the west
Still lived for one song more
In a thrush's breast.

Far in the pillared dark
Thrush music went —
Almost like a call to come in
To the dark and lament.

But no, I was out for stars:
I would not come in.
I meant not even if asked,
And I hadn't been.

Some parts of this poem are firmly anchored. The fact
that a protagonist passing by the woods hears what seems
to be a tempting invitation and rejects it is indisputable.
My image of a particular group of trees—maple and a
few dogwood, with a stream running slowly through the
group — is disputable; it is not in the poem and should
be dismissed quickly. But suppose I maintain that the
latent meaning of the poem is a part of its value, and I
note that what the poet rejects is described in heavily romantic terms. There is the dark wood, the bird is the
romantic thrush, nature is personified, and so on. I could
suggest that since all of this "romanticism" is rejected by

Frost, the real subject of the poem is the protagonist's attraction to and rejection of a certain romantic attitude toward life. I can also check Frost's other work and show, in fact, that he did reject the kind of woodsy romanticism he describes. Now, is this reading either as firmly anchored as the plot summary or as unanchored as the revery about woods-I-have-known? It obviously falls somewhere between the two. Values, then, are not all equally anchored or equally unanchored.

Actually, "anchoring" is a bipolar term relating the poem to the reader — an anchor must be fastened at both ends. To change the metaphor, the appeal of a poem is like an equation with two unknowns. To solve the equation, both $x$ (the structure of the poem) and $y$ (the context the reader provides for it) must be considered; either $x$ or $y$ may be taken as the norm and the other found thereby. Now, in critical theory it is usually more profitable and easier to work in terms of the structure of the poem, but the $y$ is always in the background, determining what may be known about $x$. Thus the sound pattern of a poem may be a relatively stable anchored value, but the weight a reader gives it in his total evaluation of the poem will depend upon the kind of reader he is.

The widespread hostility against psychologism (and subjectivism and relativism) is largely a reaction against such extreme statements as Frederick A. Pottle's "all criticism is relative to the critic's sensibility" or Margaret Macdonald's "criticism does not, and cannot, have the impersonal character and strict rules, . . . appropriate to science and mathematics." [5] Such statements grow from one insight and two fallacies. The insight, to use T. S. Eliot's metaphor, is that literary reputations fluctuate from age to age like stock listings. The fallacies are an overly simple conception of science and a failure to recognize that one can do something about his limitations. Science and mathematics are not nearly so impersonal as Miss Macdonald would have her readers believe. Wolfgang Köhler, a founder of gestalt psychology, asks: "What is our evidence for assuming that under given conditions the ultimate data of experience are the same for several persons? Unfortunately, we shall never know whether or not this is the case." [6] Simple observation cannot be guaranteed to be objective because we can never be certain that two persons calling the same object "red," for example, are experiencing the same color. And the Nobel Prize–winning physicist Werner Heisenberg has concluded that man's "science is only a link in the endless chain of discussions of man and nature, but that it cannot simply talk of nature 'as such.' Natural science always presupposes man." [7] Science and literary criticism are apparently in much the same plight.

Fortunately, both science and criticism can go far in overcoming their subjectivist limitations. If milliseconds are important, the scientist takes into account his own reaction time; or, to return to Eliot's stock market metaphor, the investor does not always have to remain an amateur. In investing in stock the professional considers current market conditions within the framework of long-term fluctuations. Nothing prevents the critic from doing the same.

Positively, I want to argue that the poem exists somewhere between the mind of the poet and the mind of the reader. In spatial terms, the area the poem occupies both includes and excludes part of the experience of the poet, and both includes and excludes part of the experience of the reader. Part of the poem, then, is not available to the poet (Coleridge's unawareness of the full archetypal implications of the scapegoat theme in *The Rime of the Ancient Mariner*, for example; after a century and a half the poem has got beyond its author, with new meanings creeping in and old meanings creeping out). Similarly, no reader fully "has" a good poem. The perceptive reader repeatedly discovers that he has missed something in his earlier readings of poems. The critic's homework is to develop his own intelligence and sensitivity so that he misses less and less of the poem, and puts less and less of himself into it. The job of criticism and literary scholarship is to help the reader develop his intelligence and sensitivity.

The basic problem of this approach is the nature and extent of the control the poem exercises. By "control" I mean the ability of the poem to force the reader to experience relatively fully all that is in the poem, the ability of the poem to direct the reader's attention toward itself. The two parts of the problem are: what in the poem exerts control? and what in the psychology of the reader permits that control? Unfortunately, the answers cannot be divided as neatly as the questions; some of the necessary concepts apply directly to the poem, some to the reader, and some to the kind of relation that exists between poem and reader. The concept applicable to the poem is a special instance of complexity that I shall call *richness*; the relational concepts are *requiredness* and *funding*; the concept applying to the reader is called, for want of a better term, *normalcy* — the tendency of men to share certain characteristics.

Taking the last first, the thoroughgoing subjectivist position is valid only if the differences between man and man are total; the thoroughgoing objectivist position is valid only if the differences are totally ignored. But similarities among persons, what Kenneth Burke has called "margin of overlap," [8] are numerous and important. The "margin of overlap" includes the life urge and its derivatives and refinements, with the correlative desires for food, procreation, security, awareness of physiological functions, and so on. Moreover, from the level of the Australian aborigine to that of the most advanced product of Western culture, the similarities on each level multiply. I am not minimizing individual differences, but rather suggesting the validity of recognizing an extensive middle ground between complete subjectivism and complete objectivism.

The odds are against our charting that middle ground because the factors involved are too varied and too subtle. Even "factors," which implies a serial addition of traits, is a dangerous oversimplification. In reality, the factors exist in varying degrees of intensity, and the presence of a factor and its intensity modifies the entire complex, so that for all practical purposes the range of human sensibilities is infinite. A reader exceptionally sensitive to rhythm might rate Shelley's "Ode to the West Wind" higher than "The Cloud" on no other basis than that the rhythm of the latter jangles. The same reader might be inclined to overlook the maudlin, "I fall upon the thorns of life, I bleed." Although what is too jangly or too maudlin is probably an unsolvable problem, the critic ought still to gauge his own responses by reasoning something like this: "True, I find Shelley's lines so strident that they ruin the poem for me, but to what extent am I normal? I'm usually at odds with my peers over matters of word music; I generally object when they approve. I'd better work a bit harder to prove my charge, or else admit to a personal idiosyncrasy." This is not timidity, but rather recognition of the element of subjectivity that enters into any critical act. Such "confessions," if published, would alert the reader to areas where the critic is likely to go astray; but much more important, published or not, they would force the critic to compare again his impression of the value of the poem, his prejudices, and the poem itself. Only then may he claim anything like objectivity. As Richards has pointed out, the rank of a critic depends as much on his ability to discount his own eccentricities as on "any hypothetical impeccability of his actual responses." [9]

The quality of the poem which makes tenable the notion of response form (the form to which the reader responds) is richness. By richness I do not mean to include any and all values a work might have — e.g., the collected works of Spenser may be used as anything from a small source of income for an editor, to a door-stop or weapon, to a source of moral satisfaction or aesthetic pleasure. I mean rather the quality Brooks attributed to Shakespeare's work when he wrote that "Shakespeare has made it relatively easy for his admirers to choose what they like and neglect what they like." [10] Axiologically, richness is the presence of diverse aesthetic values in a work; structurally, it is complexity considered as composed of strands in the poem that serve as lures for feeling.

To a certain extent, every poem is "rich." Even the most sentimental verse has a sound structure, a content, and an emotion; but a better poem will differ from an inferior one in two ways — it will have more strands that appeal and the strands will be mutually reinforcing. To repeat an example, the lines

> And his horse in the silence champed the grasses
> Of the forest's ferny floor,

have some appeal, but still fail because they offer only unintegrated values. The lines have some value as narrative, some as description, some as word music, and so on; but the description slows the narrative, the word music has nothing to do with the action, and the horse's diet has nothing to do with anything. In contrast, in a passage like,

> It is an ancient Mariner,
> And he stoppeth one of three.
> "By thy long grey beard and glittering eye,
> Now wherefore stopp'st thou me?"

we have narrative, description, and word music all tightly interwoven. The descriptive words, "ancient," "one of three," and "glittering eye" all excite interest in the narrative by creating a sense of mystery, of curiosity about what is to happen next. I could go on, but it should be sufficiently clear that the values in Coleridge's literary ballad are more integrated than those in de la Mare's; Coleridge does not stop doing one thing so that he can turn to something else.

If richness is the potentiality of a poem for arousing and satisfying various desires, funding is the process that makes it possible for the reader to grasp, eventually, the full value of the poem. The term, originally John Dewey's and developed by Stephen Pepper, accounts for the way in which aesthetic judgments are made corrigible. It recognizes two facts: any individual experience of a poem is partly subjective, and criticism must show that some experiences of the poem are more accurate than others. Since neither fact can be ignored, the critic has to reconcile them. Applied to poetry, Pepper's solution, which is designed to guarantee that the "total character [of a poem] is definable and open to verification," is to see the poem as a nest of three objects: the physical vehicle, the immediate perception of the physical vehicle, and the "funded" perception of the vehicle.[11] The last, the cumulative residue of more than one experience of the poem, is what the critic works with. Both the pure subjectivist (and the relativist) and the opponents of open form have to argue that each experience of the work is unique and independent — that my reading of Shakespeare's Sonnet 52 in May and my reading of it in June are two unrelated acts. In fact, we know that they are not. I learn something in May — perhaps it is correct, perhaps not — that is checked in my June reading. In addition, each successive reading tends to become more and more accurate and complete (the improvement is not inevitable, but highly probable) because each reading is an interplay of two factors: the poem, which is a constant, and the special and partly temporary mental set of the reader. The experience of the first reading of a poem, especially by an inexperienced reader, is likely to be loose; the residue left after reading is a confusion of ideas, feelings, and attitudes originating both in the poem and in the original mental set. But he is left with part of the poem, and when he returns to it with a different mental set, the perceptions originating in the poem are reinforced as those attributable to the former mental set are weakened. Thus with each reading a more precise and complete version of the poem emerges. (I am, of course, describing the ideal case; in practice, as a result of the development of strong special interests, for example concern with a critical problem, falling in love, etc., subsequent readings may sometimes be worse than earlier.)

The relationship between funding and richness is clear. Richness makes funding possible. The greater the range of values in a work, the more likely the reader is to get a partly different experience with each reading. Any appreciable amount of funding is impossible with inferior works either because the reader experiences all there is to experience too quickly, or because the lack of integration among the values permits no response to its total structure.

Wolfgang Köhler's concept of requiredness is too complex to be explained completely here. By placing all knowing and valuing on the phenomenological level, Köhler avoids the radical separation of kinds of knowing that Carnap, for example, made; for Köhler there are no Lockean primary and secondary qualities. Meanness, respectability, clumsiness — all such "value-qualities are found residing in . . . objects as characteristics of them." [12]

Redness, for example, is just as much — or, more accurately, just as little — a characteristic of the object as beauty. In the case of redness, neither the atomic events in space-time nor the microchemical events in the cortex explain the phenomenon of color; nor do they explain the interpretation as red, mean, and so on.[13] Value-bearing "vectors which, issuing in definite contexts, are experienced as resisting or as welcoming certain parts of a field are no less genuine facts than are those indifferent events." [14] Thus, to use the example Köhler gives, an A-minor melody has the minor pattern as part of its system. Within that system, the tonic A tends to be felt as static; given the system, the static quality is no less objective and no more objective than the number of vibrations per second that produces just that tone.

Now, it could be argued, as the relativist might, that our Western minor scale is a cultural phenomenon; Orientals have different scales and would react differently from us. But the point is that each system generates requirements that are felt as requirements by anyone familiar with the system. Requiredness, then, is both subjective and objective. For example, in scanning a telephone book for a number we have forgotten but once knew, we have only to glance at the page, totally unaware of the other numbers, to have the correct digits leap forth. The requiredness is subjective because *we* want just that series of numbers; it is objective because we must find just that series on the page. To put this in Köhler's terms, the number exists as a mental "trace" which causes the demand and determines "what is wrong and what is right with reference to that trace." [15] Applying this to poetry, we may say that a poem must satisfy both subjective and objective requirements. The subjective requirements may sometimes be aberrant, as when a sentimental reader demands that all poetry be "sincere"; but the aberrant subjective demands can be discovered because the objective requirements of the poem may be perceived by all interested readers and, for a single reader, may be repeated and "funded." Our sentimental reader, for example, may not be persuaded that Donne's "The Flea" is a worthwhile poem, but the critic can point out to him that a part of the contemporary heritage (in Köhler's terms, some "traces" in the mind of the cultivated reader) includes knowledge of the seventeenth-century literary tradition, general awareness of wit, certain more or less accurate information about Donne's style, and so on. These traces help generally to determine what is required of the poem. (This, by the way, accounts psychologically for the effect of tradition; it suggests that a modern poet dare not write like Shakespeare, even if he could, because we expect something different of him.) More closely related to form is the fact that ever more specific requirements are generated as we read. Usually we begin a poem with the most general kinds of expectations. But the first word limits the kind of word the poet will probably use next ("the" indicates that a noun-function will probably follow); these two words more narrowly limit the third, and so on. As a sound pattern starts to develop, it establishes its peculiar requiremeants, as do imagery, setting, plot, etc. If one admits that the poet, when he finishes writing a poem, or the reader, when he finishes reading it, may rightly say, "Yes, that's it; now it is done," he thereby admits that some kind of formal demand has been met; he is admitting the concept of requiredness.

It seems that we have made a long detour through psychologism merely to show that individual experiences of a poem are corrigible, a fact that practicing critics of all persuasions assume. Brooks's "ideal reader" is but a reader with fully funded perceptions. The detour was necessary, however, to show that the poem can be considered as an experience without denying its control. Later I shall consider several reasons for arguing that the poem is primarily an experience; here I want to discuss only the most important. Only by the poem's being placed in the mind of the reader can it be related to life. Only then can the diverse values found in the poem be analyzed as aesthetically operative. To put this in another way, the crux of the matter is whether aesthetic value is to be thought of as isolated from other values or as related to them. In the preceding chapters I cited three valid reasons for refusing to isolate the aesthetic: the range of aesthetic value becomes so limited that it is difficult to show why it is a value; works of art which seem consonant with such theories are usually partial failures (compare the works of Oscar Wilde and Joseph Conrad); and finally, a poem endures as a unit, not as bits and pieces of various kinds of value.

Only after a detour through psychology can a statement like "poetry tests ideas" [16] be made meaningful. Unless the critic is willing to consider the poem as an experience, unique but still an experience, the test is valueless; poetry becomes chess played with emotions and ideas — it toys with, rather than tests, ideas. By considering the poem as an experience (not loosely or vaguely stimulated by, but at least potentially determined by, the text), the critic makes the poem a part of the reader's life. Like any other experience, it is suffered and judged. I am arguing that poetry, and art in general, does actually "test" ideas (and feelings and perceptions) and that once the idea, emotion, or perception is tested it either becomes a part of the total personality of the reader or it does not. If it does not, the test, for whatever reason, has failed.

R. P. Blackmur's comments on Emily Dickinson's "More life went out" show in a specific way how a poem as structure affects the poem as experience. (Blackmur's practice here is at odds with his theory of the "dead-end symbol" — art as closed form.) First the poem:

> More life went out, when He went
> Than ordinary breath,
> Lit with a finer phosphor
> Requiring in the quench
>
> A power of renowned cold —
> The climate of the grave
> A temperature just adequate
> So anthracite to live.
>
> For some ampler zero,
> A frost more needle keen
> Is necessary to reduce
> The Ethiop within.
>
> Others extinguished easier —
> A gnat's minutest fan
> Sufficient to obliterate
> A tract of citizen.

Blackmur writes that "the order or plot of the elements of the poem is not that of a complete poem; the movement of parts is downward and toward a disintegration of the effect wanted." But a good poem ought to be ar-

ranged so that its parts "deliver or release by the psychological force of their sequence the full effect only when
the poem is done." He then remarks that the last
quatrain seems an "afterthought." The form, then, does
not adequately test the idea. Blackmur then goes on to
note that the last half of the second stanza is unintelligible.[17] To judge a passage on the basis of its intelligibility
is to judge it as an experience, for what the critic is saying
is that it does not jibe with what he knows; as a result, it
cannot be related either positively or negatively to anything he values. The point is that even an antipsycho-
logical critic such as Blackmur often finds it necessary to
explain the effect of a poem in psychological terms.

The two most important critics who have attempted
to build theories of open form are Kenneth Burke and
I. A. Richards, although each develops his theory in a way
that limits the value of its insights. Burke, as I understand his specifically literary criticism, is concerned with
what I shall call *psychological form* and *audience form*.

Burke's psychological forms are special instances (in
relation to aesthetic theory) of Köhler's concept of requiredness. Such forms as "metaphor, series, bathos,
chiasmus, . . . are implicit in the process of abstraction
and generalization by which we think." [18] Crescendo, for
example, is a psychological form or pattern that does not
exist as a "general thing," but events, including poems
utilizing the crescendo pattern, exist, as does "the potentiality for reacting favorably to such a climactic arrangement. . . . The accelerated motion of a falling body, the
cycle of a storm, the procedure of the sexual act, the
ripening of crops" are all natural embodiments of that
pattern. As a result, it requires a certain ordering of its
elements both because of the order of the crescendo in
nature and because "the work of art utilizes climactic arrangement because the brain has a pronounced potential-

ity for being arrested, or entertained, by such an arrangement." [19] In other words, psychological forms show both objective and subjective requiredness. One of the values of literature is its incarnation and refinement of forms to which life itself has conditioned the mind.

Audience form is at once a broader and a narrower concept than psychological form. Unlike the latter, it is a specifically aesthetic concept dealing with the satisfaction of expectations aroused in the audience by the work of art. After analyzing the scenes leading up to the meeting of Hamlet and his father's ghost, Burke shows that the dramatic impact results not from what Shakespeare knows about his characters, but from what he knows about his audience. The form of the opening of *Hamlet*, Burke argues, is determined not by Shakespeare's knowledge of "the psychology of the hero, but the psychology of the *audience*." [20] Form, in this sense, is the arousal, delay, and satisfaction of expectations. In the opening scenes of *Hamlet*, Shakespeare interests the audience in the meeting of Hamlet and the ghost (arousal), withholds the meeting for two scenes (delay), and finally — in the middle of a speech about the insobriety of the Danes — stages the confrontation (satisfaction) just when the audience expects it least. Even more technical and smaller elements of structure, such as rhythm, are each "a promise which the poet makes to the reader." [21]

Although Burke's work has become extraordinarily broad, the early aesthetic was quite narrow. The only aesthetic quality is "eloquence," which is the "result of that desire in the artist to make a work perfect by adapting it in every minute detail to the racial appetites." [22] In applying eloquence as an evaluative standard, however, Burke forgets the specialized definition he gave of it and uses its more normal meaning. Thus he attacks Kapek's *R. U. R.* because a scene in which the robots are to start a new race of rational beings lacks eloquence, eloquence largely in the sense of elaborate word play.[23] As happens often in the development of a critical theory, the critic begins with a valid idea, works carefully to its consequences, then dissociates the consequences from the premise that qualified them and gave them their validity.

More serious is Burke's de-emphasis of mimetic content, which, from another point of view, he calls "intrinsic interest," and which he wants "restored to its properly minor position, seen as merely one out of many possible elements of style." [24] Actually, even within Burke's theory, it should be argued that intrinsic interest is the most stable and most certain way of satisfying the expectations of the audience. To be consistent with that part of his theory I am now considering, Burke would have to rate such well-constructed trivia as Matthew Prior's "To Chloe Weeping" very highly; as a poem in the sophisticated pastoral tradition, it meets all the requirements of form except intrinsic interest. No one really cares about the lover and his cool beloved, nor about their emotional relationship, because everything is too exaggerated and too neat. It lacks the dimensions provided partly by the moral of "To His Coy Mistress," which is in much the same tradition. Prior's poem, in other words, is irrelevant to our more important experience of life; Marvell's is relevant. It is probably impossible to name a first-rate poem that does not possess intrinsic interest of some kind.

Writing of one aspect of intrinsic interest, George Santayana urged that "sensuous beauty is not the greatest or most important element of effect, but it is the most primitive and fundamental, and the most universal. There is no effect of form which an effect of material could not enhance." [25] Although critics and readers usually like to deny it, such "primitive" appeal is necessary for enduring art. It may be sensuous beauty (Keats), but it may also be erotic (Chaucer, Shakespeare, and Donne), or violent (Shakespeare), or wise (Shakespeare, Wordsworth). *Antony and Cleopatra* has greater aesthetic appeal than *All for Love* partly because Shakespeare's Cleopatra is more attractive than Dryden's stiffer queen. Visually, the bust of Nefertiti excites more admiration than any well-executed bust of Napoleon. The reason is clear. The most direct and the most basic appeal to an audience is through those things which attract it spontaneously. Such appeal may be the cheapest and, consequently, the least consciously admired, but it is therefore no less a value in art.

Logically, since form is always the form of something, any complete theory of evaluation must show the value of that something. Notions about what constitutes good form change from generation to generation; man's intrinsic interests remain fairly constant. What keeps *Hamlet* alive is not the formal standards it meets, but the fact that it has immediate intrinsic appeal on many levels. With the next revolution in taste it is likely that the stock of Henry James or Proust, Marianne Moore or William Carlos Williams, for example, will fall — probably too much unless critics learn that revolutions are short-lived to the degree that they are extreme. On the other hand, the reputations of Tolstoy, Dostoevsky, Frost, or Yeats will probably remain about constant — not only because they provide interesting forms but because they provide so much else to interest their readers and because their appeals to intrinsic interests offer a direct, enduring, and immediate source of pleasure.

The central failure of Burke's aesthetics is his failure to take advantage of his notion of form. Although he does locate it in the mind of the reader, like the critics who charge him with psychologism he has in his early and purely literary criticism refused to take advantage of the insight that poetry is somehow more than aesthetically important.

I. A. Richards has attempted to show that the poem is both an experience and yet different from ordinary experience. The latter is usually incomplete because

> the need for action, the comparative uncertainty and vagueness of the situation, the intrusion of accidental irrelevancies, inconvenient temporal spacing — the action being too slow or too fast — all these obscure and prevent the full development of the experience. . . . But in the "imaginative experience" these obstacles are removed. . . . what happens here, . . . may modify all the rest of life.[26]

Richards uses "equilibrium" to account for the prolongation of aesthetic experience; the balance of emotions and attitudes forestalls any action which would transfer the experience from the imagination to reality and so cut short the bringing "into play of all our faculties." Consequently, only through equilibrium "can the full richness and complexity of our environment be realized" and we become fully rather than partly alive.[27] Since equilibrium can be achieved whether the scales are full or empty, and since the purpose of the imaginative experience is to bring all our faculties into play, there are two aesthetic criteria: whether or not balance is achieved, and its "weight." If we ignore the special meanings of "equilibrium" or "balance," this view is probably correct. From it, we could argue that the best works of art are those which achieve the tightest organization of the greatest number of impulses; lesser works fail to the extent either that they contain unassimilated materials or that they achieve an easy organization by including less.

Nevertheless, three factors weaken Richards' theory.

176

His psychological machinery (which I have not attempted to outline here) is simply too clumsy to be of practical value. Secondly, there is an unattractive streak of the logical positivist in Richards that has led him to argue that "most critical discussion, . . . is primarily emotive with only a very loose . . . equivocal reference." [28] Yet the irritation that such critics as Ransom, Crane, and Brooks have felt with this aspect of Richards' work is only partly justified. Unlike his opponents, he has refused to avoid crucial problems. Unfortunately, his attempts at scientific criticism have only deepened the muddle. The notions of funding and objective requiredness, which Richards ignored, enable the theorist to describe the poem as an experience and the practical critic to talk about the text without overt reference to the experience and without inconsistency.

And finally, it is necessary to challenge (or at least to modify) Richards' notion of equilibrium. After using terms like "disinterested" and "detached" to describe the state of equilibrium, he concludes with the paradox, "to say that we are *impersonal* is merely a curious way of saying that our personality is more completely involved." [29] To resolve that paradox, a larger framework is needed, one that would distinguish the aesthetic experience from elements later discernible in it. It is true, in a very important sense, that the proper response to a fine poem is a state of equilibrium, or, to use Eliseo Vivas' phrase, intransitive attention; it is equally true that attention is not merely passive, emotions not merely balanced. Attention is not a staring at; it is a process in which certain feelings, ideas, and perceptions are evoked and made to constitute an experience.

Vivas' struggle with this problem is interesting because he has a rare ability to recognize the complexities of a problem and argue forcefully for the wrong solution. Although he develops the following in a discussion of Céline's novel *Journey to the End of the Night,* it nevertheless applies also to poetry. Vivas properly notes that "the act of digesting is distinguishable and often separable from the aesthetic transaction," that the reader "oscillates" between transitive and intransitive attention when reading a work such as *Journey to the End of the Night* because "what we previously knew about men instigates the need to digest the picture." [30] The perversity of Céline's theme so shocks the reader that he has to think about it; or, in formalistic terms, the structure excludes elements that it should include, so that the structure of the novel is incompatible with the structure of what may be assumed to be normal human experience. What is objectionable about Vivas' argument is the implication that superior works of art do not invite transitive attention. If I am reading Vivas correctly, transitive attention is called forth only by two kinds of art: that which contains some worthy germ of novelty, creativity, or originality (since the original cannot "jibe with what we previously knew about men"); and that which — like Céline's novel — seems contrary to actual conditions. The implication is that the only kind of work to which the reader can give purely intransitive attention is one with which he agrees perfectly, one that offers him nothing new. I doubt that Vivas meant this, but the conclusion is unavoidable.

The notion of funding, which Vivas' antipsychologistic bias keeps him from accepting, has the advantage of not forcing a distinction which it is impossible to perceive clearly. It has the further advantage both of admitting that extrinsic factors enter into the experiencing of a poem and also of accounting for their minimization. In denying that external factors enter into aesthetic experience, Vivas writes that "the poem is self-contained in the same sense that it constitutes a unified whole which supplies and controls the meaning and values which it embodies and gives them their contextual specificity." [31] Then, in a passage which must have been written in desperation, he maintains that two readers, one with little Spanish and the other a native speaker, would each get the "essential" experience of a Spanish poem. The former would get less, he admits, but all that a reader needs is a general knowledge of the language.[32] Either Vivas must assume that the "essential" poem is not much more than a rough paraphrase, or else he must assume that much in the poem is essentially irrelevant (and that it thereby lacks unity). To give an English example, can a reader who fails to sense the ambiguity of "still" and "unravished" in the first line of the "Ode on a Grecian Urn" be said to have experienced the essential poem? The concept of funding would account for the more accurate and deeper interpretation that comes with a greater mastery of the language. Funding makes possible what Vivas most desires in his poetic theory and what he fails to prove: a theoretical verification for the corrigibility of aesthetic experience.

Since the second advantage the concept of funding, and its textual equivalent, richness, has over notions of transitive and intransitive attention has been discussed before, I shall mention it only briefly now. To consider experience as now transitive and now intransitive is to consider works of art as objects with aesthetic plus other values. Funding and richness make it possible to account for the integration of various kinds of attention and to talk about the over-all value of the work.

Because the position urged here is extremely unpopular among literary critics (but less so among theorists and aestheticians), I shall restate the facts which support it. It accounts for the two most obvious facts of literary criticism: divergence of opinion about works of art and corrigibility of critical opinion. Negatively, it avoids the simplicity of the completely subjectivist position and the naïveté of the completely objectivist position. But most important, it helps bridge the gap between the formal qualities of the poem and their effect upon a reader. Poetic complexity, for example, becomes more than a formal property of the object; it becomes a source for innumerable ramifications of an initial experience which spread throughout the reader's awareness, linking his views of morality, of the physical world, of the life of his times and of other times, of all that he thinks, feels, knows, and is. A theory of open form helps to provide a broad enough framework to incorporate the insights of the mimeticists and the formalists.

# VII

## THE POEM AS SYMBOLIC FORM

Very few persons go to poems for advice about anything that matters. We know that Drs. Freud, Tillich, or Gilson, depending upon our persuasion, will answer our moral questions; social problems are left to statesmen, social workers, and chance. Cinerama does more than Wordsworth can to show off the English Highlands, and on a cold winter's night an electric blanket warms us better than "Sumer Is Icumen In." All of this is self-evident. Just what, then, is the function of literature, and especially the function of lyric poetry?

The easy answers have been found wanting. Those mimetic positions which offer the easiest and least satisfactory answer reply that poems are significant only because they are like other things that are significant. The answer fails because even if a poem represents some other thing, it is not that other thing; as a verbal construction it has its own peculiar formal requirements, and there is, despite Ransom, no valid reason for preferring imitation *qua* imitation.

Such diverse critics and theorists as Croce, Dewey, Brooks, Ransom, and Winters have from time to time adopted a more subtle variant of mimetic theory — that the poem imitates or embodies all the wonder, excitement, and value of a vividly felt particular experience. Thus Shelley's "To a Skylark" is valuable not because of what it says about skylarks, poetry, or human happiness, but because it captures a portion of Shelley's experience, solidifies it, and makes it available to readers. This approach alone cannot explain why a poem embodying the experience of an eccentric young man confronted by second-rate ideas which he only half understood and by a scene readily available elsewhere should interest a modern reader. The significance an experience has for the reader — not the significance it had for the poet — is the central question of evaluative criticism.[1]

The diametrically opposed answer, as formulated by Max Eastman and others, is no better. Arguing that poets cannot "tell us anything about life — . . . because *as poets* they don't know anything about life," [2] Eastman makes the common error of assuming a radical separation of poet as poet and poet as man. When he claims that the sole purpose of poetry is "to *heighten consciousness*," [3] he forgets that consciousness is always consciousness *of*; it must have an object. Although he is forced at this point to something like a mimetic theory, he tries to avoid it by justifying poetry on the grounds that it gives pleasure. Most readers, I believe, would want to claim that the pleasures of poetry differ from those of the movies, sex, baseball, or a cool shower on a warm day.

The most popular approach at present, the closed form kind of theory, attempts to isolate a single "aesthetic quality" — irony, tension, ambiguity, or what have you — which is structural rather than mimetic. The difficulties here are the improbability of such specific terms exhausting all possible poetic effects and the tendency to lock aesthetic and ordinary experience in separate compartments.

Specifically, the problem is to incorporate the insights of these approaches into a comprehensive and consistent literary theory. In fact, the problem has been solved haphazardly by most critics and aestheticians when they have discarded their own special theories and assumed that poetry is something for the whole man, poems something more than intermittent intellectual visions and emotional titillations. John Crowe Ransom, whose own purely theoretical work limits poetry excessively, reminds Blackmur that poetry is "more than gesture," and Blackmur in turn reminds his readers that it is more than technique; Cleanth Brooks opens up poetic form at both ends, in a footnote, and Eliseo Vivas reluctantly admits transitive attention alongside intransitive attention.[4]

Seeing the poem as a symbolic form, an interpretation of reality rather than a representation of it, is a major step in explaining both the autonomy of poems and their relation to our vital interests. Because a symbolic form is an *interpretation*, it is creative — it remakes the shape of reality; and because what is interpreted is *reality*, its consequences extend beyond itself. Thus neither mimetic accuracy alone nor internal coherence alone is the test of a symbolic form; the test is both.

I mean symbolic form here to embrace everything from the formula $E = MC^2$ through the rebirth archetype and the concept of the "economic man" to individual poems, plays, and novels. Each comes out of the world of real things, renders that world according to the proportions and laws of its peculiar perspective, and endures only so long as that rendering seems adequate. Other versions of symbolic form more popular in contemporary literary theory are more limited and lead to insoluble difficulties.

The view I am proposing could be stated in terms of Coleridge's distinction between primary and secondary imagination — between the seething, always active, always creative power of man constantly creating not reality but order-in-reality, and the secondary imagination (imaginations would be more proper) that orders reality according to specific kinds of form.[5] Hazlitt, despite his eighteenth-century ideological heritage, probably came closest to this understanding of Coleridge. At least he recognized that "if poetry is a dream, the business of life is much the same." [6] Our imagination shapes our attitude toward practical affairs no less than it shapes our poetry. Shelley also came close, if I understand rightly his statement that "poets are the unacknowledged legislators of the world." [7] Laws — whether they be laws of mathematics or of society — are made by men of vision, or else they do not endure. All the order of the world, all the multiform patterns into which we put our experience, we owe to those who codified their points of view, who, in other words, constructed a symbolic form.

But no one was able to carry on where Coleridge had left off. Emerson attempted to enforce the doctrine of symbolic imagination; and Hawthorne, Poe, and Melville utilized the aesthetic content and techniques most obviously appropriate to it. Generally, however, they left the main currents of literature undisturbed until the second decade of the twentieth century. Before the idea of symbolic imagination could take hold, practical critics and their readers needed the kind of world view Coleridge and Emerson (among the literary men) and Kant and Hegel (among the philosophers) had formulated but could not win acceptance for. The greatest spur to the required world view came, ironically, from the triumphs of science. The increasing amount and precision of scientific knowledge forced compartmentalization of the different sciences and the abandonment of what had been long accepted as universal truths. In fact, scientists came to recognize that the entire methodology of modern science is designed to provide the "right" or laboratory conditions, the purified set of occasions for which the hypothesis should hold true. Scientific laws, then, are contextualistic rather than universal. A hydraulics engineer, a physicist, and a chemist all see water as something different; and if a chemist or his associate in another science is thirsty, it is still something else. Thanks to the compartmentalization of science, we habitually view any given object from a variety of vantage points and move easily from one such point to another. In other words, we no longer ask, "What is this?" but rather, "Given this formulation of its properties, what follows?" Only after the realization that science does not tell the whole truth could the symbolist outlook be taken seriously by persons less mystic than Emerson and less philosophical than Kant. As long as science (or religion, or whatever) was thought to show reality as it exists, talk about the symbolic imagination and its interpretations of reality seemed somehow beside the mark.

Actually, the old clear-cut distinction between reason and imagination has crumbled, as has the distinction between those two and perception. What we see and hear is not what is out there, but what is out there as transformed by our receptors. What we reason out with painstaking care has been transformed any number of times by our senses and our memories and imaginations; and the reasoning itself is largely a removal of the material from its rich entanglement with reality. Although this new outlook is especially advantageous for both poetry and poetics, contemporary critics have not yet taken full advantage of the gift they have been offered. As a result, even those critics most aware of symbolism (in our sense) demand at once too much and too little of poetry. On the one hand, they want the aesthetic unrelated to the practical, the moral, the philosophic, and so on; on the other, with equal frequency and fervor, they would argue that only the imagination knows reality.

I. A. Richards' sharp distinction between statements and pseudo-statements set the pattern of discussion for a long time. For a while after the distinction was made, it seemed that the imaginative and rational modes of understanding could never be reconciled. Working within the framework of logical positivism, the notion of poetry as pseudo-statement was all but inevitable. Actually, however, "pseudo-statement" for Richards was in no sense a pejorative. It simply meant that statements that might be true or false in prose gained nothing by being considered as true (or false) in poetry. Consequently, in poetry "words are so used that their meanings are free to dispose themselves: to make up together whatever they can." [8] This is an overstatement, for the ultimate source and final resting place of poetry is reality as transformed by the human mind; words, therefore, are not "free" in any real sense. To assume that they are leads to the kind of silliness Blackmur committed when he had Lear saying "Always, always, always." Even so fine a theoretician as D.G. James makes the same error. Writing of the prosaic diction of lines like:

> O, reason not the need: our basest beggars
> Are in the poorest thing superfluous: —

James remarks that "these prosaic associations are controlled and expelled"; the poet is not "limited by previous associations; rather he is able to destroy those associations from our minds, and in the act of stripping the words of all but their bare meaning, enriches them with a new context of association." [9] The issue is whether or not the prosiness is really "expelled" — whether the "meanings are free to dispose themselves." I should prefer to argue that the prose associations are directed instead of destroyed, that the prosy reality does get into the poem and operates there in an altered but real way. If the poetic context does expel and destroy the customary associations of words, then the connection between poem and world is lost. The poem becomes thing, not symbol.

After Richards cut the poem off from the world, he naturally attempted to relate it to the reader, so that the value of the poem is its value for adjusting the reader's attitudes by inducing those mental states

> which involve the widest and most comprehensive co-ordination of activities and the least curtailment, conflict, starvation, and restriction. States of mind in general are valuable in the degree in which they tend to reduce waste and frustration.[10]

This is extremely wise, but "frustration" in relation to what? One answer is that the attitudes poetry sets in motion should not be mutually frustrating, that they should achieve a balance after only temporary frustration. But, as we have seen earlier, if we admit balance as a standard, we are unable to explain the full effects of poetry. Precisely because the poem incites attitudes, however, and because attitudes are mental, another kind of frustration is possible — the frustration caused when the attitudes generated by the poem conflict with those generated by the reader. Strictly applied, Richards' theory does not admit this kind of frustration because, theoretically, those attitudes evoked by reference and those evoked by pseudo-reference should never meet.

Practically every major critic has noted Richards' weakness on this issue and produced his own evasion of it. The usual evasion is to accept the poem as not immediately applicable to real conditions but as some kind of "test" of ideas. Ransom, for example, sees the poem as "a place where fact is turned loose, to see what it will do, in the laboratory of the scrupulous imagination"; but the experiment is always "slightly rigged" because "faith is brought into the poem a little bigger than natural." [11] On the contrary, within a satisfactory poem there is no fact and no laboratory; they are one. The fact and the laboratory both are products of the imagination, and the entire poem is the incarnation (to use a term from another phase of Ransom's criticism) of that fact in that context as expressed in that language.

Nor should we attach much importance to the "rigging" of the experiment. Ransom implies that the poem is a serious experiment that cannot be taken seriously because it is slightly dishonest; the implication is that a real scientific experiment is not rigged — we can trust it. This is Richards' error once more, the easy assumption of the objectivity of science. As I have argued, the entire methodology of the exact sciences is aimed at rigging, at least in the sense that the scientist simply cannot test his hypotheses with the necessary precision in the complex and messy real world; he must limit the "world" of his experiment to what is relevant to his inquiry. The artist does much the same, except that, according to Christopher Caudwell, science is a kind of physical experimenting, and art is "affective experimenting." [12] Both the artist and the scientist may be said to test a hypothesis about reality by creating a situation in which only relevant data may operate. The results of a poetic experiment, then, should be as binding as the results of any scientific experiment. A successful poem forces the reader to a new integration of experience.

Cleanth Brooks has suggested as much in a rather indecisive passage in which he makes a valuable distinction between judgment by coherence (structural relationships) and judgment by correspondence (mimesis). He argues first that we want judgment by coherence, not by correspondence, then states that "the coherence of parts in a literary work depends upon our belief in the plausibility of certain actions and reactions, responses and valuations. In these we must 'believe' or the work of art is indeed incredible and monstrous." Coherence, then, would seem to be judged in relation to the norm of correspondence. "But," Brooks adds, "the correspondence to reality that a poem achieves is mediated through its special kind of structure. And that fact has to be given due weight." [13] Although Brooks is trying hard to assert the primacy of coherence as an aesthetic standard, I cannot quite see the difference between a coherence to "our basic pattern of human nature" and correspondence. There is no need to choose between coherence and correspondence if one admits a special category of creative correspondence, or *congruence*.[14] Brooks probably had some such notion in mind when he wrote that Keats,

> like all other poets, is really building a more precise sort of language than the dictionaries contain, by playing off the connotations and denotations of words against each other so as to make a total statement of a great deal more accuracy than is ordinarily attained.[15]

Brooks' general theory does not permit him to explain "accuracy" — accurate in relation to what? Only by considering the poem as a symbol system within the larger symbol system of language can the question be answered adequately.

The first critic to approach such an understanding of poetry and to exploit it systematically was Kenneth Burke, especially in the sections of his later work that are devoted to literature. "Poetry," he writes, "or any verbal act, is to be considered as 'symbolic action.'" Man, with his unique ability to avoid real action, may instead engage in symbolic action and enjoy the *"dancing of an attitude"*; instead of getting married, he may write a poem about getting married.[16] Although Burke's basic conception of symbolic action has not changed greatly, the values he finds in it have. The early Burke, arguing that "an ability to function in a certain way implies gratification in so functioning," found an intrinsic appeal in symbolic action resulting simply from man's ability to act symbolically.[17] The previously examined notions of form and eloquence were the results of such an approach.

Yet even as early as *Counter-Statement* (1931), Burke's notion of literature was not quite so simple. Eloquence not only satisfies *per se*, its "primary purpose . . . is to convert life into its most thorough verbal equivalent." He hastened to add, however, that "the categorical appeal of literature resides in a liking for verbalizations as such." [18]

As Burke's general philosophy developed, the notion that literature can transform life because it begins in the life of the poet and ends in the life of the reader became more important. Although this sounds like personality theory, it is not. In the first place, Burke's theory is too broadly conceived to be so easily classified; and secondly, he is willing to give more attention to technique and form than personality theory would permit. The notion of "associational clusters," [19] for example, is typical of the complexity of Burke's thought. Such clusters arise from the tendency of a poet to link together certain words, emotions, images, etc. Whether conscious or unconscious, they are the verbal shape of his emotion; they are also a large part of the shape of the poem. The "tactics of expression, . . . organize a work technically *because* they organize it emotionally." [20] Because of this double emphasis upon both the technical and the experiential,

Burke is able to account for the significance, the uniqueness, and the unity of the poem. To simplify greatly, a successful poem is significant because of its source in transpersonal experience; it is unique because it is its own particular cluster of techniques and meanings; and it is unified because the structure of *an* experience (in John Dewey's sense) has given structure to the poem.

Continuing for a moment with the notion of associational clusters, Burke remarks that he had long been troubled by the phrase "silly buckets" in *The Rime of the Ancient Mariner*. The adjective seemed "surprising, picturesque, and interesting" but inexplicable, until Burke realized that the *silly* buckets, filled with curative rain, are part of the cluster containing the "greybeard *loon*" and the Pilot's boy, "who now doth *crazy* go." (Italics mine.) The Pilot's boy, Burke argues, is a scapegoat, "a victimized vessel for drawing off the most malign aspects of the curse that afflicts the 'greybeard loon.' " After becoming aware of the cluster,

> the structure itself became more apparent: the "loon"-atic Mariner begins his cure from drought under the aegis of a moon that causes a silly rain, thence by synecdoche to silly buckets, and the most malignant features of this problematic cure are transferred to the Pilot's boy who now doth crazy go.[21]

A part of the previously hidden meaning is now manifest. Burke believes that through such clusters the critic can show the covert interests of the poet and, conversely, a knowledge of the interests of the poet can help the critic discover the more important clusters.

I should emphasize here that in a successful poem the clusters are not mere groups of personal associations made by the poet. They are a part of the poem, which Burke describes as a proverb "writ large," whose function is "to chart, . . . 'type' situations." [22] The situation is significant precisely because it is typical; the result, the poem as chart, is significant precisely because it is a way of experiencing that situation. The structure of the poem is the structure of the experience that motivated the poem; thus the study of either leads to an awareness of the other.

How can an experience be both unique and typical? If we mean by typical that one thing is the equivalent of another, the question obviously cannot be answered. But if typical means simply analogous to, there is no problem. Because a poem is a working out of a typical situation, it is also a filling out — that is, a concrete embodiment. What is typical about a situation may be expressed in any number of ways; but the typical can be expressed only by the addition of nontypical material. To state this in another way, the typical situation is an abstraction that can only be expressed by materials which make it concrete. Thus there are any number of ways of filling out the typical emotion expressed by "Glory be to God for dappled things." We may wax theological, reflecting on the power and glory of God in creating beauty, the necessity of human gratitude for such beneficence, and even the nature of creativity. We could, in other words, write a piece in the manner of St. Augustine. Or we could stress the "dappled" and write an essay on the beauty of colors. Or we could do what Hopkins did and write a poem. In any case, the typical situation — a wonder at a certain kind of beauty — is realized and made convincing only by the addition of nontypical details. [23]

I do not want to imply that the essay in the manner of the Bishop of Hippo would state precisely what the Hopkins poem states. Each context for a typical situation generates its own particular requirements, and the more full the treatment of the situation, the richer the presentation, the greater the difference in the full implications of the statements made. To translate this from Burke's terminology to the terminology used here, a poem is a symbol which, like all symbols, is coherent and congruent. It is congruent because as a symbol it is communicative; it shares meaning with the reality in which it originated and with its reader. It is coherent because it has that tight specificity of relation of part to part required of any embodiment. And furthermore, a realized symbolic form is unique because the requisite tight specificity can be duplicated only by repetition of the pattern.

Burke's analysis of Keats's "Ode on a Grecian Urn" is perhaps his best and most fully developed later criticism. The analysis, which he calls "dramatic," is designed to make clear the "symbolic action" of the Ode. Like other actions, a symbolic action has its origin in the mind of the poet, in this case in a kind of tension he feels in the opposition between truth and beauty. Their separation is an irritant which creates a "fever"; the romantic poet simply cannot surrender truth to science and leave art with only beauty. The motive of the action, then, is the need to build a reality in which truth and beauty are one, which as Burke points out they are not at the start of the poem. To rid himself of the fever (and here I am oversimplifying Burke greatly) Keats goes through his symbolic act. The first stage is the separation of the "malign" physical from the "benign" spiritual realm, so that the latter can transform the former. In the second stanza the spiritual begins seeking its own truth. It discovers, among other things, that it has left the physical behind. The poem is not complete when the spirit escapes the body, for now the spirit becomes (in Burke's terminology) an actor with no scene in which to act. Keats now has to build a "scene," a world, for the spirit; he does so by creating a universe in which "the laws of contradiction no longer prevail." [24] He may now honestly make the predication whose denial caused his earlier agitation; he has created a universe (of discourse, at least) in which truth and beauty are reunited.

We should look a bit more closely at what has happened. First, the situation (the poet's agitation and presumably the reader's over the split between truth and beauty — or science and art) is a typical and therefore communicable situation. The origin of the poem is neither a private nor even a narrowly aesthetic emotion; it is rather an awareness of a condition which must be overcome. Moreover, the situation is typical for all who experience it; but the poet as poet is not concerned with its typicality. His only proper concern is the expansion of the situation into a form. If the situation is neither typical nor potentially typical, it will not vitally interest the reader. Fortunately, however, words themselves are the bearers of the typicality since what they express is precisely the sharable part of experience. As poet, then, Keats's only concern is to use his words to build a coherent system.

The same point may be made more generally by noting that the typical situation is a constant; the symbol is its unique and dynamic realization. The symbol equals the typical situation in the same sense that $2 + 2 = 4$; in either case the equality is not simple identity — if we can accept Whitehead's word for the mathematical part.[25] The left and right hand sides of the equation are rather based on two separate points of view; there are any number of ways of realizing four, but only one four. Two plus two is merely one of its possible realizations; as *that* realization it requires a specific, unique operation with specific but not unique materials. All of this is quite ordinary. For example, I teach a class of twenty students. I can think of it as a class of twenty, and let it go at that;

but then I have to treat the group in a certain way. Or I can think of it as composed of two scholars and eighteen clods, or of eighteen students who need special assistance and two who can work independently, and so on. But no matter how I think of the class, each way of thinking of it presupposes a special way of handling it. I am suggesting here that the two plus two that equals four is not identical with the four, and that the laws governing the two plus two are laws of coherence, laws of internal order and organization. But when I think in terms of the four, I am thinking in terms of congruence, in terms of simple comparison of this four with other fours. The analogy should not be pushed too far, but it is significant that most persons can think of the same object — whether mathematical, human, or aesthetic — in diverse ways. To return to poetry, the only factor which determines whether one talks about the fully embodied symbol or the typical situation is the point of view and interest at the moment.

What is brilliant about Burke's analysis of the "Ode on a Grecian Urn" is neither the details nor the terminology. He manages to suggest forcefully both the typical situation upon which the Ode is based and which gains for it a serious reading, and the rich realization of the symbol. The poem emerges from the unassimilated flux of reality through the poet and into its incarnation in the poem; but because of its origins, it is equipped to shed itself of the splendor of its embodiment and to take its chance as experience.

Unfortunately, however, Burke slights the formative powers of language itself.[26] The poet, I should argue, both co-operates with and fights against his language; he can do nothing which it will not permit. Because language is by definition communal, it always strains toward the typical situation. Ultimately, the poem begins and ends in reality; but mediately it begins and ends in language. As the poet attempts to organize reality (or his experience of it) verbally, he is also forced to organize it in the mode of his medium, to follow those laws of organization common to those who use his language. Thus not only the experience of the poet, but the method of expression, both begins and ends in the great world and is designed to empty out into it.

I am here trying to avoid the intentionalism of Burke not because it is invalid but because it is irrelevant for evaluation. It may be possible for a poet to "solve" a problem of which he is not aware. Thus it is not necessary to assume, as Burke does, that Keats understood or even felt the divorce of science and art; perhaps the problem and its solution were implicit in the language rather than in the poet's experience.

Poe's "To Helen" might provide a better illustration of the point I am making. It is that, regardless of the overt experience of the poet, language itself may work to build a symbol which is both coherent and congruent. "To Helen" is challenging because it at once invites and resists facile interpretation. Moreover, the usual assumption is that the poem stands out among Poe's works because for once Poe has not overdone his technical effects. The result, so the easy explanation runs, is that "To Helen" is merely the best of the poems composed according to Poe's usual formula. There may be something more in the lyric:

> Helen, thy beauty is to me
>   Like those Nicéan barks of yore
> That gently, o'er a perfumed sea,
>   The weary, way-worn wanderer bore
>   To his own native shore.

On desperate seas long wont to roam
　　Thy hyacinth hair, thy classic face,
　　Thy Naiad airs have brought me home
　　　To the glory that was Greece
And the grandeur that was Rome.

Lo! in yon brilliant window-niche
　　How statue-like I see thee stand!
　　The agate lamp within thy hand,
Ah, Psyche, from the regions which
　　Are Holy-Land!

The most obvious feature about the development of this lyric is the apotheosis of Helen from woman, to symbol, to Psyche. This is the same kind of transformation (a typical situation) undergone in Keats's Ode, although the elements differ. There is no reason for believing that the experience behind this lyric was any more intense than Poe's experience behind other lyrics (compare, for example, the maudlin "Anabelle Lee," also inspired by the death of a young woman). But there is something in the poem, and it almost comes off; I want to suggest that what happens is largely an accident of language — that Poe put his usual stock of words and themes together, but got something special.

How? The poem begins tritely enough, with the beauty of Helen compared with the beauty of other sensuous things. But hardly is the simile under way when a metaphor begins to grow. The Nicéan barks of the simile suggest traveling, and the persona of the poem is a wanderer. Without this suggestion of movement, the poem would seem a jerky jumbling together of Nicéan barks, Greece, Rome, and the Holy Land. Moreover, by the end of the first stanza the magic in the name of Helen has begun its work. The persona is now transformed from a nameless traveler into a timeless and placeless combination of Ulysses and Paris, a man somehow beyond mortal men. Helen is also transformed; she is both vehicle (bark) and goal. Poe keeps the two functions nicely separated but imaginatively joined — within the simile she is vehicle, outside, goal; within she is a ship wandering the seas; outside, she is immobile. All of this grows naturally out of the simile. It is the language, not the poet, that has developed the symbol.

The poem stands out among Poe's work for two reasons, both closely related. (I shall not go into matters of technique here, although I believe that they are the clues to what I shall say about the poem.) Perhaps the two reasons could best be stated as cause and effect: the situation is typical (despite the usual untypicality of Poe's themes) because he permits language to work; or, because he permits language to work more or less on its own, instead of bending it in his usual direction, the situation is typical. For the practical critic there is no difference between these two statements, for the practical critic works with the poem, the product of the process.

As suggested above, the typical situation behind "To Helen" is also that behind the "Ode on a Grecian Urn" — the transformation and consequent equivalence of different orders of experience. Helen the woman becomes Psyche not because she is woman but because she is symbol, and as such is both the vehicle for the understanding of the experience and the mediate end of that experience. The poem works as well as it does because by an accident of language the central figure conveys all this. Because the figure works the way it does to transform Helen to Psyche, the poem, at least in its rough outlines, meets the test of coherence, the first test of a symbolic form. More importantly, however, because the situation is typical, it manages (unlike the situations in most of Poe's work) to meet the test of congruence. To put this in terms of value, the poem succeeds because it provides a realization of an experience that can be accepted within the larger framework of human knowledge and feeling.

Most theorists' work designed to show in what ways symbolic forms have value has taken one of two directions. The first was stated quite early by Burke, who "would not for the world make literature and life synonymous since, by comparison in such terms, the meanest life is so overwhelmingly superior to the noblest poem that illiteracy becomes almost a moral obligation." [27] The strongest statement of the second is by Vivas: "if literature does not give us knowledge, it ought to be recognized that it is prior in the order of logic to all knowledge, since it is constitutive of culture, which is one of the conditions of knowledge." [28] Although this problem of the relation of poetry to knowledge has run throughout most of this study, I want to approach it more directly this time. Burke's "typical situation" is one way of getting literature involved with life and yet keeping some distance between them, but more common is the attempt to stake out an "aesthetic" area with a "poetic" subdivision.

Recently, with the work of Philip Wheelwright and Northrop Frye in particular, the aesthetic area has been closely linked with the notion of archetypes. Both Wheelwright and Frye see archetypes as extensions of the Jungian concept more or less freely adapted especially to literature. Conceived broadly enough, and disregarding man's natural admiration for technical virtuosity, they are the chief source of our delight in poetry; they are "typical situations" in their most primitive form and so "closer to man's natural human vision than are the products of brain-ingenuity." [29] Their natural mode of expression is myth and art.

The difficulty is that archetypes are not usually thought of so broadly, and most properly are occasional instruments of critical investigation rather than critical principles. But before proceeding, I should note once more that the idea of the archetype goes well with the symbolic nature of literature to the extent that the archetype may (for literary purposes) be described as a potentially communicable and valuable occasion of experience which lends itself to innumerable incarnations. Nevertheless, even when specifically adapted to literature, archetypes do present grave difficulties. As Wheelwright admits, archetypes are not the only product of the literary imagination; in addition to the archetypal imagination there are also the stylistic imagination, the confrontive imagination, and the metaphoric imagination; [30] and four kinds of discourse (literal, meaningless and nonemotive, ejaculative, and expressive or poetic), with only the expressive both emotional and referential.[31] It is somewhat disconcerting to learn later that there are eight "principles of expressive language." [32] By this time, it would seem that Wheelwright's analysis has been carried too far for practical criticism; not that it is necessarily invalid, but the profusion of divisions and subdivisions discourages criticism. Accepting Wheelwright's framework loosely, we have a series of occasionally usable insights; accepted rigidly, it is unworkable because one mode of discourse can never completely accommodate another, and the more rigid the one, the more violence it does to the other. Further, precisely what is the difference between archetypal and metaphoric imaginations? The former "sees the particular object as embodying and adumbrating suggestions of universality" and the latter "fuses heterogeneous elements into some kind of unity." [33] But to fuse such elements into a unity is to create the universal under which they are united, and to see the particular as universal is precisely to fuse heterogeneous elements. The distinction dissolves because the notion of the archetype, which seems the basic concept in Wheelwright's work, is too narrow. By the time he finishes bridging it out, it is at once too complicated for practical use and too rigid for application.

Specifically, "archetype" carries with it certain psychological connotations which too radically limit the kind of situation with which poetry may deal. Because Wheelwright sees the archetype as an essential element in literature, he keeps literary truth unrelated to other kinds of truth. Wheelwright writes that:

> the poet stakes out his context, the "world" of his poem, with his imagination audaciously alive and responsive; that is the way toward the regaining of the Terrestrial Paradise. . . . The ground-bass of poetic truth is the truth, contextual but real, of man's possible redemption through the fullest imaginative response.[34]

Wheelwright is probably correct; but I should rather emphasize that there is a truth apart from poetic truth, and that while the immediate business of the poem is to be true poetically, in the long run it must provide an experience which is at least potentially congruous with rational and practical experience. I should, in other words, rather link the poem to the real world than to a problematic terrestrial paradise.

Northrop Frye's work fares better because it is developed more broadly and not so rigidly. Archetypes, for Frye, make it possible to "conceive the possibility of a self-contained literary universe" and so "to prevent the analogies supplied by convention and genre from being an endless series of free associations, perhaps suggestive, perhaps even tantalizing, but never creating a real structure." [35] Frye avoids the psychological implications of the notion of archetype and uses it as a kind of bare literary pattern, a symbol "which connects one poem with another and thereby helps us to unify and integrate our literary experience." [36] Unfortunately for our purposes, Frye is more concerned with relating individual poems to the whole of poetry than with relating them to experience. Although he is not unaware of the more important relationship, he minimizes it by arguing that

> whenever we read anything, we find our attention moving in two directions at once. One direction is outward, or centrifugal. . . . The other direction is inward or centripetal. . . .
>
> In all literary verbal structures the final direction of meaning is inward. In literature the standards of outward meaning are secondary, for literary works do not pretend to describe or assert.[37]

Although we may agree that meanings come from the outside and work inwards through the poem, should we not also go further? Should we not also maintain that once the words are controlled within the poem, once they make up the poem, the poem itself becomes a total symbol which, when realized in the reader's experience, is directed outside itself? D. G. James, for example, points out that art "at once provides the will with a clear and lucid situation in which to act, and facilitates the action of the will by the diminution of the power of disturbance of emotional-conative activity." [38] But art does even more; it provides data for other modes of experience. The various modes of experience — aesthetic, scientific, practical, social, and so on — are not as autonomous as Wheelwright, Frye, and others contend. The classic example is the influence of Wordsworth's poetry on Mill. Whitehead has observed that

> both Shelley and Wordsworth emphatically bear witness that nature cannot be divorced from its aesthetic values, and that these values arise from the cumulation, in some sense, of the brooding presence of the whole on its various parts. Thus we gain from the poets the doctrine that a philosophy of nature must concern itself at least with these six notions: change, value, eternal objects, endurance, organism, interfusion.[39]

Poetry is related to other modes of experience because, as Whitehead suggests in his discussion of the relation between philosophy and science, all modes of experience are rooted in the experience of concrete fact.[40]

Earl R. Wasserman gains an advantage over Frye's view by keeping poetry within the spectrum of language, rather than myth, and thereby keeping poetry within the range of ordinary human experience. Wasserman sees practical and poetic discourse as opposites, with individual poems falling somewhere in between; the extremes are ideals of definition rather than realizable conditions. Practical discourse is chiefly referential, poetic discourse chiefly intrareferential, or constitutive, or (the term Wasserman prefers) syntactical. By "syntax" Wasserman means "the interactive capacities of any of the properties of words," including reference in all its forms, "position and repetition; word order, sound; rhyme, even orthography." Any and all of these relations "may work syntactically, thickening and concretizing the tenuous language of discourse." [41] The special value of poetry is that, by calling upon syntactical means beyond those of grammar, poetry establishes a new syntax and hence establishes a new set of presuppositions in its language. . . . the extraordinary syntactical possibilities of poetry create a new syntactical order and therefore a new organization of reality.[42]

As a result of its unique order, poetry loses its ability to assert but gains the ability to affirm. It creates, in other words, a poetic cosmos in which the concept it bears is "true." The following is important because it shows an unusually fine understanding of the way the poem, the symbol out of reality and raised beyond it, returns to operate in that reality:

> Language advances beyond its own systematic preconceptions by the exploration of their permutations. It is the limits of these explorations that are the limits of our customary world. The poetically constituted reality, however, releases the possibility of exploring by poetic logic, or imagination, the consequences of the newly realized conceptions. The special integrative, or constitutive, act of poetry, that is, not only may realize a special cosmos but also thereby opens the opportunity for further conceptual discoveries in that cosmos.[43]

My only reservation concerning Wasserman's statement is a doubt about the implications of "further conceptual discoveries in that cosmos." If the discoveries are conceptual, they should also function outside of and beyond the "special cosmos" created by the poetic imagination. To the extent that man's personality is an integrated whole, any new organization of reality that he experiences will in some way force a total reorganization of all his experience. Hence the cross-fertilization of modes of experience (the kind of mutual influence that poetry, philosophy, and science have had on each other) is possible.

Before turning from literary theorists to aestheticians, it is necessary to consider the work of Ernst Cassirer. The discussion should place much of the above in order and also provide a basis for examining further the work of Vivas and Susanne K. Langer, both of whom are indebted to Cassirer.

My interpretation of Cassirer's thought is, to my best knowledge, unorthodox in that it stresses the relation of the aesthetic and other realms. For Cassirer, the basic symbolic forms are myth and religion, language and art, science and history.[44] Followers of Cassirer usually treat them as relatively autonomous, and Cassirer himself sometimes writes as if they were — on the methodological principle, I believe, that analysis precedes synthesis. Cassirer has written that the achievement of each of the symbolic modes "must be measured by itself, and not by the standards and aims of any other." He did not live to answer his own question, "whether and how all these forms of conceiving the world and the I are compatible with one another." [45] I feel some justification, therefore, in maintaining that Cassirer conceived of the symbolic forms as mutually relevant.

Because Cassirer's philosophy is the result of close and complex reasoning based upon an abundance of empirical data, I cannot hope to present it convincingly. At best, I can outline the system, hoping by the way to show its unusual consistency and richness, but concentrating on its value to poetics. The first problem is the relation of the kinds of symbolic form to reality — or rather, the relation between the ego and reality as mediated by such forms. Like Köhler, Heisenberg, and Whitehead, Cassirer argues that "objects are not 'given' to the consciousness in a rigid, finished state, in their naked 'as suchness.' "

What we ordinarily call reality "is the product of a formative operation effected by the basic instrumentality of consciousness, by intuition and pure thought." [46] For reasons which I cannot explore now, certain fairly well-defined modes of consciousness tend to develop — the artistic, scientific, and religious consciousness. Each is a way of objectifying reality, of forming it so that it may enter significantly into the consciousness of man.

The most far-reaching effect of this view is to dethrone reason as queen of the faculties. Reason still enters into other modes of awareness, just as the aesthetic and the religious enter into the realm of reason; nevertheless, rationality is no longer the primary way of knowing. "Reason," Cassirer writes,

> is a very inadequate term with which to comprehend the forms of man's cultural life in all their richness and variety. But all these forms are symbolic forms. Hence, instead of defining man as an *animal rationale*, we should define him as an *animal symbolicum*. By doing so we can designate his specific difference, and we can understand the new way open to man — the way of civilization.[47]

Most of the applications of this view for literary theory have been noted earlier. It makes the old reference-pseudo-reference terminology (and its derivatives) unnecessary. No symbolic form has a direct claim on reality or on any segment of it, though each symbolic form has a claim on an area of reconstituted reality. Also, it makes impossible the *direct* criticism of one mode by another. Thirdly, just as art is no longer subordinate to science, so science cannot be subordinate to art. The symbolic forms "enjoy equal rank as products of the human spirit." [48] Thus on the one side poetry is freed from the bonds of direct mimetic responsibility, and on the other from the imposition and criticism of other forms. And still further, it is freed from the responsibility of being, as latter-day Shelleyians claim, "the unacknowledged legislator of the world." But this is not to say that poetry is freed from indirect mimesis, that other forms are irrelevant to it, or that it is irresponsible.

Before resolving these near contradictions, I should sketch briefly the way in which, according to Cassirer, a symbolic form works. In the beginning was not the word, but the ego and the world. The word-symbol developed as a mediator between the two, but with the development of the symbol a new factor entered the relationship. The symbol generates its own objective requirements, its own mode and sphere of operation, which in its turn becomes a part of the data of experience. Language has for man

> the same "objectivity" as the world of things. Like the world of things, it confronts him as a whole, possessing its own self-contained nature and laws, in which there is nothing individual or arbitrary.[49]

Thus the laws of language differ from the laws of both science and ritual. Symbolic forms are not vacuous or inchoate mediators, but mediators possessing a given structure and molding reality to that structure. For this reason imitation of material in one medium by means of another medium is, strictly speaking, impossible.

Just as the major symbolic forms have their own principles, so their individuations proceed in accord with principles which are semiautonomous within the major form. Consequently, neither the physical properties of words (their sound and look) nor their meanings enter into a poem without being altered and, if all is going well, enhanced by their context; this is why no poem is simply the sum of its parts.[50] A word — or, for that matter, a sentence, phrase, or any unit of discourse — must meet three sets of requirements when used in a poem. As meaningful language, it must ultimately refer back to the world; it must do so in accord with the general principles of the major symbolic form of which it is a part; and it must do so in accord with the specific principles of that individual work of art. No matter how tight the context provided by the poem, the individual units of meaning must always harken back to the laws of language and to the general principles covering the interpretation of reality by symbolic construction.

It is now possible to indicate the peculiar nature of the responsibility of art, and also to indicate the relationship between art and other modes of knowing. Art is a means for knowing reality, but it is incomplete. The other symbolic modes are necessary, and together all of the symbolic modes are for the human mind reality at that given moment. "At that given moment" is an essential qualification because the constant activity of the symbolic imagination ceaselessly pushes on, sharpens, clarifies, and makes more consistent man's knowledge of reality.[51] Consequently, "empirical reality, the constant core of objective being," is not dependent on any particular sense impression, nor on any particular form of apprehension, but on confirmation "by experience as a whole." [52] Ideally, then, because all symbolic forms begin and end in the same ground, they must be congruent despite their differences. That is, the total import of a poem must not defy the interpretations of reality given by other modes. It is no accident, for example, that Swinburne's unacceptable attitude toward reality produced (despite his technical mastery) poetry less significant *as poetry* than Wordsworth's, which embodies an attitude somewhat more congruent with reality as known. Nevertheless, to say that the implications of symbolic forms must be congruous with one another is an exaggeration.

The "must" indicates a hope rather than a fact, a never-to-be-realized ideal in which readers are simultaneously aware of the totality of actual and potential human experience.

There are two other sources of the incongruity of some works of literature with our experience. The first is the valuable novelty or originality that arises because symbols tend to be creative. Each really new symbol creates a vision of reality which, were it not for man's limited vision, would compel immediate revisions in other symbolic modes. In such a case the incongruity is only temporary; psychology, for example, is finally catching up with Shakespeare, and urban sociology with Dostoevsky. Or the incongruity may be felt simply because the symbolic form has failed or has outlived its relevance, much as the old faculty psychology has now become incongruous with what other symbolic forms tell us about man's mind. This explains why, for example, sentimentality is an aesthetic vice: the sentimental experience is out of line with the majority of other modes of experience.

The most elaborate attempt to apply Cassirer's work to art in general and to literature in particular has come from Susanne K. Langer. Despite her impressive credentials, her departures from the master's system nullify the gains he made. She insists that the kinds of symbolic forms are mutually independent; the result is that art becomes for her what it was for Cleanth Brooks — not a true test of ideas, but a kind of inconsequential window-shopping. She writes that

> a poet usually builds a philosophical poem around an idea
> that strikes him, at the time, as true and important; but
> not for the sake of debating it. He accepts it and exhibits
> its emotional value and imaginative possibilities. Consider
> the Platonic doctrine of transcendental remembrance in

Wordsworth's "Ode: Intimations of Immortality": there are no statements pro and con, no doubts and proofs, but essentially the experience of having so great an idea — the excitement of it, the awe, the tinge of holiness it bestows on childhood, the explanation of the growing commonplaceness of later life, the resigned acceptance of an insight. But to cite Wordsworth as the proponent of a bona fide philosophical theory is a mistake; for he could not and would not have elaborated and defended his position. The Platonic doctrine to which the poem commits him is actually rejected by the Church whose teachings he professed. As he presents it in the Ode, however, it has nothing to do with any further theology; it does not go beyond the poem.[53]

Miss Langer follows Cassirer in asserting that Wordsworth did not attempt to propound a philosophy, but departs from his view in asserting that the poem has nothing to do with theological experience. She seems to assume, as Cassirer did not, that man is made up of discontinuous phases of experience which flit on and off in his consciousness. To argue that the poet could express "so great an idea" and yet ignore it in part of his life comments upon the poet, not the poem. Such discontinuity may indeed be a part of the unfortunate condition of man, but it is precisely that misfortune that the symbolic imagination attempts to overcome. Theology and poetry are grounded in the same empirical reality; if a poem and a theology disagree, the poet or the theologian should examine what he has done.

Having disconnected poetry not only from other symbolic modes but also from reality, Miss Langer is unable to see that the experience embodied in the Ode is not the experience of "having so great an idea" as "the Platonic doctrine," but rather a more direct experience of reality.

What is embodied in the Ode (whether intentionally or
not, whether actually experienced by Wordsworth or
not) is what Kenneth Burke called a "typical situation."
The situation is that the luster of childhood leaves life
and is replaced by a less exciting but more gratifying wisdom. As such the situation is not Christian, not Platonic,
not romantic, not Wordsworthian, and not even particularly poetic; it is rather a common human experience
which may appear in any doctrine, in any form. The
Platonism is not so much a theme as a setting; perhaps it
is merely a strategic exaggeration to drive home the
nearness of the child to a certain kind of joy and perception.[54]

Poems for Miss Langer are not so much interpretations of reality (and hence connected with it) as they are
illusory events having

> no core of actuality that allows them to appear under
> many aspects. They have only such aspects as they are
> given in the telling; they are as terrible, as wonderful, as
> homely, or as moving as they "sound."
>
> > Tyger, tyger, burning bright
> > In the forests of the night —
>
> At once the "tyger" exists as a supernatural animal, not
> a beast for British sportsmen to hunt and have skinned. A
> common tiger would prowl in a dark jungle, not burn in
> "forests of the night." The turn of phrase: "forests of the
> night" makes the place as unrealistic and symbolic as
> the creature himself.[55]

The problem here is the familiar one of how much the
word brings into the poem. I would maintain that the
tiger of the poem and the tiger of the British hunter are
the same beast, but seen in different guises, under different symbolic forms. The tiger is a fitting symbol of the

experience Blake describes largely because of what British hunters, and those who read about them, know of tigers — their fierceness, the brilliance of their eyes in the dark, their beauty and majesty, their cunning, their awesome power, their association with the mysterious jungle, and so on. The British tiger hunter may see the beast as a rug, but if he wants to survive he had also better feel its terror. I am contending, to put this in more general terms, that what Cassirer calls "empirical reality" has supplied a basis for a multiplicity of interpretations of the tiger and that although these interpretations proceed in widely divergent directions, they are not mutually unrelated. If one assumes they are, he may try reading, "Hoot owl, hoot owl, burning bright / In the forests of the night." The effect is not quite the same.

Because Miss Langer denies the relevance of the poem to reality, she concludes that "the vision of such a tiger is a virtual experience." [56] But is not the phrase "virtual experience" misleading? Granted that Blake's tiger is only a virtual tiger, the experience Blake conveys is quite real — which is another way of saying that it is congruent with our general attitudes toward tigers and lambs of whatever ontological status, and with our knowledge of one of the basic concerns of philosophy and theology — the problem of evil.

What, then, is the value of art for Miss Langer? It is threefold:

> (1) Art makes feeling apparent, objectively given so we may reflect on it and understand it; (2) the practice and familiar knowledge of any art provides forms for actual feeling to take, as language provides forms for sensory experience and factual observation; and (3) art is the education of the senses to see nature in expressive form.

Thereby the actual world becomes in some measure symbolic of feeling . . . and personally significant.[57]

Cassirer's philosophy would require that one more value be added, perhaps the most important: precisely because art is objective, it is a ground for further symbolic interpretations of reality, some of which will be aesthetic and some of which probably will not be.

Eliseo Vivas presents two views which should be considered before ending this chapter. Both are relatively common, and both create difficulties that Cassirer's epistemology can solve. Vivas makes two unjustified claims for art: he claims the objectivity of art without admitting the consequences thereof, and he assigns art a central role in the formation of culture. The last has been discussed earlier and may be treated very briefly here. Vivas claims that "art *creates* culture: it creates the values and meanings by which a society fulfills its destiny." [58] If Vivas is correct, the alternatives are somewhat confusing. We must either deny that our culture is the product of laws, scientific theories, moral and religious views, folkways, and so on, or we must argue that Andrew Jackson, Pavlov, Bentham, the Wesleys, Billy the Kid, and a host of other unlikely candidates were actually artists. The third possibility, limiting "culture" to the aesthetic, makes a tautology of Vivas' statement. The major difficulty with the kind of exaggeration Vivas makes is that it confuses two things which had better be seen in their proper relations: it confuses the symbolic imagination with one of its modes (or, in another terminology, it fails to distinguish between the primary and secondary imaginations).

More practically, if art is to be placed on a pedestal above other ways of knowing, it tends also to be elevated above life. In writing of William James's criticism of his brother Henry's novels — William felt that the novels were lifeless — Vivas contends that "life can also legitimately refer to the thrill that comes from acuity of perception organised by the intellect into self-contained form." He goes on:

> Life is consciousness crowded with discriminations of subtle shades of character and mood, temperament and attitudes. But the passion and the thrill are there. As in a quiet auction, where a nod of the head or a hand almost imperceptibly raised is a gesture which conceals anxiety and anticipates the exultation of success or the inward vacuum of defeat, so in Henry James.[59]

Precisely. The "hand almost imperceptibly raised" does just what Vivas claims for it — it conceals; but the function of the symbol is to make manifest. Only by revealing the content of the symbol can art return through human experience to operate in reality. To translate this into terms used earlier, the argument that art is superior to life tends to establish coherence as the sole end and test of art.

In the preceding chapter I argued that the real poem is partly a construct by the reader, and I cited Vivas as one of the opponents of such a view. His position is fundamentally inconsistent with his basic approach to art. On the one hand he claims that "the mind is constitutive of the world," and on the other that the aesthetic experience is " 'pure' to the extent that in the intensity of apprehension of the object before us it appears as self-sufficient, that it excludes all conscious reference." [60] If "the mind is constitutive of the world" there can be no "pure" experience. If the poem is an object, it cannot for that very reason be treated objectively. As a piece of reality, the poem is subject to the same kind of interpre-

214

tation that the mind makes when it deals with other objects. Its only advantages are its relatively tight organization and the strong communal forces of language — both of which limit but do not prevent the mind's reshaping it.

If the preceding is correct, then the philosophy of Cassirer is (for the present) the only adequate tool that criticism has for discussing the value of the experience of art. A sound literary theory and a responsible criticism must be based upon a just estimate of art, upon an understanding that art is not inferior to other modes of knowing and feeling, not superior to them, and not isolated from them. The symbolic function of art is to provide a new perspective from which to view empirical reality; the "truth" lies not in art, not in science, not in myth, not in any particular way of apprehending, but in the entire range of such perspectives. Cassirer's philosophy does justice both to the mimetic and to the formal claims of art; it recognizes art as mimetic because its ultimate source is reality as experienced, and it recognizes art as formal because the experience is meaningful only to the extent that it imposes a shape upon reality.

The effects of such a view on practical criticism could be far-reaching, but I prefer here to draw attention to just one—the problem of the various functions assigned to poetry. More often than not, revolutions in both poetic technique and poetic theory are chiefly conflicts concerning the kind of truth poetry should or should not embody, and the appropriate means for displaying a particular view of reality. Coleridge's attempts to establish the primacy of imagination over fancy may be thought of as an effort to change the "object" which poetry should imitate, the "truth" it should reflect. Matthew Arnold's description of poetry as "high seriousness" is another such attempt, as is T. E. Hulme's plea for literal accuracy of description. Winters wants one kind of symbol, one kind of form; Ransom demands a different kind of structure imposed upon a different slice of reality. The revolutions and skirmishes which comprise the bulk of literary history are, if viewed from the perspectives of time and a broad theoretical framework, merely shifts of emphasis. There is ample reason to believe that Pope, Wordsworth, and T. S. Eliot each thought his kind of poetry alone could artfully reflect what is important to man. From the vantage point of a philosophy of symbolic forms, discussions about what poetry should or should not imitate are futile. Such a view recognizes no priority among kinds of truth, among the various descriptions of empirical reality. It is, therefore, pointless to contend that poetry should be true to religion, science, nature, philosophy, psychology, or wildflowers; a poem may start by imitating whatever it can imitate. More important, however, is the fact that the function of any symbolic form is both to reflect and to create truth. A poem — or, on a larger scale, a type of poetry — in effect opens up virgin territory for the mind. To proscribe the limits of that territory before it is charted, to mark off in theory what can be known only through long and careful exploration, is simply not wise. The notion of symbolic form, as developed by Cassirer, marks no boundaries in advance. Because of its inclusiveness, it permits the critic to follow the poem through the thickets of human experience without radically altering either the poem or the general theory. It permits the critic to do his most important job: to discover what the poem has to offer and to comment upon that in an orderly way. How he does this will be taken up in the next chapter.

216

# VIII

## THE POEM AS VALUED

In the preceding chapter I maintained that a symbolic form may be judged either by its internal coherence or by its congruence with other elements of experience. Without coherence it is not a *single* form; without congruence it is not relevant to anything else and so not symbolic. Happily, there should be no conflict between the requirements of coherence and congruence because, with certain exceptions (music and mathematics, for example), most of our thinking is done with language and our symbolizations thereby share a double reference. All deal in some way with empirical reality and most deal with it according to accepted traditions of language. Our philosophy, our religion, our sociology, our poetry are all ultimately referable back to reality; but further, our development of these symbolic modes is largely according to the laws of language — the habits of expression and therefore the habits of mind we have acquired. I do not want to imply that there are no differences between, say, philosophy and poetry; but I do want to argue that both the philosopher and the poet take their material from this welter of a world and organize it according to the broadest conventions of language. We do not necessarily expect them to talk about the same things in the same way, and we should not; but neither should we expect them to contradict each other, nor should we tolerate it. I am arguing that the humanistic disciplines, including literature, have roughly the same kind of family relationships as the sciences. I should assume that if a chemist, running a qualitative analysis, reaches a conclusion that contradicts his mathematics — in other words, if his chemistry and his mathematics are incongruent — he inquires into the internal organization — the coherence — of his analysis or of the pertinent mathematical theorem. I should expect, if we all functioned as wholly as we should at all times, that the same cross-checking between poetry and other disciplines would be appropriate. Ideally, a coherent poem should not contradict what we know from other coherent systems. If we find a poem coherent, then, we should also find it congruent with our beliefs; and, up to a certain point, the terms describing that coherence and congruence should be convertible.

Although the notions of coherence and congruence are not new, modern poetics has tended to separate them as widely as possible. We have seen Northrop Frye, speaking for many of the most influential contemporary critics, make the separation and place himself firmly on the side of coherence by arguing that in all works of literature the "final direction of meaning is inward." [1] And when T. S. Eliot sets up the criterion of maturity, he announces his position on the side of congruence. If we were perfect beings, either standard alone would suffice; we could then automatically assume that the value of an object *per se* is precisely its value in our experience of it; but as we are, some cross-checking seems in order. Both the internal structure of the poem and its implications are significant in our evaluation. The poem cannot be judged solely on its compatibility with other systems, for the

218

problem at hand is the value of the *poem;* nor can it be judged solely in terms of the poem, for value is known only by the experience that results. The critic can adequately fill out the poem only by recognizing that the poetic material is imported from experience and only by placing the experience got from the poem alongside other experiences, but he can discover accurately what the poem is only by structural analysis. The problem of literary theory is to find a way of making both judgments and of demonstrating their identity.

Perhaps William Wimsatt has come closest. The following passage shows his ability to pick his way through a number of tangled theoretical problems:

> Actual disvalue in poetry arises when some abstractly true assertion or correct attitude is blurred or garbled in symbolic or stylistic incoherencies, or (more flagrantly) when some false assertion or attitude is invested with specious forms of coherence. A sentimental, that is an excessive or oversimplified, feeling about an object can be endowed, for instance, with such a pattern of coherence and suggestion of deep resonance as the metrical and rhyming scheme of a sonnet. The very fact that a poem is a sonnet may create a greater opportunity for badness than if it were a ramble in free verse. Or again, a poem can be given an illusion of depth through the introduction of apparently real but actually phantasmal or irrelevant symbols. In such cases explication reveals disvalue by explicating the absence of the truly explicable. In such cases, there is more (and less) than mere lack or meagerness of meaning. There is positive and active carelessness and self-deception of the human will and imagination. This is disvalue and from it comes our experience of displeasure.[2]

The fine thing about this is Wimsatt's realization of the subjective-objective nature of evaluation, his awareness of the importance both of the elements outside of the poem and the elements inside it. Reading Wordsworth's "Ode: Intimations of Immortality," for example, a modern reader (and, I should think, a reader in Wordsworth's day) would feel something in the poem break when he comes to the line in which the child is hailed as "Thou best Philosopher." The description does not jibe with what most persons know about children, so in the terminology I am using here it would be incongruous with normal experience. Looked at more closely, the line is incoherent; it is not consistent with the rest of the poem. Within the meaning structure of the Ode itself we find that Wordsworth wants to attribute one set of virtues to childhood, another set to maturity; but it so happens that the virtues he assigns the child are specifically nonphilosophical. The virtues he finds in childhood are exuberance, intuitive rightness, freedom from sober and chilling reflection — none of which are the typical philosophic virtues. In fact, the conclusion of the Ode is that the adult is the better philosopher; the adult is better able than the child to reflect upon life and to reach mature conclusions. Whether the reader first notes the incongruity and then discovers the incoherence, or vice versa, makes no real difference; after noting one, the other becomes apparent.

Or, a more positive example. For a long time I knew that the following lines expressed an experience quite well (that they were congruent); yet I was unable to understand their coherence:

> Whenas in silks my Julia goes,
> Then, then (methinks) how sweetly flows
> That liquefaction of her clothes.

"Liquefaction" was troublesome, although obviously right. I knew it to be the perfect word for its place in the poem, although I could not say why. It seemed pulled from the wrong kind of vocabulary — too precise, too scientific sounding for such a small and personal poem. But if one looks at the structure, the patently rationalistic "whenas this, then that" pattern, he sees that such precision is appropriate. "Liquefaction" not only sounds right, but it also carries through the note of reason and practicality Herrick sounded in the first word, "whenas." Now that I know the stanza is coherent, I can feel its congruence (its relevance to other experience) in good conscience.

The correlation of congruence and coherence is not limited to literature; it is characteristic of all art and of all symbolic experience. As Alfred North Whitehead has shown, any symbolic form is made up of "components of experience" (hence referring outside the form), each of which "by its very nature stands in a certain potential scheme of relationships to the other components. It is the transformation of this potentiality into a real unity which constitutes that actual concrete fact which is an act of experience." [3]

Despite the theoretical importance of coherence and congruence (or some such pair of terms indicating internal consistency and external reference), the two terms are hardly adequate for the evaluation of poetry; at most, they indicate the minimal requirements of any satisfactory symbolic form. It is necessary to have terms that permit the critic to discuss the intensity and quality of the coherence, and the range and quantity of the congruence. Thus any poem that does at least one thing adequately — present an argument, communicate an emotion, give an accurate description — is a coherent symbolic form; if a poem, however, does a number of things well, and if those things seem mutually relevant, we shall say that it has more or less *integrity*. It also has more or less *complexity* by virtue of the fact that it is doing more than one thing. If we can specify the peculiar kind of complexity and integrity poems have, these two terms may provide a basis for the evaluation of poetry.

The terms themselves, however, are not important; what is important is that they do not limit unnecessarily what the critic may find in the poem. Among the acceptable substitutes for *complexity* are richness, multivalence, scope, width, etc. In place of *integrity* we could use depth, intensity, narrowness, power, etc. The individual terms in each set probably suggest differences of application; I prefer complexity and integrity because the more specific connotations of the other terms may be subsumed under them. The use of the two terms is, of course, hardly original, and it is better that it is not. After a period of innovation in criticism and a proliferation of specialized vocabularies, each of which deals with only that part of the poem in its range, it is wise to return to fundamentals. Ambiguity, paradox, meters activated, tension, motive, irony — almost the entire lexicon of contemporary criticism — may be brought into play as special instances of complexity or integrity. The advantage of the general terms is that they do not force any special interpretation of the poem; a poem without paradox, for example, may still interest if it has some other kind of complexity. Also, because the terms are general, they demand some diligence on the part of the critic. It is easy to write off Milton's "Cyriak, this three year's day, though blind" if we are looking only for paradox; but even a critic who does not like Milton's sonnet might hesitate before dismissing it because it is not sufficiently complex. Wimsatt makes an especially valuable comment in this connection: "At higher levels of abstraction, certain terms by which poetry has been defined have tended to lose all specific coloration and to become value predicates nearly if not quite synonymous with the subject 'good poetry.' " [4] Equally as important, because the terms I have suggested are not absolutes, they make possible a loose ranking of poems. The danger of absolutes like "organic form," "unity," "intransitive attention," "autonomous meaning," and so on, is that they force the critic to make an either-or judgment — either the poem has the required quality (or produces the right response) or else it is not a poem.[5] The corollary is that all good poems are equally good, which is obviously false. We know that "Poor Soul! the center of my sinful earth" is a better poem than "Ozymandias," just as we know that the latter is better than Drayton's "To nothing fitter can I thee compare."

The best poem is simply the one which exhibits the most complexity and integrity. Either quality alone is fairly easy to attain and is more readily available outside art than inside it. A glance from the living room window gives the eye more complexity than it can master in a whole afternoon; the dripping of a faucet at night offers greater integrity of sensation than many persons can bear. But because literature is an art, it finds means for overcoming the natural antagonism of complexity and integrity.

The peculiarity of poetry, and especially of lyric poetry, is that the entire object is offered for appreciation. This is the real significance of the truism that poetry is less abstract than other forms of discourse. Because a poem is a symbolic form it is by its very nature an abstraction, a consideration of something from a set vantage point; but in ordinary discourse (practical, scientific, or even philosophical) both speaker and listener are conditioned to make a further abstraction — to abstract only a part of the material presented. If someone says "Sister Susie is sitting on the sofa sewing" we pay no attention to the alliteration (or else we feel a bit annoyed by it) because we know that it distracts us from the meaning we are interested in. If someone asks, "Is the library to the left?" and the reply is "Right," we normally remove the ambiguity as quickly as possible. But in poetry the entire potential of words is expected to function. This is why a poem like Ransom's "Go and ask Robin to bring the girls over / To Sweetwater, said my Aunt" will not completely satisfy despite its merits; it is as if the poet had forgot for a moment that words have sounds. In Ransom's "Survey of Literature" ("A better man was Aristotle, / Pulling steady on the bottle") meanings are ignored. But the effect of the following lines (from Ransom's "Piazza Piece") is much better:

> —I am a gentleman in a dustcoat trying
> To make you hear. Your ears are soft and small
> And listen to an old man not at all.
> They want the young men's whispering and sighing.
> But see the roses on your trellis dying
> And hear the spectral singing of the moon;
> For I must have my lovely lady soon,
> I am a gentleman in a dustcoat trying.

This is not major poetry, but it is poetry of considerable merit. The piece is superior because all the elements of each of the words are used; in the terminology developed here, it has a greater amount of relevant complexity than is found in the other two poems. It is integrated because it presents a single experience, complex because it uses the fullest possibilities of its words.

Before going on with the discussion of form in literature, a brief survey of form in general is in order. An abstract analysis of form in terms of complexity and integrity will, I believe, show what may be said about the formal value of poems. The following is derived largely from the work of Alfred North Whitehead, whose gen-

224

eral and special theories of aesthetics seem to be especially applicable to poetry.

The basis for a theory of form in Whitehead's philosophy is the notion of contrast. Each being and each combination of beings exists to feel and be felt, e.g., to be related to other beings. Now, the value of an object depends upon the subjective intensity that it generates in itself for its own reiteration or endurance, or upon its ability to serve as an object generating more or less intensity in the subjective form of another object. The latter is the value of art objects, whose worth depends largely upon their ability to bring specific feeling into experience. "Heightening of intensity," Whitehead writes, "arises from order such that the multiplicity of components in the nexus can enter explicit feeling as *contrasts*, and are not dismissed into negative prehensions as incompatibilities." [6] This is the general case of influence, including sensory perception and intellection. But a poem, as a work of art, exhibits more than mere contrast of compatibles; it exhibits patterned contrast, and patterned contrasts of contrasts. An iambus, for example, is a contrast; an iambic pentameter line is a pattern of five such contrasts. But when the pattern is filled in, other contrasts appear — the normal tension between rhythm and meter, the slow or fast cadence of individual words, the interrelationships of meanings and grammatical functions, etc. In the following, for example, F. R. Leavis is considering such contrasts:

> Consider, . . . the way in which Donne here, playing his sense-movement across the rimes, controls his tone and gets his key stresses, coming finally down with retarded emphasis on "damn'd":

> Are not heavens joyes as valiant to asswage
> Lusts, as earths honour was to them? Alas,
> As wee do them in meanes, shall they surpasse

Us in the end, and shall thy fathers spirit
Meete blinde Philosophers in heaven, whose merit
Of strict life may be imputed faith, and heare
Thee, whom he taught so easie wayes and neare
To follow, damn'd?

> . . . For all their apparent casualness, the rimes, it should
> be plain, are strictly *used*; the couplet-structure, though
> not in Pope's way, is functional. If, for instance, "asswage"
> had not been a rime-word, there would not have been
> quite that lagging deliberation of stress upon "lusts." [7]

In other words, Donne's lines are effective because the
contrasts have been so patterned that, when experienced,
they produce further contrasts which enter into still further combinations. In this way a poem becomes "a feat
of style by which a complex meaning is handled all at
once." [8]

As the patterned contrasts become progressively more
numerous, however, and the pattern itself more complex, the danger of loss of integrity becomes progressively
greater. The more varied the elements constituting the
experience, the less any one element is likely to be felt;
and as the outlines of the individual elements blur, the
entire group comes to be felt as one rush of events. Complexity requires contrasts patterned so that the details of
the individual members are emphasized; integrity requires that the details be emphasized as belonging to
that particular pattern. "A pattern," Whitehead writes,

> is the "manner" of a complex contrast abstracted from the
> specific eternal objects which constitute the "matter" of
> the contrast. But the pattern refers unselectively to any
> eternal objects with the potentiality of being elements in
> the "matter" of some contrast in that "manner."
> . . . The *manner* of a pattern is the individual essence

of the pattern. But no individual essence is realizable apart from some of its potentialities of relationship, that is, apart from its relational essence.[9]

By *manner* Whitehead means what most critics call "form"; fourteen lines of iambic pentameter, for example, constitute one manner of the sonnet form. The interplay of meanings and specific combinations of sound make up the matter or content of that pattern. I should like to reserve the term *form* for the over-all complex of patterns, and reserve *pattern* to mean an abstractable grouping of contrasts of a certain kind. A poem, then, may show any number of patterns within its over-all form. To return to the example of the sonnet, fourteen lines is merely a spatial arrangement of words on paper, that is, a spatial pattern; iambic pentameter is a pattern of accentual relationships. In any given sonnet a pattern of relative pitch may be abstracted with more or less accuracy, as may semantic, rhythmic, metaphoric, and other patterns. In a genuine work of art the patterns which make up the form do not inhibit each other appreciably.

The opening lines of Keats's "La Belle Dame Sans Merci" provide a quick and familiar example:

> O what can ail thee, Knight at arms,
>   Alone and palely loitering?
> The sedge has withered from the Lake
> And no birds sing!

The iambic tetrameter metrical pattern would quickly prove monotonous. Within the first two lines, however, an interesting rhythmic complexity occurs: the first five syllables of each line move fairly slowly, the last three so much faster that the endings have a quasi-feminine sound. The unstressed "can" is probably more heavily accented than the stressed "arms," and certainly more so than the "-ing" in "loitering." This is a relatively simple case of functional patterned complexity. More than this is happening, obviously, but I want to keep the analysis elementary. In the third line nothing much more is done with the rhythm; the most striking feature is the definite assertion of the basic tetrameter pattern, even to the point of the conventional strong masculine ending. Then, suddenly, in the fourth line, we see the purpose of all this preparation. The four-beat pattern has been so strongly established that it carries over, provoking four equal stresses on "And no birds sing." The metrical pattern has reinforced the pattern of meaning. At first the condition of the knight was merely asserted; in the last line an objective correlative which establishes the mood is found and underlined by the unavoidably heavy rhythmic structure. Although the correlative is stated both in the third and fourth lines, only in the last is it actually realized, for only then is all the oppressiveness of the knight's loneliness felt. The rhythm — the forced unnatural reading of the four equal stresses — does not of itself account for the effect, but it is an important element therein. A pattern of rhythm has become a pattern of experience, and from awareness of the latter may emerge a pattern of meaning. The meter helps to give the lines their integrity, their status as form; the variations introduce a note of complexity which not only relieves the monotony of the repetition but also reacts upon the meanings of the words to enhance the total effect.

Rhythmic complexity is, of course, not the only kind of complexity; it is simply one of the easiest to illustrate. T. S. Eliot's "Gerontion," with its contrasts of wet and dry, past and present, reality and imagination, shows a different type of patterned complexity:

Here I am, an old man in a dry month,
Being read to by a boy, waiting for rain.
I was neither at the hot gates
Nor fought in the warm rain
Nor knee deep in the salt marsh, heaving a cutlass,
Bitten by flies, fought.

The most interesting thing here is what I am tempted to call a threat of complexity which, because it is never fulfilled but yet in the background, adds an impressive dimension. After the matter-of-fact dryness and halting progress of the first two lines, the narrator attempts flamboyance. The reader is led to have visions of death and battle, of men in armor scaling walls, and of all the usual detail of a romanticized description of conquest; the hero, very likely with the Spanish in Central America, may even risk slow death by disease. This, or something like it, is the expected complexity — the threat of another detailed description of a battle; but Eliot quickly lets the whole structure come thudding down. Suddenly, the imagination of the narrator gives out; the worst he can imagine is to be pestered by flies, the best he can do to finish the heroic scene is to repeat himself, using the colorless verb "fought." The peculiar suspended structure of the sentence and the stressed anticlimax refer back to and reinforce the old-dry pattern of meaning started in the first line. What Eliot gives the reader, then, is a group of patterns — in this case the most prominent are the patterns of metaphor, anticlimax, and sentence structure — which so support each other that the effect of the lines is truly greater than the sum of their parts.

To return to the abstract description of form, relevant complexity or significant intensity of all parts characterizes the form of any aesthetic object. In great art, form is felt as a formal intensity generated by a complex of patterns — thus Whitehead's definition of beauty as "the mutual adaptation of the several factors in an occasion of experience." [10] The adaptation must be complete, so that "if you single out one moment of a poem, all the other moments automatically become its context." [11] From this starting point, any work of art has two possible sources of disvalue. Following Whitehead, I shall call them triviality and vagueness, although again the meanings are more important than the terminology.

"Triviality," according to Whitehead, "arises from lack of cooperation in the factors of the datum, so that no feeling arising from one factor is reinforced by any feeling arising from another factor"; it is, in our terminology, a result of unintegrated complexity. The particular cause of a feeling of triviality may be a discordant sound in the poem, a discrepancy between the connotations and the denotations of the words, and so on. Vagueness, on the other hand, is simply undifferentiated complexity, or an excess of integrity.[12] It describes what happens when a reader finds that the words in the poem he is reading blur, so that the eyes scan the page but the mind finds nothing to grasp firmly. The possible technical reasons are many: the meter may be too regular, as in Bryant's

> O fairest of the rural maids!
> Thy birth was in the forest shades;
> Green boughs, and glimpses of the sky,
> Were all that met thine infant eye.

Or the whole sound structure may be monotonous, as in Poe's

> At midnight, in the month of June,
> I stand beneath the mystic moon.

> And, softly dripping, drop by drop,
> Upon the quiet mountain top,
> Steals drowsily and musically
> Into the universal valley,

Or the idea may be repeated too frequently, as in Blake's

> A Robin Red breast in a Cage
> Puts all Heaven in a Rage.
> A dove house fill'd with doves and Pigeons
> Shudders Hell thro' all its regions.
> A dog starv'd at his Master's Gate
> Predicts the ruin of the State.

What happens is that the parts get lost in the whole, so that nothing, not even the whole, stands out clearly. It would be incorrect to imply that repetition, in any form, makes a poem worthless; but such determined insistence upon keeping to a single pattern throughout a poem tends to turn it into a mere *tour de force*.

The task of the poet, then, is complicated. To write well, he must introduce into the poem as much complexity, as much quantitatively, as his talent can manage; he must also provide for the integrity of the piece so that each contrast at once emerges vividly and also takes its place in the total structure. The job of the critic is to demonstrate the poet's success or failure.

Of the two elements of pattern and their resultant control of experience, complexity is the easier to demonstrate. It takes no great skill to make up a list of the patterns present in a poem and to show that they all are active. Nor should it take extraordinary persuasive powers to show that, other things being equal, a more complex poem is better than a less complex poem. I. A. Richards' axiom that men want as many kinds of value as they can get is sound; it explains why most readers return to an imperfect but relatively complex piece such as "Tintern Abbey" more frequently than to the perfect, delightful, and simple "Jenny Kissed Me." The Wordsworth poem engages the reader's whole attention not only by making him respond to some finely wrought passages, but also by making him experience a relatively complex set of emotions and indulge in some relatively abstract thought. Wordsworth's poem reverberates deeply in man's experience; Hunt's titillates the top of it. Just as a contrast is trivial if it does not significantly combine with other contrasts in the object, so a poem is trivial if it fails to combine significantly with a wide and deep range of human experience.

The effects of the integrity of the poem upon the experience of the reader are more complicated. When contrasts are overly integrated, the effect is the vagueness or monotony noted earlier. But the chief disvalue of too much integrity is narrowness. Probably the most common kind of narrowness is simply the absence of sufficient complexity; in more ambitious poems it is often the result of forcing the poem to mean less than it should. In Robert Frost's "The Tuft of Flowers," the concluding lines present the moral:

> "Men work together," I told him from the heart,
> "Whether they work together or apart."

The moral is not only gratuitous, it limits the poem by telling the reader that it means just that and nothing more. The brilliance of the other elements is tarnished and becomes vague; the poem itself is likely to get lost among other statements of the same general message.

The critic's most difficult task here, however, is to demonstrate that individual contrasts are not lost within the integrity of the poem. It is one of those more or less situations in which the only guide is experience and good taste. Without repetition there is no pattern; with too much, there is no interest. The critic can judge only on the basis of broad experience and his reaction as controlled by the poem. Consider the following passage by Whitman:

Poets to come! orators, singers, musicians to come!
Not to-day is to justify me and answer what I am for,
But you, a new brood, native, athletic, continental,
    greater than before known,
Arouse! for you must justify me.

I myself but write one or two indicative words
    for the future,
I but advance a moment only to wheel and
    hurry back in the darkness.

I am the man who, sauntering along without fully
    stopping, turns a casual look upon you
    and then averts his face,
Leaving it to you to prove and define it,
Expecting the main things from you.

May not a legitimate prejudice of the reader refuse this? The prejudice is not a demand for rhyme, meter, or symbolism, but rather a demand for something more than the will of the poet to tighten and bind the poem.

Poe, on the other hand, uses all the familiar devices of poetry and still fails to achieve more than specious integrity in most of his work. The following stanza will do for illustration:

Thus I pacified Psyche and kissed her,
    And tempted her out of her gloom —
    And conquered her scruples and gloom;
And we passed to the end of the vista,
    But were stopped by the door of a tomb —
    By the door of a legended tomb;

233

> And I said — "What is written, sweet sister,
>     On the door of this legended tomb?"
>     She replied — "Ulalume — Ulalume —
>     'Tis the vault of thy lost Ulalume!"

Both the Whitman and the Poe passages are extreme cases of the misuse of poetry; despite their antipodal technical qualities, both fail because in neither are the "parts" important. They are used, but not integrated. Despite the fact that each seems repulsively egocentric, the essential "I" is in the background when it should be in the foreground — which is another way of saying that integrity fails because an essential element in the complexity is lacking. If Whitman expects us to do the "main things" for him, he ought to convince us here that he is worth our effort; if Poe wants us to feel the impact of the situation in "Ulalume," he must convince us of the reality of the narrator. Because the parts of both poems add up to so little and because certain key parts are missing, the experiences they offer are relatively valueless.

Shakespeare's "Poor Soul, the center of my sinful earth" is more successful because it never gets away from a central point (a point indescribable exactly in any other form), but instead seems to direct the entire capabilities of words toward one significant range of feeling and meaning. The initial contrast in the sonnet, at least the first striking contrast, is between the materialistic "Poor," with its economic implications, and the spiritual "Soul." The reconciliation takes place almost immediately, with the quick acceptance of "Poor" in the metaphorical sense of "unfortunate." But then things start happening. The soul is a "center," hence spatial and therefore material, so that it seems for a moment as though the materialistic implications might win out, except that the soul is the subject and the material metaphors are used adjectively. The same kind of contrast occurs in the next line, with "soul" maintaining its spiritual influence while contrasting and yet uniting with the notion of materiality. Moreover, an interesting minor contrast occurs in the alliteration of the $p$'s in "Poor" and "powers." This minor contrast does not end as mere technical display, however, but builds further by the material-spiritual ambiguity of the two words; and the contrast builds still further, for within the sonnet "Poor" and "power" are antonyms. Thus everything about the words miraculously focuses upon the poem's major obsession, the relation between the material and the spiritual. It would not be accurate to claim that this analysis explains the total effect of either the sonnet or its first two lines. But it should be noted that the analysis has not exhausted the ramifications of the two basic terms, complexity and integrity. I have already mentioned the ambiguity of the passage; irony is also present. The notion that the soul is poor is itself ironic, as is the implication that the active principle of man is dominated by the desires of the passive flesh. But the height of the irony occurs when the reader understands that it is the narrator's intellect that is being critical: the soul is criticizing the soul. The contrasts I pointed out before center around the material-spiritual relationship; these around the relationship between understanding and morality. Within the integrated human personality, however, both sets of relationships merge; and the lines convey this quite well by the simultaneity (an aspect of integrity) of the various suggestions. The irony, note, is only one element in the complexity of the lines, although it is itself complex. I could go on in the manner of Winters, Burke, Ransom, Brooks, et al., but I should merely be underscoring special instances of integrated complexity.

In itself such analysis may not prove the value of the

lines; but assuming that the rest of the sonnet lives up to its early promise, the critic can show that it exhibits a high degree of complexity with an abnormal amount of mutual reinforcement among the elements in that complexity. And if the poem has those qualities, the experience — if the reader is reading aright — should have also.

The kind of analysis I have suggested may seem petty, but a word should be said in favor of pettiness in criticism. Literary critics generally seem reluctant to discuss the details of poems; or, when they do so, they usually stop at mere enumeration, as Empson does throughout most of his *Seven Types of Ambiguity*. Critics of painting, on the other hand, are eager to discuss such minutiae of style as brush strokes, which in apparent pettiness is comparable to the poet's use of consonants. Leo Stein somewhere tells how Matisse changed a single line by a sixteenth of an inch, a change which altered the entire composition of his painting. In a very real sense the effect of a work of art is the effect of an accumulation of details; it is often a brush stroke, an extra fraction of an inch, a few vibrations per second, or a slight tonal variation which makes or mars an art work.

I should like to make a relatively brief comparison of two passages, both of the same general type, in order to show what kinds of discriminations are possible within the system I have outlined. I have not chosen lyrics, because I want to show that the system is applicable to other types of poetry.

> Awake, my St. John! leave all meaner things
> To low ambition, and the pride of Kings.
> Let us (since Life can little more supply
> Than just to look about us and to die)

> Expatiate free o'er all this scene of Man;
> A mighty maze! but not without a plan.

And:

> You, who the sweets of rural life have known,
> Despise th'ungrateful hurry of the town;
> In Windsor groves your easy hours employ,
> And, undisturb'd, yourself and Muse enjoy.
> Thames listens to thy strains, and silent flows,
> And no rude wind through rustling osiers blows,
> While all his wond'ring nymphs around thee throng,
> To hear the sirens warble in thy song.

Assuming that most readers would prefer the first by Pope to the second by Gay, the problem is to account for the difference in quality. A critic who deals only in large-scale effects will not be able to justify his preference. Both depict versions of the good life; the former emphasizes rationality, the latter quietly busy contentment. Furthermore, both are conventional dedications. Yet Pope's lines come alive; they are more complex and yet better integrated than Gay's. Gay refers the reader to the narrow pastoral tradition, thus limiting the associations that may appropriately be brought to bear on the poem; Pope refers the reader to reality, or at least to a significant segment of it. Moreover, the first passage is dramatic, the second is not; and because drama is movement and movement is change, there is likely to be "more" in a dramatic situation than in a static one. Looking more closely, we find that Pope's lines provide not only the drama of awakening and self-realization, but also introduce a new realm of complexity by use of a flight and exploration metaphor, the operative terms of which are "Awake," "leave," "low," "look," "Expatiate," "free," "o'er," "scene," and "maze." The implied image is that of a creature which, disturbed, climbs upward for a general view of its surroundings. In addition, each of the operative words in the metaphor also functions in the dedication — as flattery to St. John for being a person capable of climbing — and on the more prosaic level of introducing the subject. Much is done, nothing is wasted. The metaphor not only adds a value, it combines with other elements to deepen the total value of the passage.

Gay's lines are adequate, in the sense that they give some pleasure, but just barely adequate in the sense that a close reading shows that the contrasts cancel each other out. In lines one and two "sweets" contrasts with "ungrateful hurry," although the only relation between the two is the general notion of pleasantness and unpleasantness. The only connection between "easy" and "employ" is alliteration; if Pope and Gay had not been on such good terms, the master would likely have pointed out that poetry is not the result of "easy," leisure hours. More importantly, though, Gay's use of the pastoral tradition seems to interfere with his subject — praise of Pope. For whatever reason, Gay seems able to make Pope a conventional pastoral figure only by falsifying his subject. The Pope that Gay praises is a fictional creation who has retired to the country to delight in the sweets of rural life and, from time to time, to jot down a poem. This Pope is not only different from the real Pope, he is much less interesting. The real Pope was a thoroughly social man, extremely interested in London life, and the hard-working author of *An Essay on Criticism* and *The Rape of the Lock*; he was, in addition, preparing for the immense labor of translating *The Iliad*. We can, of course, admire the strategy of Gay's transformation of Pope into a conventional pastoral figure as a clever thrust in the war of the pastorals; but the lines are difficult to admire as anything more than a graceful and shrewd use of poetic convention.

This again brings up the problem of congruence — the ability of the poem to create an experience which can be assimilated into other experiences and be verified by comparison with other symbol systems. In these terms Gay's lines are verifiable only in relation to his use of the pastoral tradition, Pope's in relation to a much larger area of experience. As soon as we attempt to put Gay's lines in any wider context than the poem, we sense their falsity. Now, there are two chief disadvantages of falsity in a poem; both stem from the fact that the real form of the poem exists only in the fully funded experience of a reader. The form of the artifact is a seed which grows and blossoms only when fertilized by contact with a responsive mind. The first disadvantage of falsity, then, is that it is a distraction, and as such it tends to prevent the form from being completed adequately in the experience. At this level, falsity encourages the reader to say, "Ah, but this is not so; the situation is really . . ." Then, of course, the reader is off on his own train of thought, a train set in motion but not guided by the poem. When this happens, the reader is unable to experience the integrity of the form; the poem is a failure because it stimulates an undirected reaction. A poem succeeds only when it creates, with the co-operation of the reader, a specific experience rigidly determined by its formed content.

Second, falsity also narrows the possible range of complexity. Falsity is a dead end; it prevents the reader from going further in building the poem from his own stock of related attitudes. The richness of the perceived patterns is directly dependent upon the range of associations (always limited by the entire context of the poem) which can be brought into play. Falsity, when noticed, makes it impossible for the reader to provide the relevant material for the enrichment of the bare content presented by the words of the poem.

In the preceding pages I have sketched certain aspects of poetic pattern and the effects of an experience of that kind of pattern. One more piece remains to be placed — the nature of the experience itself. Congruence is, after all, realized only as an effect of the aesthetic experience; it broadens the experience, but is recognized only after reflection. On the other hand, the contrasts making up the poem cause a certain kind of experience, but are not themselves that experience. Just what, then, is the aesthetic experience? Rather than describe some problematic ideal, as theorists usually prefer to do, I shall describe the relatively satisfactory kind of experience that the critic most often has to communicate.

An aesthetic experience occurs when the bulk of the data provided by an object determines and limits the direction of the experience. Two factors are involved: the data are almost the entire sensa of the poem and the data are of sufficient breadth to fill the attention. "Sensa" here is used very broadly; it includes sound-look (the pattern of words on the page, visual and aural rhyme, tonal quality, alliteration, rhythm, meter, and so on) and all the raw material that words usually suggest to the mind. To the extent that some of the sensa are unused, the experience is simply nonaesthetic. Thus when Burns writes, "My luve is like a red, red rose," almost all of the sensa are relevant to the experience; but when a young man says, "My girl's cheeks are red," only a literal meaning is presented. The hearer has a choice in the latter of attending either to what the words say or to their sound; in a prosaic statement one can experience the tone or the meaning, but not both as an integrated experience. Burns permits the experience of both simultaneously because

tween tone and meaning, or disproportionate length, or delicately poised symmetry, or a certain functional harshness. It is here, with his initial reaction to the poem — whatever that reaction may be — that the critic begins. Before he has finished, he must work his way through the poem, pushing meanings, visualizing, listening, unweaving and reweaving the strands of the poem until he is satisfied that he has earned all that is in the poem — not in terms of his theory, but in terms of what the poem has to give.

# NOTES

NOTES TO CHAPTER I, PP. 3–19

1. T. S. Eliot, "The Perfect Critic," *The Sacred Wood* (New York: Alfred A. Knopf, 1930), pp. 11, 14.

2. William Empson, *Seven Types of Ambiguity*, 3rd ed. (New York: Meridian Books, 1955), p. 174.

3. Mortimer Adler, *Art and Prudence* (New York: Longmans, Green and Co., 1937), esp. pp. 458–9; D. W. Gotshalk, *Art and the Social Order* (New York: Dover Books, 1962), esp. pp. 186–7; I. A. Richards, *Practical Criticism* (New York: Harvest Books, 1958), esp. p. 10; and Randall Jarrell, *Poetry and the Age* (New York: Vintage Books, 1955).

4. *Poetry and the Age*, p. 80.

5. Thomas Clark Pollock, *The Nature of Literature* (Princeton: Princeton University Press, 1942), p. xviii.

6. See, for example, Rudolph Carnap, *Philosophy and Logical Syntax* (London: Kegan Paul, Trench, Trubner & Co., 1935), p. 24.

7. C. K. Ogden and I. A. Richards, *The Meaning of Meaning* (New York: Harcourt, Brace & Co., 1960), p. 125.

8. John Crowe Ransom, *The World's Body* (New York: Charles Scribner's Sons, 1938), pp. 309–10.

9. Helen Gardner, *The Business of Criticism* (Oxford: At the Clarendon Press, 1959), p. 13.

10. Kenneth Burke, *The Philosophy of Literary Form* (Baton Rouge: Louisiana State University Press, 1941), p. 22.

11. *The World's Body*, p. 173.

12. 'The Perfect Critic," *The Sacred Wood*, p. 15.

13. Among the better critic-by-critic surveys of practical criticism and literary theory are Ransom's *The New Criticism* (Norfolk, Conn.: New Directions, 1941); Stanley Edgar Hyman's *The Armed Vision* (New York: Alfred A. Knopf, 1948); Murray Krieger's *The New Apologists for Poetry* (Minneapolis: University of Minnesota Press, 1956); and Richard Foster's *The New Romantics* (Bloomington: Indiana University Press, 1962).
14. William Hazlitt, *Lectures on English Poets and The Spirit of the Age* (New York: Everyman's Library, 1951), p. 3.
15. F. R. Leavis, *Revaluation* (London: Chatto & Windus, 1936), pp. 204–6; and René Wellek in *The Importance of Scrutiny*, ed. Eric Bentley (New York: George W. Stewart, Publisher, 1948), p. 26.
16. *The World's Body*, p. 206.
17. Richard Foster argues very persuasively for the essential romanticism of the new critics in *The New Romantics*, esp. Chapter II.
18. Jacques Maritain, *Creative Intuition in Art and Poetry* (New York: Meridian Books, 1955), pp. 188–9 and 52–3.

NOTES TO CHAPTER II, PP. 20–41

1. *The Works of Lyof N. Tolstoi*, trans. Aylmer Maude (New York: Thomas Y. Crowell Co., 1899), VIII, 443–4; Charles Baudelaire, *The Mirror of Art*, trans. and ed. Jonathan Mayne (Garden City: Doubleday Anchor Books, 1956), p. 234.
2. Eugene Veron in *A Modern Book of Esthetics*, ed. Melvin M. Rader (New York: Henry Holt and Co., 1951), p. 97.
3. Henri Bergson, *The Creative Mind*, trans. Mabelle L. Andison (New York: The Wisdom Library, 1946), pp. 32, 42.
4. Benedetto Croce, *Aesthetic*, trans. Douglas Ainslie (New York: The Noonday Press, 1958), p. 1.
5. Ibid., pp. 15–16, 52–3, 80–81, 50–51.
6. John Dewey, *Art as Experience* (New York: Capricorn Books, 1958), p. 65.
7. Ibid., pp. 75, 325.
8. Samuel Alexander, *Art and the Material* (London: Longmans, Green & Co., 1925), pp. 11–12.
9. Jacques Maritain, *Creative Intuition in Art and Poetry* (New York: Meridian Books, 1955), p. 3.

10. I. A. Richards, *Practical Criticism* (New York: Harvest Books, 1958), p. 236.
11. Herbert Read, *The Nature of Literature* (New York: Grove Press, 1958), p. 23.
12. Thomas Clark Pollock, *The Nature of Literature* (Princeton: Princeton University Press, 1942), p. 141.
13. Herbert Read, *English Prose Style* (New York: Henry Holt and Co., 1928), pp. ix–x. In *The Nature of Literature*, pp. 41–2, Read defines poetry as a "transcendental quality" which differs from prose by its "essence."
14. Read, *The Nature of Literature*, pp. 29–30.
15. Jean-Arthur Rimbaud, letter dated 13 May 1871, quoted in Stephen Spender, *The Creative Element* (New York: The British Book Center, 1954), p. 45.
16. Read, *The Nature of Literature*, pp. 119–21.
17. Ibid., p. 100.
18. Ibid., pp. 95–6.
19. Ibid., p. 132.
20. Ibid., p. 70.
21. Ibid., p. 138.
22. Ibid., p. 68.
23. Herbert Read, *In Defense of Shelley and Other Essays* (London: William Heinemann, 1936), p. 213.
24. Pollock, *The Nature of Literature*, p. 96. In this and subsequent quotations from Pollock's book, I have removed the symbols (L) and (E) which appear consistently after the words "literature" and "experience."
25. Ibid., p. 10.
26. Rudolph Carnap, *Philosophy and Logical Syntax* (London: Kegan Paul, Trench, Trubner & Co., 1935). Pages 27–9 state fully but briefly Carnap's distinction between expressive and representative uses of language.
27. Pollock, *The Nature of Literature*, p. 96.
28. Ibid., pp. 112–13.
29. Ibid., pp. 179–80.
30. Ibid., pp. 192, 205.
31. Ibid., p. 191.
32. Ibid., p. 200.
33. Ibid., pp. 202–3.
34. Kenneth Burke, *Counter-Statement* (Chicago: University of Chicago Press, 1957), p. 53.

35. Murray Krieger, *The New Apologists for Poetry* (Minneapolis: University of Minnesota Press, 1956), p. 35. Yvor Winters is much more severe with Eliot. His comment that Eliot "can speak with equal firmness and dignity on both sides of almost any question, and with no realization of the difficulties in which he is involved" is harsh but largely accurate. *In Defense of Reason* (New York: Swallow Press and Wm. Morrow & Co., 1947), p. 466.
36. T. S. Eliot, *Selected Essays* (London: Faber and Faber, 1953), p. 18.
37. Ibid., p. 20.
38. Ibid., p. 20.
39. "John Ford," *Selected Essays*, p. 203.
40. T. S. Eliot, "Yeats," *On Poetry and Poets* (London: Faber and Faber, 1957), p. 255.
41. John Crowe Ransom, *The World's Body* (New York: Charles Scribner's Sons, 1938), p. 2.
42. Ibid., p. 38.
43. *The Selected Letters of John Keats*, ed. Lionel Trilling (New York: Farrar, Straus and Young, 1951), p. 4.

NOTES TO CHAPTER III, PP. 42–75

1. Alfred Kazin, review of *The Letters of William Blake* in *The New York Times Book Review* (Jan. 27, 1957), p. 1.
2. George Orwell, *A Collection of Essays* (Garden City: Doubleday Anchor Books, 1954), p. 230.
3. Austin Warren, *Rage for Order* (Chicago: University of Chicago Press, 1948), pp. 15–16.
4. Randall Jarrell, *Poetry and the Age* (New York: Vintage Books, 1955), p. 41.
5. David Daiches, *A Study of Literature* (Ithaca: Cornell University Press, 1948), pp. 81–2.
6. Yvor Winters, *In Defense of Reason* (New York: Swallow Press and Wm. Morrow and Co., 1947), p. 364.
7. Eric Gill, *Beauty Looks After Herself* (New York: Sheed & Ward, 1933), p. 245.
8. T. S. Eliot, *On Poetry and Poets* (London: Faber and Faber, 1957), pp. 169–70.
9. Samuel Alexander, *Beauty and Other Forms of Value* (London: Macmillan and Co., 1933), pp. 137–9.

10. D. W. Gotshalk, *Art and the Social Order* (New York: Dover Books, 1962), pp. 222–3.
11. Mortimer Adler, *Art and Prudence* (New York: Longmans, Green and Co., 1937), p. 194.
12. John Dewey, *Art as Experience* (New York: Capricorn Books, 1958), pp. 130–31.
13. Ibid., pp. 270–71.
14. Ibid., p. 150.
15. Ibid., p. 133.
16. Ibid., p. 254.
17. Ibid., p. 15.
18. Jacques Maritain, *Creative Intuition in Art and Poetry* (New York: Meridian Books, 1955), p. 80. Jacques and Raïssa Maritain make the same point in *The Situation of Poetry* (New York: Philosophical Library, 1955), p. 8.
19. *Creative Intuition in Art and Poetry*, p. 221.
20. Jacques Maritain in *A Modern Book of Esthetics*, ed. Melvin M. Rader (New York: Henry Holt and Co., 1951), p. 213.
21. Murray Krieger, *The New Apologists for Poetry* (Minneapolis: University of Minnesota Press, 1956), p. 14.
22. T. S. Eliot, "Shelley and Keats," *The Use of Poetry and the Use of Criticism* (London: Faber and Faber, 1933), p. 91.
23. T. S. Eliot, "Charles Whibley," *Selected Essays* (London: Faber and Faber, 1953), p. 495.
24. "Milton I," *On Poetry and Poets,* pp. 139–40.
25. "The Metaphysical Poets," *Selected Essays*, p. 287.
26. "Shakespeare and the Stoicism of Seneca," *Selected Essays*, p. 135.
27. "Dante," *Selected Essays*, pp. 248–9.
28. "Milton I," *On Poetry and Poets*, p. 144.
29. "Shakespeare and the Stoicism of Seneca," *Selected Essays*, pp. 136–7.
30. "Conclusion," *The Use of Poetry and the Use of Criticism,* p. 144.
31. F. O. Matthiessen, *The Achievement of T. S. Eliot* (Boston: Houghton Co., 1935), p. 113.
32. "Shelley and Keats," *The Use of Poetry and the Use of Criticism*, p. 96.
33. William Empson, *Seven Types of Ambiguity* (New York: Meridian Books, 1955), p. 275.

34. I. A. Richards, *Principles of Literary Criticism* (New York: Harcourt, Brace & Co., 1925), pp. 32–3.
35. Ibid., pp. 61–2.
36. Ibid., p. 32.
37. John Crowe Ransom, *The World's Body* (New York: Charles Scribner's Sons, 1938), pp. 118, 130.
38. Herbert Read, *The Nature of Literature* (New York: Grove Press, 1958), p. 110.
39. *The World's Body*, p. 349.
40. Frederick A. Pottle, *The Idiom of Poetry* (Ithaca: Cornell University Press, 1941), pp. 75, 99.
41. Allen Tate, *Reactionary Essays* (New York: Charles Scribner's Sons, 1936), p. xi.
42. Ibid., p. 12.
43. Ibid., pp. 14–15.
44. Allen Tate, *Reason in Madness* (New York: G. P. Putnam's Sons, 1941), p. 129.
45. Ibid., p. 128.
46. Interestingly, Tate does not bring into play here his notion of irony (a quality in the expression of an idea that implies a criticism of that idea). Hardy's poem, with its emotional protest against the philosophical position it takes, seems to have the kind of irony Tate usually admires; Miss Dickinson's poem lacks it.
47. E. M. Tillyard, *Poetry Direct and Oblique* (London: Chatto & Windus, 1948), pp. 48–9.
48. Ibid., pp. 9–10.
49. Irving Babbitt, *On Being Creative* (Boston: Houghton Mifflin Co., 1932), pp. 119–20.
50. W. K. Wimsatt and Monroe C. Beardsley, *The Verbal Icon* (Lexington: University of Kentucky Press, 1954), p. 258.
51. Ibid., p. 79.
52. Ibid., pp. 79–80.
53. Yvor Winters, *The Function of Criticism* (Denver: Swallow Press, 1957), p. 26.
54. *Four Poets on Poetry*, ed. Don Cameron Allen (Baltimore: The Johns Hopkins Press, 1959), p. 71.
55. *The Function of Criticism*, pp. 107–8.
56. *In Defense of Reason*, p. 56.
57. Ibid., p. 505.

58. See especially his very fine comments on Wallace Stevens' "Sunday Morning," ibid., pp. 476–7.
59. *The Function of Criticism*, p. 68.
60. *In Defense of Reason*, p. 502.
61. Ibid., p. 533.
62. Ibid., pp. 18–19.
63. René Wellek and Austin Warren, *Theory of Literature* (New York: Harvest Books, 1956), p. 112.
64. Alfred North Whitehead, *Adventures of Ideas* (New York: Mentor Books, 1955), p. 265.

NOTES TO CHAPTER IV, PP. 76–106

1. A. B. Lunacharsky, *Stati o sovetskoi literaturye* (Moscow: Government Press, 1958), p. 63. Unless otherwise noted, the Russian translations are my own.
2. Ibid., p. 3.
3. Ibid., p. 19.
4. Ibid., pp. 191–2.
5. Ibid., p. 109.
6. Ibid., p. 192.
7. Pavel G. Antokolsky, *Poeti i vremya* (Moscow: Government Press, 1957), pp. 5–16.
8. *Stati o sovetskoi literaturye*, p. 431.
9. Ibid., pp. 112–13. Probably the fullest and certainly the most interesting attempt to develop a Marxist literary theory is found in Christopher Caudwell's *Illusion and Reality* (New York: International Publishers, 1947). I do not discuss it here because Caudwell's aesthetics seems unrelated to his Marxism. Except for the insistence upon the social and economic implications of art, which seem to me largely irrelevant to his general literary theory, his work resembles that of such neo-Hegelians as Cassirer and Miss Langer.
10. Granville Hicks, *The Great Tradition* (New York: The Macmillan Co., 1933), pp. 125–7.
11. Erich Auerbach, *Mimesis* (Garden City: Doubleday Anchor Books, 1957), p. 9.
12. Kenneth Burke, *Counter-Statement* (Chicago: University of Chicago Press, 1957), p. 107.
13. Allen Tate, *The Forlorn Demon* (Chicago: Henry Regnery Co., 1953), p. 129.

256

14. R. P. Blackmur, *Language as Gesture* (New York: Harcourt, Brace and Co., 1952), p. 59.
15. The titles alone are sufficient to illustrate the point: F. R. Leavis, *Revaluation: Tradition and Development in English Poetry* (London: Chatto & Windus, 1936); Cleanth Brooks, *Modern Poetry and the Tradition* (Chapel Hill: The University of North Carolina Press, 1939); and Gilbert Murray, *The Classical Tradition in Poetry* (New York: Vintage Books, 1957).
16. John Crowe Ransom, *The New Criticism* (Norfolk: New Directions, 1941), p. 141.
17. T. S. Eliot, "Tradition and the Individual Talent," *Selected Essays* (London: Faber and Faber, 1953), p. 15.
18. I. A. Richards, *Principles of Literary Criticism* (New York: Harcourt, Brace and Co., 1925), pp. 117–18.
19. Ibid., p. 137.
20. Ibid., p. 248.
21. Vernon Lee in *A Modern Book of Esthetics*, ed. Melvin M. Rader (New York: Henry Holt and Co., 1951), pp. 305–6.
22. *Revaluation*, pp. 201–2.
23. Sigmund Freud in *A Modern Book of Esthetics*, p. 72.
24. René Wellek and Austin Warren, *Theory of Literature* (New York: Harvest Books, 1956), p. 71.
25. Susanne K. Langer, *Philosophy in a New Key* (New York: Mentor Books, 1954), p. 168.
26. Carl Gustav Jung, *Two Essays on Analytical Psychology*, trans. H. G. and C. F. Baynes (New York: Dodd, Mead and Co., 1928), pp. 67–8.
27. Lionel Trilling, *The Liberal Imagination* (Garden City: Doubleday Anchor Books, 1953), p. 60.
28. Carl Gustav Jung, *Psyche and Symbol*, ed. Violet S. de-Laszlo (Garden City: Doubleday Anchor Books, 1958), p. 27.
29. Maud Bodkin, *Archetypal Patterns in Poetry* (New York: Vintage Books, 1958), pp. 52–3.
30. T. E. Hulme, *Speculations*, ed. Herbert Read (New York: Harcourt, Brace and Co., 1924), pp. 134–5.
31. Ibid., p. 162.
32. Ibid., p. 132.
33. T. E. Hulme, *Further Speculations*, ed. Sam Hynes (Minneapolis: University of Minnesota Press, 1955), p. 138.

34. John Crowe Ransom in *Lectures in Criticism* (New York: Pantheon Books, 1949), p. 24.
35. John Crowe Ransom, *Poems and Essays* (New York: Vintage Books, 1955), p. 171.
36. John Crowe Ransom, *The World's Body* (New York: Charles Scribner's Sons, 1938), pp. 196–7.
37. Ibid., p. 138.
38. T. S. Eliot, "Milton I," *On Poetry and Poets* (London: Faber and Faber, 1957), pp. 139–40.
39. Wallace Stevens, *The Necessary Angel* (New York: Alfred A. Knopf, 1951), pp. 94–5.
40. Ibid., pp. 129–30.
41. Ibid., p. 130.

NOTES TO CHAPTER V, PP. 107–55

1. Murray Krieger, *The New Apologists for Poetry* (Minneapolis: University of Minnesota Press, 1956), p. 129.
2. José Ortega y Gasset, *The Dehumanization of Art* (Garden City: Doubleday Anchor Books, 1956), p. 69.
3. Elizabeth Sewell, *The Structure of Poetry* (New York: Charles Scribner's Sons, 1952), esp. Chs. XII and XIII.
4. Cleanth Brooks, *The Well Wrought Urn* (New York: Reynal & Hitchcock, 1947), pp. 228–9. For an unusually clear exposition of the nature of closed form by a sympathetic critic see Murray Krieger's *The New Apologists for Poetry*, pp. 20–22.
5. Max Eastman, *The Enjoyment of Poetry* (New York: Charles Schribner's Sons, 1939), p. 20.
6. See below, Chapter VII.
7. T. S. Eliot, "The Social Function of Poetry," *On Poetry and Poets* (London: Faber and Faber, 1957), p. 19.
8. T. S. Eliot, "Introduction," *The Use of Poetry and the Use of Criticism* (London: Faber and Faber, 1933), p. 25.
9. "Milton II," *On Poetry and Poets*, p. 154.
10. "Matthew Arnold," *The Use of Poetry and the Use of Criticism*, pp. 118–19.
11. "The Social Function of Poetry," *On Poetry and Poets*, p. 20.
12. See Max Eastman's *The Enjoyment of Poetry* and Owen Barfield's *Poetic Diction* (London: Faber and Faber, 1952).

13. William Hazlitt, *Lectures on English Poets and the Spirit of the Age* (New York: Everyman's Library, 1951), pp. 12–13.

14. René Wellek, *A History of Modern Criticism* (New Haven: Yale University Press, 1955), II, 170.

15. John Crowe Ransom, *The World's Body* (New York: Charles Scribner's Sons, 1938), p. 349.

16. John Crowe Ransom, *The New Criticism* (Norfolk: New Directions, 1941), pp. 316–17.

17. *The World's Body*, p. 236.

18. Ibid., p. 349.

19. *The New Criticism*, p. 271.

20. *The Poems of Robert Frost* (New York: Modern Library, 1946), pp. xx–xxi.

21. *The New Criticism*, pp. 280–81, 330.

22. *The World's Body*, p. 348.

23. Ibid., pp. 130–33.

24. *The New Criticism,* p. 30.

25. John Crowe Ransom, *Poems and Essays* (New York: Vintage Books, 1955), pp. 156–7.

26. *The New Criticism*, pp. 273–4.

27. Allen Tate, *Reason in Madness* (New York: G. P. Putnam's Sons, 1941), p. 62.

28. Ibid., p. 76.

29. Ibid., p. 64.

30. William Empson, *Seven Types of Ambiguity*, 3rd ed. (New York: Meridian Books, 1955), p. 5.

31. Ibid., p. xiv.

32. *The New Criticism*, pp. 128–9.

33. *Seven Types of Ambiguity*, pp. 96–7.

34. Ibid., p. 224.

35. R. P. Blackmur, *Language as Gesture* (New York: Harcourt, Brace, and Co., 1952), p. 6.

36. Ibid., p. 3.

37. Ibid., p. 13.

38. Ibid., pp. 35–7. Here and later (p. 171) I have cited the text of a Dickinson poem used by the critic rather than the more recent and standard texts established by Thomas Johnson and printed in *The Poems of Emily Dickinson* (Cambridge: Harvard University Press, 1955) and in the shorter edition published by Little, Brown, and Co.

39. R. P. Blackmur in *Lectures in Criticism* (New York: Pantheon Books, 1949), pp. 203–6.
40. It is difficult to recognize the Brooks of *The Well Wrought Urn* either in his and William K. Wimsatt's *Literary Criticism: A Short History* (New York: Alfred A. Knopf, 1959) or in his *The Hidden God* (New Haven: Yale University Press, 1963.).
41. *The Well Wrought Urn*, p. 230.
42. Ibid., p. 162.
43. Ibid., pp. 5–6.
44. Cleanth Brooks, *Modern Poetry and the Tradition* (Chapel Hill: University of North Carolina Press, 1939), p. 16.
45. *The Well Wrought Urn*, p. 161.
46. Cleanth Brooks, "The Formalist Critics," *Kenyon Review*, XIII (1951), p. 72.
47. *The Well Wrought Urn*, pp. 229–30.
48. *Modern Poetry and the Tradition*, p. 111.
49. Ibid., p. 113.
50. *The Well Wrought Urn*, pp. 141–2.
51. Ibid., p. 152.
52. Ibid., p. 87.
53. Ibid., p. 27.
54. R. S. Crane, *The Languages of Criticism and the Structure of Poetry* (Toronto: University of Toronto Press, 1953), p. 13.
55. Ibid., p. 32.
56. Ibid., p. 180.
57. Ibid., p. 56.
58. Ibid., p. 143.
59. Ibid., pp. 166–7.
60. Ibid., pp. 20–21.
61. Yvor Winters, *The Function of Criticism* (Denver: Swallow Press, 1957), p. 21.
62. *The Languages of Criticism*, p. 60.
63. Ibid., p. 161.
64. W. K. Wimsatt and Monroe C. Beardsley, *The Verbal Icon* (Lexington: University of Kentucky Press, 1954), p. 50.

NOTES TO CHAPTER VI, PP. 156–80

1. Monroe C. Beardsley, *Aesthetics* (New York: Harcourt, Brace, and Co., 1958), p. 232.

2. Cleanth Brooks, "The Formalist Critics," *Kenyon Review,* XIII (1951), p. 75.

3. Cleanth Brooks, *Modern Poetry and the Tradition* (Chapel Hill: University of North Carolina Press, 1939), Ch. 3.

4. Murray Krieger, *The New Apologists for Poetry* (Minneapolis: University of Minnesota Press, 1956), pp. 160–61. In *A Window to Criticism* (Princeton: Princeton University Press, 1964), Krieger modifies his earlier position to stress the "miracle" by which poetry, through the tightness of its structure, loosens out onto the world.

5. Frederick A. Pottle, *The Idiom of Poetry* (Ithaca: Cornell University Press, 1941), pp. 16–17; and Margaret Macdonald, in *Aesthetics and Language,* ed. William Elton (Oxford: Blackwell's, 1954), pp. 128–9.

6. Wolfgang Köhler, *Gestalt Psychology* (New York: Mentor Books, 1959), p. 12.

7. Werner Heisenberg in *Symbolism and Religion in Literature,* ed. Rollo May (New York: George Braziller, 1960), p. 221.

8. Kenneth Burke, *Counter-Statement* (Chicago: University of Chicago Press, 1957), p. 78; see also John Dewey, *Art as Experience* (New York: Capricorn Books, 1958), pp. 245–6.

9. I. A. Richards, *Principles of Literary Criticism* (New York: Harcourt, Brace, and Co., 1925), p. 224.

10. Cleanth Brooks, *The Well Wrought Urn* (New York: Reynal & Hitchcock, 1947), p. 27.

11. Stephen C. Pepper, *The Work of Art* (Bloomington: Indiana University Press, 1955), pp. 29–33.

12. Wolfgang Köhler, *The Place of Value in a World of Facts* (New York: Meridian Books, 1959), p. 78.

13. Ibid., pp. 412–13.

14. Ibid., p. 84.

15. Ibid., p. 332.

16. *The Well Wrought Urn,* pp. 229–30.

17. R. P. Blackmur, *Language as Gesture* (New York: Harcourt, Brace, and Co., 1952), pp. 40–41.

18. *Counter-Statement,* p. 142. For an excellent study of the complexity of Burke's many-faceted thought with special emphasis on literature, see William H. Rueckert's *Kenneth Burke* (Minneapolis: University of Minnesota Press, 1963).

19. Ibid., p. 45.

20. Ibid., p. 31.

21. Ibid., p. 140.
22. Ibid., p. 41.
23. Ibid., p. 38.
24. Ibid., p. 34.
25. George Santayana, *The Sense of Beauty* (New York: Modern Library, 1955), p. 80.
26. *Principles of Literary Criticism*, pp. 237–8.
27. C. K. Ogden, I. A. Richards, and James Wood, *The Foundations of Aesthetics* (London: George Allen & Unwin, 1922), p. 91.
28. *Principles of Literary Criticism*, p. 225.
29. Ibid., pp. 251–2.
30. Eliseo Vivas, *Creation and Discovery* (New York: The Noonday Press, 1953), p. 113.
31. Ibid., p. 168.
32. Ibid., p. 169.

NOTES TO CHAPTER VII, PP. 181–216

1. I do not deny that it is necessary to understand the initial poetic experience in order to account for the complete poetic process of creation, transmission, and effect; but for reasons that should be clear by now, evaluation need concern itself with only the final two stages.
2. Max Eastman, *The Literary Mind* (New York: Charles Scribner's Sons, 1931), p. 158.
3. Ibid., p. 170.
4. John Crowe Ransom, *Poems and Essays* (New York: Vintage Books, 1955), p. 102; R. P. Blackmur in *Lectures in Criticism* (New York: Pantheon Books, 1949), pp. 203–6; Cleanth Brooks, *The Well Wrought Urn* (New York: Reynal & Hitchcock, 1947), p. 229; Eliseo Vivas, *Creation and Discovery* (New York: The Noonday Press, 1953), pp. 113–14.
5. Samuel Taylor Coleridge, *Biographia Literaria*, ed. J. Shawcross (London: Oxford University Press, 1949), I, 202.
6. William Hazlitt, *Lectures on English Poets and the Spirit of the Age* (New York: Everyman's Library, 1951), p. 3.
7. *Shelley: Selected Poems, Essays, and Letters*, ed. Ellsworth Barnard (New York: The Odyssey Press, 1944), p. 568.
8. I. A. Richards, *Speculative Instruments* (London: Routledge & Kegan Paul, 1955), pp. 147–9.

9. D. G. James, *Scepticism and Poetry* (London: George Allen & Unwin, 1937), p. 94.
10. I. A. Richards, *Principles of Literary Criticism* (New York: Harcourt, Brace, and Co., 1925), p. 59.
11. *Poems and Essays*, p. 107.
12. Christopher Caudwell, *Illusion and Reality* (New York: International Publishers, 1947), pp. 267–8.
13. Cleanth Brooks in *Literature and Belief* (New York: Columbia University Press, 1958), p. 71.
14. The difference here is a matter of emphasis and direction. If the critic admits, as Brooks does, the effects of "congruence," then it would seem that he would have to work both ways — both toward the internal structure of the poem and toward its external implications. Brooks usually wants to do only the former.
15. Cleanth Brooks, *Modern Poetry and the Tradition* (Chapel Hill: University of North Carolina Press, 1939), p. 16.
16. Kenneth Burke, *The Philosophy of Literary Form* (Baton Rouge: Louisiana State University Press, 1941), pp. 8–9.
17. Kenneth Burke, *Counter-Statement* (Chicago: University of Chicago Press, 1957), p. 142.
18. Ibid., p. 167.
19. *The Philosophy of Literary Form*, p. 20.
20. Ibid., p. 92.
21. Ibid., pp. 288–9.
22. Ibid., pp. 296, 294.
23. In *Hamlet*, for example, we cannot predict with certainty what the "Hamlet" type will say or do. We can, however, say that because the type is meditative, the author has to show him thinking, and that the thought will probably be subtle, with a peculiar blend of selflessness and selfishness. But we cannot predict in advance what the thoughts will be, what images will be used, nor the way they will be expressed. These are all particulars necessary for the embodiment of the type, even though in themselves they are not "typical."
24. Kenneth Burke, *A Grammar of Motives* (New York: Prentice-Hall, 1945). For his analysis of "Ode on a Grecian Urn" see pp. 450–62.
25. Alfred North Whitehead, *Modes of Thought* (New York: Capricorn Books, 1958), pp. 132–3.
26. If I read Burke correctly, which is no easy task, he slights

the formative powers of language only when dealing with literature; otherwise he treats language as a creative element in human awareness.

27. *Counter-Statement*, p. vi.
28. *Creation and Discovery*, p. 127.
29. Philip Wheelwright, *The Burning Fountain* (Bloomington: Indiana University Press, 1954), p. 92.
30. Ibid., p. 78.
31. Ibid., pp. 49–50.
32. Ibid., pp. 60–75.
33. Ibid., p. 78.
34. Ibid., p. 302.
35. Northrop Frye, *Anatomy of Criticism* (Princeton: Princeton University Press, 1957), p. 118.
36. Ibid., p. 99.
37. Ibid., pp. 73–4. Despite the mechanism Frye offers, I do not see how he can go from the position stated here to his later statement (p. 125) that "the study of literature takes us toward seeing poetry as the imitation of infinite social action and infinite human thought"; but see Frye's *Fables of Identity* (New York: Harcourt, Brace & World, 1963), p. 58.
38. *Scepticism and Poetry*, p. 124.
39. Alfred North Whitehead, *Science and the Modern World* (New York: Mentor Books, 1948), p. 89.
40. Ibid., p. 89.
41. Earl R. Wasserman, *The Subtler Language* (Baltimore: The Johns Hopkins Press, 1959), pp. 7–8.
42. Ibid., p. 9.
43. Ibid., p. 10.
44. Ernst Cassirer, *An Essay on Man* (Garden City: Doubleday Anchor Books, 1953), p. ii of an unnumbered preface.
45. Ernst Cassirer, *Philosophy of Symbolic Forms* (New Haven: Yale University Press, 1953–57), I, 91.
46. Ibid., II, 29.
47. *An Essay on Man*, p. 44.
48. *Philosophy of Symbolic Forms*, I, 78.
49. Ibid., I, 117.
50. Ibid., I, 94.
51. For a detailed yet fairly simple description of the operation of a mode of knowing, see ibid., III, 478–9.
52. Ibid., II, 31.

53. Susanne K. Langer, *Feeling and Form* (New York: Charles Scribner's Sons, 1953), p. 219.
54. For Miss Langer's attempt to relate art to life see *Problems of Art* (New York: Charles Scribner's Sons, 1957), pp. 53–4, and "The Cultural Importance of Art," *Philosophical Sketches* (Baltimore: The Johns Hopkins Press, 1962).
55. *Feeling and Form*, p. 214.
56. Ibid., p. 215.
57. *Problems of Art*, p. 73.
58. *Creation and Discovery*, p. x.
59. Ibid., pp. 16–17.
60. Ibid., p. xii.

NOTES TO CHAPTER VIII, PP. 217–49

1. Northrop Frye, *Anatomy of Criticism* (Princeton: Princeton University Press, 1957), p. 73.
2. William R. Wimsatt and Monroe C. Beardsley, *The Verbal Icon* (Lexington: University of Kentucky Press, 1954), p. 242.
3. Alfred North Whitehead, *Symbolism* (New York: Capricorn Books, 1959), p. 86.
4. *The Verbal Icon*, p. 251.
5. The point is interesting and deserves more attention than it can be given here. The standard practice of theorists is to use an absolute, such as "autonomy," and to deny much of its force. Eliseo Vivas, for example, asks whether any "responsible aesthetician" has ever claimed "that the artist can dissociate himself from all other aspects of his society than the artistic?" He then suggests "self-sufficient" as a replacement for "autonomous," but admits that neither is satisfactory. Partial autonomy, or partial self-sufficiency, is a contradiction. If a critic wishes to be taken seriously, he must explain away the contradiction, and to do so is to explain that he did not really mean "autonomous" or "self-sufficient" at all. See Vivas' *Creation and Discovery* (New York: The Noonday Press, 1953), p. 166.
6. Alfred North Whitehead, *Process and Reality* (New York: The Humanities Press, 1955), p. 128.
7. F. R. Leavis, *Revaluation* (London: Chatto & Windus, 1936), pp. 11–12.

8. *The Verbal Icon*, p. 4.
9. *Process and Reality*, p. 175.
10. Alfred North Whitehead, *Adventures of Ideas* (New York: Mentor Books, 1955), p. 250.
11. Kenneth Burke, *A Grammar of Motives* (New York: Prentice-Hall, 1945), p. 490.
12. *Process and Reality*, pp. 170–71.
13. Leo Stein, *The ABC of Aesthetics* (New York: Boni and Liveright, 1927), p. 156.
14. *Process and Reality*, pp. 170–71.

# INDEX

acceptability, 55–6
Addison, Joseph, 16, 44
Adler, Mortimer, 4, 48
aesthetic distance, 83, 118, 139
aesthetic experience, 12, 33, 35, 38, 49–50, 179, 240–41, 246
Alexander, Samuel, 24, 30, 47
ambiguity, 64, 130–34, 139–40, 150, 222, 247
anchored values, 159–61
"Annabel Lee," 197
anonymity, 38–9, 123
Antokolsky, Pavel, 78–9
appreciation, 9–10
Aquinas, St. Thomas, 16, 48, 50–51, 69
*Archetypal Patterns in Poetry*, 93–4
archetype, 94–5, 200–203
Aristotle, 13, 16, 44, 99, 154
Arnold, Matthew, 22, 98, 215
associational clusters, 190–91
attention, transitive *and* intransitive, 107, 177–8, 179, 183, 223
audience form, 172, 173
auditory imagination, 53–5, 114–17
Auerbach, Erich, 81–2
"Auguries of Innocence," 45, 231

Babbitt, Irving, 65, 69
balanced poise, 88, 176–7, 187
"Bare ruined choirs," 131–2
Barfield, Owen, 117–18
Baudelaire, Charles, 22, 27
"Bear, The," 69
Beardsley, Monroe C., 157
beauty, 3, 71–5, 230
"Because I could not stop for death," 61–2
belief, 56–9, 189
Berenson, Bernard, 108
Bergson, Henri, 13, 22–3, 108
Blackmur, R. P., 11, 85, 134–8, 171–2, 183, 186
Blake, William, 29, 45, 211–12, 231
Bodkin, Maud, 93–4
Book of Job, 81–2
"Bought," 115–16
Bradley, A. C., 22
"Break, break, break," 13, 145
Brooks, Cleanth, 15, 85, 86, 110, 139–50, 158–9, 165, 170, 177, 181, 183, 188–9, 209, 235, 246
Browning, Robert, 22
Bryant, William Cullen, 230
"Burden for Critics, A," 138
Burke, Kenneth, 10, 36, 82–3,

"Elegy X," 157
Eliot, T. S., 3, 11, 13, 15, 31, 36–8, 39, 44, 52–6, 57, 84–6, 103–4, 109–10, 113–17, 161–2, 216, 218, 228–9
eloquence, 173–4, 190
Emerson, Ralph Waldo, 184–5, 244–5
emotion, 24, 26, 28, 39, 54, 67–8, 128, 130, 171, 190–91, 221, 232
emotive language, 59
Empson, William, 4, 44, 56–7, 130–34, 139–40, 144, 236, 246
equilibrium, *see* balanced poise
*Essay on Man, An*, 45, 236–9
"Eve of Saint Agnes, The," 112
experience, 21, 22–4, 32–3, 37, 48–50, 53–4, 67–8, 110, 143–4, 166–7, 170, 172, 179, 191–2, 195–6, 198, 202, 214, 216, 221, 232, 235, 240, *see also* aesthetic experience *and* virtual experience

falsity, 239–40
Faust, 26–7
"Fog," 117
form, 23, 24, 29, 30, 47, 50, 53, 157, 175, 227–8, 229–30
formalism, 15, 17–19, 43, 96
Forster, E. M., 73
Freud, Sigmund, 28, 87, 91–5, 181
Frost, Robert, 16, 43, 69, 70, 121–2, 126, 146, 159–61, 175, 232
Frye, Northrop, 6–7, 199, 201–3, 218
funding, 163, 166–7, 170, 177, 178–9
fundamental attitudes, 82–3

Gardner, Helen, 9
Gay, John, 237–9
German Idealism, 27, 44–6
"Gerontian," 228–9
gestalt psychology, 162
gesture, 134–8, 150, 183

Gill, Eric, 43
"Glory be to God for dappled things," 192
"God Is Good: It Is a Beautiful Night," 99–100
Gotshalk, D. W., 4, 47–8
Gray, Thomas, 153–4
great commonplaces, 64–5
great tradition, 84–6

*Hamlet*, 34, 88–9, 173, 175
Hardy, Thomas, 62–3, 85
Hawthorne, Nathaniel, 184
Hazlitt, William, 15, 118, 184
"He 'digesteth harde yron,' " 104
Hegel, G. W., 184
Heisenberg, Werner, 162, 205
Herbert, George, 21, 27, 51–2
Herder, J. G., 22
Herrick, Robert, 86, 122, 220–21, 241–3, 244
Hicks, Granville, 79–81
Homer, 4, 34, 57, 81
Hopkins, Gerard Manley, 8, 35, 67–8, 192
Horace, 16
Hulme, T. E., 97–8, 215
Hunt, Leigh, 232
"Hymn to Light," 127–8

ideal reader, 158, 170
*Idylls of the King*, 54
*Iliad*, 4, 238
illusion of density, 125
images, 24, 28, 29, 141–2
imagination, 18, 44, 91, 184
imitation, *see* mimetic theory
indeterminate meaning *and* sound, 120–22
"Indian Serenade, The," 110–11
integrity, 8, 70–75, 111, 167, 221–3, 224, 232, 235, 247, 248
intensity, 72–5, 111, 221, 225, 229–30
intention, 34, 143, 152
intuition, 22–5, 30, 50, 108, 152–3

269

narrowness, 232–4
Nashe, Thomas, 129–30
"Nature's Questioning," 62–3
neo-Aristotelian, 151–5
"No worst, there is none," 67–8
normalcy, 163–5
"Not marble nor the gilded monuments," 88
"Note on Ontology, A," 122

"O fairest of the rural maids," 230
objective correlative, 54
objectivity, 5, 7, 14, 19, 35, 157, 162, 163–5, 180, 188, 208, 213, 214–15, 219–20, 246–8
oblique poetry, 64
"Ode: Intimations of Immortality," 210–11, 220
"Ode on a Grecian Urn," 144–5, 146–9, 179, 193–6, 197, 198, 246–7
"Ode to a Nightingale," 154–5
"Ode to Autumn," 12, 99
"Ode to the West Wind," 17, 164
Odyssey, 34, 81
Ogden, C. K., 5–6
"On first looking into Chapman's Homer," 66
On Poets and Poetry, 113
open form, 19, 156–80
organic form, 18, 51, 223
Ortega y Gasset, José, 49, 108
Orwell, George, 42–3
"Ozymandias," 75, 223

paradox, 64, 139–45, 222, 247
"Passionate Shepherd to His Love, The," 34, 76
pattern, 156–7, 226–7, 232–6
perception theory, 17, 28, 95–106
personality theory, 17, 20–41, 44
physical poetry, see pure poetry
"Piazza Piece," 224
Plato, 16, 21, 44, 210–11
Platonic poetry, 59–60

Poe, Edgar Allan, 22, 84, 122, 184, 196–9, 230–31, 233–4
"Poets to come," 233–4
Pollock, Thomas Clark, 5, 25, 30–36, 42
"Poor Soul, the center of my sinful earth," 32, 58, 223, 234–6
Pope, Alexander, 16, 21, 29, 45, 216, 236–9
Pottle, Frederick A., 60, 161–2
Prelude, The, 20–21
Principles of Literary Criticism, 58
Prior, Matthew, 174
"Provide, provide," 43
pseudo-statement, 186–7
psychoanalytic theories, 87, 91–5
psychological form, 172–3
psychological theories, 87–95
psychologism, 158–9, 161–2, 171–2, 175
psychology, 13–14, 30, 58–9, 163, 177
"Pulley, The," 51–2
pure poetry, 18–9, 59–60, 91
purpose, see intention

Ransom, John Crowe, 7, 11, 15, 17, 36, 38–9, 59–60, 69, 85, 91, 96, 98–103, 118–19, 128, 132, 153, 177, 181, 183, 188, 216, 224, 235
Read, Herbert, 25–30, 36, 40, 42, 49, 50, 59–60, 91
recurrent emotions, 82–3
relativism, 158–9, 161–2, 167
"Renunciation," 136–8
requiredness, 163, 168–70, 173, 177
Reynolds, John, 46
rhythm, 88
Richards, I. A., 4, 5–6, 22, 24, 31, 57–9, 62, 87–9, 159, 165, 172, 176–7, 186–8, 231
richness, 163, 165–6, 167, 179, 222, 239
Rilke, Rainer Maria, 27

Rimbaud, Arthur, 27, 68
*Rime of the Ancient Mariner,
The,* 65, 93–4, 95, 162–3, 166,
191
R. U. R., 173–4
*Rural Sports,* 237–9
Rymer, Thomas, 16

*Sacred Wood, The,* 3
Sandburg, Carl, 117
Santayana, George, 120, 174–5
scholarship, 6–8
semantics, 30
*Seven Types of Ambiguity,* 236
Sewell, Elizabeth, 108–9
Shakespeare, William, 6, 7, 12, 16,
24, 29, 32, 34, 55, 58, 85, 88–9, 98, 103–4, 131–2, 133, 134–6, 146–7, 149–50, 165, 167,
169, 173, 175, 186, 209, 223,
234–6
Shelley, Percy Bysshe, 13, 17, 21,
29, 52, 55, 75, 86, 110–11, 164,
182, 184, 203, 207, 223
Sidney, Philip, 16, 34, 85
"Sleeper, The," 230–31
social theories, 76–84
"Song for St. Cecilia's Day," 133–4
sound, 53–5, 115–16, 119–20,
157, 169
statement, 186–7
Stein, Leo, 236, 241
Stevens, Wallace, 13, 97, 99–102,
104–6
stimulus theory, 87–91
"Strange fits of passion have I
known," 90–91
structure, 119–20, 126–7, 128,
150, 153, 178, 189, 216, 218,
231
"Study of Two Pears," 97, 100–102
subjectivism, 5, 14, 19, 28, 35,

157, 158–9, 161–2, 163–4, 166–7, 180, 219–20
"Sumer Is Icumen In," 40, 181
Swinburne, Charles A., 22, 27,
122, 208
symbolic form, 19, 66, 70, 138,
157, 181–216, 217–18, 221–2
symbolism, evocative, 31–2
symbolism, referential, 31–2, 58–9, 111–13, 203–4
syntax, 203–5

Tate, Allen, 15, 60–64, 85, 127–30
Taylor, Edward, 43
Tennyson, Alfred, 8, 13, 22, 54,
102–3, 145
tension, 127–30, 150, 222, 247
test of ideas, 60–64, 170–71, 188,
209
texture, 119–20, 126–7, 128, 153
Thomas, Dylan, 126
Tillyard, E. M. W., 64–5
"Tintern Abbey," 4, 33, 55, 232
tissue of irrelevance, 60, 119–20
"To a Skylark," 182
"To Chloe Weeping," 174
"To Helen," 196–8
"To His Coy Mistress," 13, 153,
174
Tolstoy, Leo, 22, 73, 175
"Tradition and the Individual
Talent," 37
tradition theory, 84–6, 169
"Trees," 4, 154
Trilling, Lionel, 40, 92
triviality, 230–31
truth, 12, 22, 38, 43, 44, 46, 50,
55–9, 204, 215, 218
"Tuft of Flowers, The," 232
"Two Tramps in Mud Time," 146
"Tyger, tyger," 211–12
typical situations, 192–3, 199, 211

"Ulalume," 233–4
unanchored values, 159–61

unconscious mind, 28–9, 91–5,
  108–9
unity, 119, 139–40, 150, 223

vagueness, 230–31, 232
valuation, *see* double valuation
Verlaine, Paul, 22, 68
Veron, Eugene, 22
virtual experience, 212
Vivas, Eliseo, 107, 159–61, 177–
  80, 183, 199, 205, 213–14


"Wanted: An Ontological Critic,"
  122
Warren, Austin, 43, 92
Wasserman, Earl R., 203–5
*Waste Land, The,* 31
Wellek, René, 17, 71, 92, 118
Wheelwright, Philip, 199–201,
  203
"When I have fears that I may
  cease to be," 89

"Whenas in silks my Julia goes,"
  220–21, 241–3
Whitehead, Alfred North, 31, 71–
  5, 194, 203, 205, 221, 224–30,
  242–3
Whitman, Walt, 81, 223–4
Wilde, Oscar, 22, 170
Williams, William Carlos, 13, 97,
  175
Wimsatt, William K., 66, 155,
  219–20, 222
Winters, Yvor, 15, 43–4, 65, 66–
  70, 128, 153–4, 181, 215–16,
  235
wisdom, 43, 72–5
wit, 64, 139–45
Wordsworth, William, 4, 8, 11,
  16, 20–21, 27, 29, 33, 46, 83,
  90–91, 140–43, 175, 181, 203,
  208, 209–11, 216, 220, 232
*World's Body, The,* 39

Yeats, William Butler, 81, 175